Norman E. Wegmeyer
716 Marshall Ave
Rockville, Maryland   June, 1961

luther
on the
christian
home

william h. lazareth

luther
on the
christian
home

An Application of the Social Ethics of the Reformation

MUHLENBERG PRESS   PHILADELPHIA

DEDICATION

To my Mother and Father, for providing their grateful children with everything Luther hoped for in his liberation of the Christian home.

Preface

Medieval life was colored by many lurid superstitions. One of
the more fantastic of these old wives' tales was the prediction
that the Antichrist would be born from the union of a renegade
monk and an apostate nun. It is little wonder, therefore, that
many a breath was held—among friend and foe alike—when
the news spread abroad like wildfire that on the evening of
June 13, 1525, ex-monk Martin Luther and ex-nun Katherine
von Bora were joined in holy matrimony.

Little did the sixteenth-century world realize the tremendous
significance—both religious and social—of this simple and
reverent ceremony in the backwoods of rural Germany. The
union of Martin and Katie was not cursed with the birth of the
Antichrist. Instead, it was blessed by God with the birth of the
Protestant parsonage and the rebirth of a genuinely Christian
ethos in home and community. Luther's marriage remains to this
day the central evangelical symbol of the Reformation's liberation and transformation of Christian daily life.

What lay behind Luther's dramatic act? Eight long and
eventful years had passed between his divorce from Rome and
his marriage to Katie. As will be shown in a biographical first
chapter, Luther clearly did not break with Rome in order to
marry. Why then did he do as late as 1525 what he could have
done as early as 1517? Taking Luther at his word, that he
married in order to ". . . confirm what I have taught by my
example," we shall examine just what it was that he had taught

between 1517 and 1525 which he felt needed his own public testimony of faith.

Our aim in the first part of this study will be to develop the theological heart of Luther's social ethics, namely, that a living faith in Jesus Christ frees us from the bondage of our selves for the service of our neighbors. Our chief task here will be to demonstrate the dialectical way in which Luther relates personal love to social justice for realistic Christian action. Then, on this solid foundation, we shall trace how Luther's theology gradually infused and shaped his views on marriage, family, home, and society as he progressed from celibate monk to married reformer. In his ethics as well as his doctrine, Luther had to learn the painful lesson that "Not reading and speculating, but living, dying, and being condemned makes a real theologian."[1]

But this study is not aimed merely at exploring a dark and often misunderstood and misinterpreted corner of Reformation theology for the benefit of professional students and scholars—though this would be a welcome and salutary by-product. Ours is a much more practical mission in "applied Christianity." We shall search Luther's writings because we are badly in need of his help. Our contemporary marriages, homes, and society at large are in grave danger of disruption, and the church is obligated to gather all the resources at its disposal to meet this growing social crisis. While our corporate service to the neighbor and the neighborhood is not the church's primary task, it is certainly inseparable from our commission of evangelism, and is "like unto it." Our goal is not to save America's homes and society, but to serve God's kingdom within them, and this surely is a vital part of our Christian social responsibility.

To help meet this challenge, we will try to disclose the secret of Luther's abiding value for all Christians—the reason why every great theological age, like our own, must always rediscover him for itself. Since Luther was a sixteenth-century man, most of what he said on concrete social issues is historically dated

[1] *WA* 5, 163.

and largely irrelevant for us. Yet Luther was also a profound and dedicated Christian; knowledge of why and how he addressed God's Word to the many social problems of his day, therefore, may well offer constructive guidance for our own contemporary witness in society. Essentially it is this *evangelical spirit and stance* in Luther's ethics which we wish to recapture. For this could be of great benefit to us in strengthening the foundation of our own social order—the Christian home and all that it stands for in a responsible society under God.

*   *   *   *

In its present form, this study is a condensed adaptation of a doctoral dissertation approved in 1958 by the joint faculties of Columbia University and Union Theological Seminary. Professor Wilhelm Pauck provided the guidance for this research in his own inimitable fashion. He has already inspired a whole generation of young American theologians to face both the anguish and the thrill of serious Luther research.

I wish also to acknowledge my indebtedness to the Samuel Trexler Fellowship Committee of the United Lutheran Synod of New York and New England for having supplied the funds necessary for graduate study both in this country and abroad at the Universities of Tübingen, Germany, and Lund, Sweden. My colleagues on the faculty of the Lutheran Theological Seminary at Philadelphia next deserve my thanks for permitting me the time and facilities needed to complete this work. Professors Martin J. Heinecken and Theodore G. Tappert have been especially generous in sharing their time and talents with me. They alone know how much I owe them for all the coffee and theology I have consumed at their expense. Dr. Tappert also read the entire manuscript at a critical stage of its development and offered many valuable suggestions for its improvement. It is also a pleasure to express appreciation to my wife, Jacqueline, for all that she has meant to me and done for me during the writing of these pages.

The numerous quotations in this book are purposely limited almost exclusively to Luther's own collected works. Wherever possible I have used the English translations listed in the following table of abbreviations. Many such quotations, however, have been altered freely and without notation for the sake of accuracy or style. Where English translations of German or Latin works were nonexistent, I have made my own. Biblical citations are generally given in the Revised Standard Version, except where violence is done to peculiarities in Luther's exegesis of earlier translations. In short, the constant aim has been to let Luther speak for himself.

January 29, 1959   William H. Lazareth

Table of Contents

Abbreviations

BA   Luther, Martin. *Werke*. Herausgegeben von Buchwald, G., Kawerau, G., u.A. 8 vols. Berlin: Schwetschke, 1905ff.

BA, Er   *Ibid.*, 2 supplementary volumes.

EA   ——. *Sämmtliche Werke*. 67 vols. Frankfurt u. Erlangen: Heyder, 1826-57.

LW   ——. *Works*. American edition. Edited by Pelikan, Jaroslav and Lehmann, Helmut. Philadelphia and St. Louis: Muhlenberg and Concordia, 1955ff.

MA   ——. *Ausgewählte Werke*. Herausgegeben von Borcherdt, H., u. Merz, Georg. 6 vols. München: Kaiser, 1937ff.

MA, Er   *Ibid.*, 2 supplementary volumes.

PE   ——. *Works*. 6 vols. Philadelphia: Muhlenberg, 1915-43.

Sm   Smith, Preserved. *The Life and Letters of Martin Luther*. Boston: Houghton Mifflin, 1911.

SJ   Smith, Preserved, and Jacobs, Charles (eds.). *Luther's Correspondence and Other Contemporary Letters*. 2 vols. Philadelphia: Lutheran Publication Society, 1913-18.

St. L.   Luther, Martin. *Sämmtliche Schriften*. Herausgegeben von Walch, Johann. Neue revidierte Stereotypausgabe. 23 vols. St. Louis: Concordia, 1880-1910.

Ta   Tappert, Theodore (ed.). *Luther: Letters of Spiritual Counsel*. Library of Christian Classics. Vol. 18. Philadelphia: Westminster, 1955.

WA   Luther, Martin. *Werke; Kritische Gesamtausgabe*. 58 vols. Weimar: Böhlau, 1883ff.

WA, Br   ——. *Werke; Kritische Gesamtausgabe. Briefwechsel*. 11 vols. Weimar: Böhlau, 1930ff.

WA, TR   ——. *Werke; Kritische Gesamtausgabe. Tischreden*. 6 vols. Weimar: Böhlau, 1912ff.

CHAPTER ONE

Testimony of Faith

Actions speak louder than words. An act of commitment can often dramatize a message in such a way that it becomes fixed indelibly in the hearts and minds of its viewers. The Bible is filled with accounts of the mighty acts of God in history which demonstrate his love for mankind far more convincingly than words ever could. There always have been many pious Christians who have not been able to comprehend the theological subtleties of John 1 or Romans 8, but for whom the religious drama so vividly enacted in the manger at Bethlehem and the cross of Calvary means more than life itself.

In his own marriage Luther was practicing what he had preached. It is for this reason, as well as to provide us with the historical setting of his message, that our theological study begins with a brief review of the main events in the early domestic life of the Reformer. Strictly speaking, of course, the biblical validity of Luther's views can and should be judged separately from his own personal life and work. The fact that he was first an unhappy monk and later a happy husband and father is historically important but theologically irrelevant. Nevertheless, it is no exaggeration to say that Luther's monastic revolt and subsequent marriage represent for his ethics what his nailing of the *Theses* and his defense at Worms represent for his theology. Rightly understood both are dramatic symbols of the very heart of the biblical message which was recovered by Luther in his reformation of Christian life and thought.

1

The World, the Flesh, and the Devil

Luther was born on November 10, 1483, in the little Saxon town of Eisleben. In the early, rigorous days of their marriage, Margaret and Hans Luther raised their son in a strict and frugal atmosphere aimed at meeting the rigors of everyday life which bordered on poverty. Luther later recalled how, as a little boy, he used to watch his mother carry wood on her back from the town's common forest,[1] or listen to her sing melancholy little songs as she did her housework.[2] Nor was she an exception to the rule of strict parental discipline common to the home life of late fifteenth-century Germany. "Spare the rod and spoil the child" was taken so literally by Margaret that her son in his maturity felt compelled to question the severity of her discipline, even though "her actions were always meant well."[3]

From Luther's writings, we gain the impression that the boy felt closer in spirit to his equally stern but more animated father. To be sure, beatings from his father were remembered just as vividly. "My father once beat me so severely that I ran away and was very angry with him until we were finally reconciled."[4] Nevertheless, Luther often boasted that he was "the son of a peasant" whose roots went deep into the rich brown earth of Saxony.[5] He always considered it one of the mysteries of God that a doctor of theology should ever emerge from his parents' humble homestead.[6] Even as it was, the focus of Luther's activity was heavily concentrated in Saxony despite its eventual worldwide consequences.

Luther had great respect for the dedication of his father who rose in his lifetime to comfortable circumstances on the basis of hard work and a careful budget. Before Martin reached his teens his father had become a homeowner, a small capitalist in the

[1] *WA*, TR 3, 2888a.
[2] *WA* 38, 338.
[3] *WA*, TR 3, 3566b.
[4] *WA*, TR 2, 1559.
[5] *WA*, TR 5, 5573.
[6] *WA*, TR 4, 4773.

mining industry who leased and operated local mines and furnaces, and a respected member of the town council of Mansfeld. Hans held especially high hopes for his son, to whom he gave an excellent education despite its heavy costs. Martin never forgot this and often spoke with gratitude about his father's "sweat and labor" to pay for his academic training.[7] Though he generally worked hard, Hans enjoyed relaxing over a stein of beer, sharing the laughter and companionship of his friends.[8] All in all, though never particularly religious, he and his wife lived a God-fearing and happy life together, serving God's will for their lives in the estate of holy matrimony.[9]

The most decisive event in Luther's relations with his parents occurred when he was a law student of twenty-two. He was returning to the University of Erfurt after a short visit home when he experienced a terrifying religious crisis. Imagine his parents' amazement when, shortly after his return, he informed them of his sudden vow to flee this "world" and become a monk. More than amazed, Luther's disappointed father was extremely angry at him for abandoning a law career. His parental response was swift and decisive. "When I became a monk, my father was so furious that he wrote me a very nasty letter in which he addressed me as 'thou' instead of 'you' and renounced his parental blessing."[10]

Luther himself confessed later that he had fulfilled his cloister vow only out of a sense of moral obligation and against his own free will.[11] Yet fulfill it he did by entering the monastery in Erfurt on July 12, 1505. By the end of the summer of 1506, after a satisfactory novitiate year, Luther was considered ready to take the monastic vows of poverty, chastity, and obedience, and was received into the permanent ranks of the Hermits of St. Augustine. In keeping with the rules of the Order, he solemnly swore:

[7] *WA* 30[II], 576.
[8] *WA*, TR 4, 5050.
[9] *WA*, TR 2, 1658.
[10] *WA* 49, 322.
[11] *WA*, TR 4, 4414.

I, Brother Martin, do make profession and promise obedience to Almighty God, to Mary the Sacred Virgin, and to you, the prior of this cloister, as representative of the general head of the order of Eremites of the holy bishop of St. Augustine and his rightful successors, to live unto death without worldly possessions and in chastity according to the rule of St. Augustine.[12]

In the spring of 1507, Luther was ordained a priest of the Church of Rome at the high altar in the Cathedral of Erfurt. The celebration of his first mass was set for May 2, Cantate Sunday. His experiences both during and after the mass remained vivid memories for Luther. He recalled often how he had felt such terror during the sacrifice of the Eucharist that he was tempted to flee from the altar, a desire which was checked only by the prodding of an experienced preceptor assisting him in the service.[13]

The long-awaited encounter between Luther and his estranged father took place during the social festivities which traditionally followed a priest's first mass to celebrate his entry into holy orders. The desired reconciliation was effected all right, but not without some sharp words in which old Hans proved himself well-equipped to take on his grown son, even on Martin's home ground of theology. Their ensuing conversation so impressed the young monk that he later referred to it more frequently than to any other experience he ever had with any of his family. Its most poignant description occurs in Martin's public letter to his father in 1521 which serves as the dedicatory epistle to his work, *On Monastic Vows.*

For you remember that unforgettable scene when, after we were reconciled and you were talking with me, I told you that I had been called by terrors from heaven and that I did not become a monk of my own free will and accord, still less to gain any gratification of the flesh, but that, blocked by the terror and the agony of sudden death, I took a forced and necessary vow, and then you said, "Let us hope that it was not an illusion and a deception." That word

---

[12] Quoted from the *Constitutiones Fratrum Heremitarum Sancti Augustini* in Robert Fife, *The Revolt of Martin Luther* (New York: Columbia, 1957), p. 89.
[13] *WA,* TR 2, 1558.

penetrated to the depths of my soul and stayed there, as if God had spoken by your lips, though I hardened my heart as much as I could against you and your word.

You said something else too. When in filial confidence I upbraided you for your wrath, you suddenly retorted with a reply so fitting and so much to the point that I have hardly ever in my life heard any man say anything that struck me so forcibly and stuck to me so long. "Have you not also heard," you said, "that parents are to be obeyed?" But I was so sure of my own righteousness that I heard only the words of a man and had very little regard for them, though in my heart I could not despise what you said.[14]

In interpreting the young monk's struggles with the "flesh," an area which has been marked by bitter controversy in the past, two equally false extremes are to be avoided: 1) the attacks of enemies who contend that Luther's marriage in particular and the Reformation in general can ultimately be traced back to his sexual frustration; and 2) the defense of friends who reply that Luther's monastic trials were purely religious and not at all sexual. Evidence from his own confessions would support a third position, which recognizes realistically that Luther—like his fellow monks—did, of course, suffer from some sexual frustrations; but which also contends that religious anxiety over salvation was by far Luther's primary concern, the one which was eventually to provide the driving force behind the Reformation and all of its ethical by-products.

Because Luther viewed sex life as a responsible trust from the Creator, unbridled sexual passion had for him religious significance of the first order. This would have been especially true for someone trying avidly to earn his salvation by the performance of good works, as was the case with Brother Martin. He was deeply concerned over the demands of his own flesh.

In an authorized edition of his *Treatise on Marriage* (1519), published in order to correct an earlier edition that had been circulating without his permission, Luther made certain revisions because "speaking with a living voice is very different from

[14] *Ta* 259.

writing on dead paper."[15] One of the minor peculiarities of the later edition as over against the unauthorized copy is Luther's omission of a personal reference to his own temptations in the area of sex: "Everyone knows that the flesh of youth knows no peace. I do not experience more than I can control . . . . It is good for a man to confess his uncleanness to the pure and holy God. Yet he should also petition God's help."[16]

At first glance, it might seem from this omission as if Luther was purposely trying to hide the fact that he also experienced the normal human pangs of sexual tension and desire. That this is not the case, however, is proved by the generous number of utterances which Luther made quite freely and frankly elsewhere concerning his sex life as a monk. They show that the demands of the flesh for sexual satisfaction were definitely a source of concern for the zealous young monk, particularly after the novelty of the novitiate year began to wear off.[17]

When I was a monk I thought that I was utterly damned if at any time I felt the concupiscence of the flesh; that is to say, if I felt any evil motive, fleshly lust [*libidinem*], wrath, hatred, or envy against my brother. I tried many ways, I went to confession daily, etc., but nothing helped; for the concupiscence of my flesh always returned so that I could not rest.[18]

I was a chaste monk as a young man but I also felt my old Adam at work. A pious monk would gladly not have any shameful dreams and [nocturnal] pollutions, but the flesh is still there. Consequently, when a young man sees a pretty girl he lusts after her even against his own will.[19]

As a monk I did not feel great sexual desire. I had [nocturnal] pollutions which were expressions of bodily impulses. I did not look at girls even when they made confessions, for I did not wish to know the faces of those whose confessions I was hearing. In Erfurt I heard the confessions of no girls; in Wittenberg, of only three.[20]

In like fashion, Luther's early works written during his

[15] *WA* 2, 166.
[16] *WA* 9, 215.
[17] *WA* 8, 660.
[18] *WA* 40^II, 92.
[19] *WA* 51, 52.
[20] *WA*, TR 1, 121.

monastic period include personal references testifying to the intensity of the sexual passion which overpowers even the most dedicated men. The evil thoughts a man overcomes during the day return all the stronger to plague him while asleep at night.[21] The concupiscence or fleshly self-centeredness of man forces him into all kinds of immorality and unchastity.[22] Even though "concupiscence" is described by Luther basically in terms of egoism rather than sexual lust,[23] he is still impressed by the frightening ease with which man's sinful personality can unleash such uncontrollable passions. He confesses his own weaknesses in vivid colors.[24] What is so discouraging to him, however, is that his celibate fellow monks seemed no more impervious to these sexual assaults than he was.

Then [Luther] began to complain of the horrible temptations in the cloisters with all the pollutions and defilements from which the devout fathers continually suffered. Because of this, they were often not permitted to hold their masses. Yet the number of masses assigned was so large that the prior was forced to permit masses to be held even by those monks who were bodily polluted.[25]

Against the background of all these admissions, however, Luther always insists that "outwardly I was pious and chaste."[26] That this was a real test of his mettle is confirmed by his confession, "I have been a monk and have given up sleep, fasted, prayed, castigated and tormented my body, all in order to maintain obedience and chastity."[27] There is absolutely no evidence to suggest that Luther ever engaged in any premarital relations.

One must, of course, always read Luther in context. His true position often comes to light only when framed against the background of what he is writing against. This appears to be particularly true in regard to his recollections of his sexual life in the monastery. When he is opposing the monks' obligatory

[21] *WA* 3, 423.
[22] *WA* 9, 73.
[23] *WA* 56, 275.
[24] *WA*, Br 1, 152; 2, 418.
[25] *WA*, TR 4, 3921.
[26] *WA* 47, 322.
[27] *WA* 33, 574.

vow of celibacy, Luther pictures sex as an uncontrollable tyrant whose struggles constitute a monk's chief preoccupation. "In those days I thought that there was no greater sin on earth than unchastity."[28] On the other hand, when Luther measures sexual problems against the work-righteousness inherent in the monastic order, he can relegate those problems to a quite secondary level. They are still a problem, but in comparison with the assaults of religious distrust, they are certainly no longer *the* problem. Both the "world" and the "flesh" seem relatively harmless to Luther when he is confronted by the devil himself. "And the greatest assaults of the devil occur when he says, 'God is the enemy of sinners. Since you are a sinner he hates you too.' "[29]

It is striking that whenever Luther recounts his monastic struggles, it is not the "temptations" (*Versuchungen*) of the world and the flesh which are his major concern. His confessions, for example, were "not about women, but about the really knotty problems."[30] It is rather the *Anfechtungen* of which Luther constantly complains: those aggressive assaults of the devil which terrify the sinner's conscience when he is thrust alone and unprotected into the presence of a wrathful God. Luther contends that the agony of this living hell is almost unbearable.

I knew a man who said that he had often suffered these torments in the shortest possible compass of time, so great and infernal that "no tongue nor pen can show" nor can those believe who have not experienced, so that if they were completed, or lasted half an hour, or even a tenth of an hour, he would utterly perish, and his bones be reduced to ashes. Then God appears horrifyingly angry, and with him the whole creation. There can be no flight, no consolation, either within or without, but all is accusation. Then he laments, "I am cast away from thy face; Lord, accuse me not in thy wrath!"[31]

In this state of utter abandonment, Luther conceived his chief monastic problem to lie in the "flesh"—but in the biblical sense of the word, in his being rooted in sinfulness rather than merely

[28] *WA*, TR 1, 126.
[29] *EA* 60, 1607.
[30] *WA*, TR 1, 122.
[31] *WA* 1, 557.

in creatureliness. Luther was terrified not because he lived "in the flesh," but because he continued to live "after the flesh"—in the love of self which disregards the grace of God and the needs of neighbors. Time and again throughout his life he wondered why sexual frustrations should have posed such crises in the lives of the great church fathers.

Even as an old man, St. Augustine still complained of having [nocturnal] pollutions. St. Jerome beat his chest with a stone in vain because of his powerful temptations. Yet he could not overcome the evil or drive out his inward desires for a dancing girl he once saw in Rome. St. Francis, the barefoot monk, made figures out of snow and then caressed them in order to quiet the lust which burned within him. St. Benedict threw himself into the midst of thorny bushes as a sexual remedy. Whenever he was overcome by evil lust, he stripped himself naked and crawled through thorny bushes to lacerate his body. St. Bernard pommeled himself so badly that his body just reeked and stank and nobody could remain near him. . . . I am amazed that the holy fathers permitted themselves to be plagued with such childish temptations—rather than the higher spiritual assaults—since they held such high offices as rulers of the church.[32]

Luther, on the other hand, felt much in common with the religious sufferings of Paul. "These are the high spiritual assaults which no papist has ever understood properly. These gross and untempted folk know of no other attacks than an evil disposition and lust of the flesh . . . . Oh the devil has them so firmly in hand that he has virtually forgotten the carnal unchastity!"[33] The cloisters of Rome consider sin too much in terms of external immoral acts instead of the prideful rebellion of the actor.[34] The real assaults upon one's burdened conscience and anguished soul have to do with man's relation to God (coram Deo). When Luther describes his "highest assaults," they always concern his lack of faith, his uncertainty of salvation, his alienation from a loving and gracious God.

[32] WA, TR 3, 3777.
[33] WA, TR 4, 5097.
[34] WA 34[1], 253.

Man's hardest and highest assaults and suffering take place when God occasionally tests his saints by the threat of withholding his grace from them [*desertionem gratiae*]. Then man feels as if God and his grace have rejected and deserted him. In this crisis man knows nothing but wrath and horror. But such intensive assaults are not experienced by everyone and no one can understand them who has not personally experienced them. It takes strong and powerful spirits to withstand such assaults.[35]

When we remember that it was precisely Luther's aim "to get a gracious God" by the sacrifices of cloister life, it becomes clearer why he found such demands so fruitless in meeting his real need. In a spirit which reveals more of disappointed futility than either malice or conceit, Luther recalls the frantic extremes to which he voluntarily subjected himself in the hopeless quest for self-sanctification. Never knowing how much was necessary to placate an angry God, the zealous young monk went far beyond the prescribed norm in his diligent pursuit of meritorious good works. As an industrious monk who had not joined the order merely "for the sake of his belly," Luther was not at all averse to stating that he led his monastic life in strict conformity to the Augustinian Rule, indeed even more strictly than did his fellow monks.[36]

I was a monk myself for twenty years and mortified my body with prayers, fasts, watches, and exposures to the cold. This cold alone was enough to kill me. I did myself more harm and danger than I ever could again even if I wanted to. And why did I do all this except in search of God? I wanted him to see how well I obeyed my order and how strictly I lived my life. I succumbed completely to my own dreams and idolatry for I did not truly believe in Christ.[37]

Such confessions testify to the really crucial dilemma of Luther's monastic days. Though he had entered the cloister to earn salvation, his experiences inside convinced him only of his damnation. "With all my masses, prayers, fasts, watches, and chastity, I still could not bring myself to say, 'Now I am finally

[35] *WA* 17[II], 20.
[36] Cf. *WA* 33, 433; 38, 143; 40[I], 134; 41, 15; 47, 92; 51, 34.
[37] *WA* 45, 482.

certain that God is gracious to me.' "[38] His only help at this time came from the pastoral counsel of his district vicar and personal friend, John von Staupitz. If Brother Martin's life was hell behind the monastic walls, Staupitz consoled him with the assurance that this too must have a meaning and a purpose in God's providence. It was only much later in life, however, that Luther was able to see that he had to share the experience of his religious mentor, Paul, in order to be permitted also to speak with the authority of an ex-"Pharisee of the Pharisees" (Acts 26:5).

Luther became convinced that God had made him walk that same painful road from "Saul" to "Paul" in order that the work-righteousness of Rome could be rejected with passion once there had been revealed to him the righteousness of God's grace through faith alone. "It was the Lord's will (as I now see) that I should become acquainted with the wisdom of the schools and the sanctity of the monasteries on the basis of personal and reliable experience (that is, through many sins and impieties) in order that wicked men might not have a chance, when I became their adversary, to boast that I condemned things I knew nothing about."[39] The law-bound life of the cloister had been Luther's bitter "custodian" to prepare him for the sweetness of the gospel of Christ (Gal. 3:24).

Two Become One

Luther entered the monastery in 1505, broke with Rome in 1517, and married in 1525. His monastic experience and biblical studies convinced him that marriage is the holy estate in which God wishes the vast majority of his children to live in mutual love and fidelity. He always allowed the possibility, however, that God grants "supernatural gifts" to some of his children in order to empower them to remain unmarried and yet chaste. Luther numbered himself among this minority group right up to

[38] *WA* 36, 505.
[39] *Ta* 260.

a week before his own marriage.[40] It is really not surprising that Luther married after he arrived at theological clarity on an evangelical marriage ethic. What is surprising, however, is the unusual set of circumstances which led up to his marriage, and the suddenness with which he finally decided to "take God's gift on the wing."[41]

Luther's correspondence took an unexpected turn toward the distaff side in April of 1523. In a personal note to Wenzel Link, he declared very matter-of-factly, "Today I took in nine nuns from the convent at Nimbschen, among whom there are two von Zeschaus and a Staupitz."[42] On the next day, April 10, he wrote a fuller explanation to his friend, George Spalatin, in which he included a request for some public funds to help in the temporary support of his uninvited but welcome guests.

Nine apostate nuns, a wretched group, have been brought to me by honest citizens of Torgau (that is, by Leonard Koppe and his nephew and Wolf Dommitzsch) and there is no reason to suspect hostile action. I feel very sorry for them, but most of all for the many others who are perishing everywhere in their cursed and impure celibacy. This sex, which is so very weak by itself and which is joined by nature, or rather by God, to the other sex, perishes when it is so cruelly separated. O tyrants![43]

His plans for their welfare were simple and practical. "First I shall inform their relatives and ask them to take in the girls. If they are unwilling, then I shall have the girls provided for elsewhere. Some families have already promised to take them. For others I shall get husbands if I can."[44] Then, with characteristic lack of proportion, Luther goes on in this letter to discuss the possible hiring of a worthy but unemployed minor public official named Sebastian von Kötteritzsch. If Luther is sexually excited about the arrival of this ill-fated "harem" of his, he certainly does a fine job of hiding it! Actually, of course, his

[40] *WA*, TR 3, 883.
[41] *WA*, Br 3, 886.
[42] *SJ* 2, 179.
[43] *Ta* 172.
[44] *Ibid.*

main concern is obviously financial: "I pray that you also do a charitable work and beg some money for me from your rich courtiers in order that I might support the girls for a week or two until it is convenient for me to turn them over to their kinsmen or to those who have promised to provide for them."[45]

Of special interest is "the miraculous way" in which these nuns escaped from their cloister in the name of their Christian freedom. Luther was beginning to feel that the time was growing ripe for the many social reforms which he believed necessary in the clericalized society of his day. The purified Word of God had been proclaimed now for over six years and its social fruits were long since in seed. Luther himself was already wearing civilian dress at home although he did not yet see fit to go into the chancel without his monastic cowl until October of 1524. Socially conservative as he was, Luther believed that the enforced celibacy of monks and nuns within Roman Catholic cloisters was one of the first major social evils which had to be remedied.

The Cistercian convent "Marienthron" at Nimbschen in Saxony was destined to provide the setting for Luther's initial direct intervention. He had long been advising monks and nuns to abandon their vows of celibacy on theological grounds, but never before had he become personally involved in their actual liberation. The near-by town of Grimma had already become an Evangelical center and Luther's teachings were beginning to reach the nuns in the convent. Some were influenced enough to desire to leave the cloistered walls but found that friends and relatives were too afraid or were unwilling to help them. Besides the social stigma involved, such actions could be punished by death according to medieval canon and civil law.

Appealing at last directly (but secretly) to the Reformer himself, a dozen like-minded nuns soon found Luther's love of neighbor at their command. He arranged at once for some stalwart citizens of Torgau to effect their escape. The respected

[45] *Ta* 173.

fifty-nine-year-old merchant and *Ratsherr*, Leonard Koppe, was chosen as leader because, as the commercial supplier of the convent's fish and beer, he had free access to the convent grounds. On the night of April 4, 1523, taking advantage of the special arrangements being made by the busy sisters for their Easter celebration, the hidden party rode off quietly in the merchant's wagon and made their escape to freedom. Three of the twelve fugitives returned at once to their homesteads. The remaining nine, fearing to go back to homes in Duke George's Catholic territory, were brought by Koppe directly to Luther for his counsel and help.

One of Luther's first acts after their arrival was to issue a public letter in which the "godly action" and its justification were openly and unashamedly proclaimed. Entitled *That Maidens May Honorably Leave Their Cloisters* (1523), Luther's tract makes clear at the outset that it was the will of Almighty God, and not the whim of public opinion, which inspired the freeing of the nuns. It is to be expected that the Evangelical cause will now suffer all the more scorn and derision. This has always been true of Christ and his cross-bearing disciples. Men under bondage to the law cannot bear to see others live under the freedom of the gospel. Yet, rightly understood, the theft at the convent is a fitting celebration of the liberating victory of Christ on Easter morn.

Here you will probably say: That was certainly done secretly and involved betrayal and payment. Undoubtedly the whole cloister at Nimbschen is enraged at Luther, now that they know that he was the robber. I answer: Truly a blessed robbery, just as Christ was also a robber when his death stole from the princes of this world their armor and fortress and he cast them all into prison. We have also liberated these poor souls from the human tyranny under which they suffered. Properly and significantly, it has taken place at Easter when we celebrate Christ's capture of his own captors.[46]

Luther goes on to cite three reasons why he has chosen to make

[46] *WA* 11, 394.

14

this a matter of public knowledge.[47] First, "Our actions have been undertaken in the Lord and we are not afraid of the light of day." Second, "We wish to preserve the honor and reputation of these poor children and their kin." Third, "We wish to provide an example for pious rulers and people so that they will also help other nuns to be released without fear of conscience or consequence." Recognizing full well that centuries of folk superstition and church tradition were against him, Luther placed all his confidence in the emancipating power of the Word of God. He was certain that his words and deeds in witness to the Word would not return unblessed: "In time, things will be a lot better."

Proclaiming that this daring action has been taken "for the honor of God and the service of our neighbors," Luther proceeds to spell out more fully its theological justification. He explains first how he intervened on the nuns' behalf "out of duty in Christian love to save their souls and their consciences," only after their own friends and relatives had left them helpless and forsaken.[48] In the second place, he considers it pastorally wrong to expect any young women to maintain their chastity without the guidance and aid of God's Word. The continual struggle for sexual continence is not one in which one can engage unarmed, and yet this is precisely what Rome demands of its nuns. "For it is well known that in most cloisters—and especially in the nuns' convents—the Word of God is no longer read and studied daily, and in some of them it has disappeared altogether. They are now concerned primarily with the laws and works of man."[49]

In the third place, Luther reiterates his constant insistence that there can be no enforced and unwilling divine service. That there is "scarcely one in a thousand" nuns who is joyful and loving in her daily tasks shows that the Holy Spirit is not operative in the convents with the multitude of his gifts. "Since God only accepts service which is voluntary and joyful, it follows that no

[47] *Ibid.*, 395f.
[48] *Ibid.*, 396.
[49] *Ibid.*, 397.

vows should be kept or taken any longer. The Holy Spirit is certainly not at work where there is no love or joy and such works are neither recognized nor accepted by God."[50]

Finally, celibacy is declared to be so rare a gift of God that it should never be made obligatory and institutionalized as it now is in the convents. Basing his argument on the familiar passage in Genesis, Luther cannot conceive of a valid vow which purposely flaunts God's own blessed ordinance of marriage.

It is impossible that the gift of celibacy is as common as the cloisters are. For a woman's body is not created to remain virgin but to bear children (Gen. 1:28). God spoke to Eve as well as to Adam when he said, "Be fruitful and multiply." This is clearly witnessed to by the way in which God has created the woman's body. And this command is not given only to the first wife but to all women everywhere. And should there be any exceptions to this rule, they should come not from our human vows and free will, but from the exercise of God's own divine will and command. Normally, however, a woman should obey God's will that she marry and have a family full of children.[51]

In the face of God's Word, the Roman Catholic arguments that religious vows are inviolable and that such vows are in keeping with long-standing tradition and custom in the church are quickly dismissed. The ordinance of God, the testimony of Christ, and the Ten Commandments are incontestable biblical bulwarks for the divine institution of marriage against the human institution of celibacy. Young girls, therefore, should be permitted to decide in free conscience whether they should become or remain nuns. Church and society should acknowledge their Christian freedom in such matters and force them neither to enter nor to leave. The nine (named) nuns who have just chosen to leave should be respected and held in honor by all for their courageous decision.[52]

Having settled the formality of a public declaration to their satisfaction, Luther and his friends set about making the less

[50] *Ibid.*
[51] *Ibid.*, 398.
[52] *Ibid.*, 400.

dramatic but far more necessary arrangements for the care and safekeeping of the fugitive nuns. One by one, the nine nuns were settled in local homes, six of them to await eventual marriage and the establishing of homes and families of their own. Destined to become the most famous of them was the twenty-four-year-old woman of noble birth who was sent to the home of the ex-mayor of Wittenberg, Master Philip Reichenbach. Her name—before she exchanged it for Mrs. Martin Luther—was Katherine von Bora.

Born in the town of Lippendorf in January, 1499, Katie was sent off to the convent at Nimbschen at the age of ten with the full consent of her father and new stepmother.[53] The young girl was educated in the convent school until she was fifteen. At that time she began her novitiate year, and on October 8, 1515, she was consecrated as a full-fledged nun (*virgo religiosa*) at the tender age of sixteen.

Very little is known of Katie's life during the nine years she was a nun. There is certainly no evidence to suggest that she shared any of the brutal experiences which the apostate nun Florentina von Oberweimar suffered under the fanatical mother-superior Katherine von Watzdorf at the cloister "Neuenhelfta." Luther helped to circulate her tragic story for the benefit of the naive and inexperienced.[54] On the contrary, the abbess of Nimbschen, Margaret von Haubitz, is described as "an honorable, pious and understanding woman," and, even as late as 1540, Katie could still recall with admiration the intensity of the prayer life which she and her fellow sisters enjoyed within the convent walls. The basic fact remains, however, that Katie voluntarily assumed the risk of breaking her vow and escaping from the convent. To take so bold and drastic a step, her inner turmoil must have been very great indeed.

While in Wittenberg, Katie must have been an apt and

---

[53] Biographical details on Luther's wife in the following pages are taken from Ernst Kroker, *Katherina von Bora* (Leipzig: Haberland, 1906).
[54] *WA* 15, 86-94.

diligent pupil of Frau Reichenbach's domestic arts if her later performance as mistress and overseer of the Luther household is any indication. She seems to have lived a happy life with the Reichenbachs, slowly mollifying the curious combination of convent shyness and aristocratic haughtiness which gave her the aloof air that even her closest friends often found difficult to penetrate. One young man who was quite successful in this feat, however, was a law student of the Nürnberg nobility named Jerome Baumgärtner.

Although her contemporaries did not find Katie a particularly attractive person, Jerome fell in love with her on a visit to Wittenberg in late 1523 and promised to return to marry her. They were never formally engaged, however, and apparently Jerome's parents saw to it that his relationship would never reach that stage with an apostate nun. Whatever the reasons, Jerome never returned to Wittenberg; eventually he married fourteen-year-old Sybilla Dichtl and became a leading figure in Nürnberg social and political affairs.

Katie was so heartbroken over the whole affair that she became ill. Feeling a moral obligation to look after the welfare of those nuns who had left their sheltered existence on the basis of his teachings, Luther took it upon himself to write to Baumgärtner in October, 1524, to determine the young patrician's intentions toward Katie. "If you want your Katie von Bora, you had best act quickly, before she is given to someone else who wants her. She has not yet conquered her love for you. I would gladly see you married to each other."[55]

Jerome never responded to this letter and Luther and his friends began to stump for the "someone else" mentioned here; namely, Dr. Kasper Glatz, onetime rector of Wittenberg University. Katie, however, considered Glatz an impossible choice, and freely said so to Luther's friend, Dr. Nicholas Amsdorf, in order that he might persuade the Reformer that such a match would be extremely unhappy for her. When Amsdorf suggested

[55] *SJ* 2, 258.

that she was being unreasonable about her marriage, Katie hinted broadly that it would be quite a different matter if, for instance, Amsdorf were to speak up for himself—or even for Dr. Martin Luther! It is hard to say whether Katie was at her outspoken best here, or whether these two names suggested themselves to her because of their unlikelihood. Far beyond the customary age for marriage in the Middle Ages, Amsdorf and Luther were both over forty when the twenty-six-year-old Katie made her shocking "proposal."

Luther seems honestly to have entertained no serious thoughts of marriage up to this time. During his first years out of the monastery he could not theologically justify the marriage of monks, even though he saw no objection to the marriage of priests (cf. ch. 6). In the middle of 1521, for example, when Karlstadt and his party were insisting that it was the duty of monks as well as priests to marry, Luther exclaimed, "Good God, will our Wittenbergers give wives even to the monks? But they will never thrust a wife on me!"[56]

Even after Luther arrived at evangelical clarity on the permission of monks to marry if they wished, the course of events in the Reformation made his own marriage a very remote possibility. "Because I daily expect the death decreed to a heretic," Luther felt that he could not conscientiously take on the responsibilities of a home and family life in his precarious situation.[57] This conviction remained set in his mind even after the totally unexpected arrival of the fugitive nuns of Nimbschen. Rumors to the contrary notwithstanding, Luther wrote to Spalatin less than five months before Katie's conversation with Amsdorf that although a theoretical possibility for his marriage always existed —"for I am neither wood nor stone"—it was certainly not very likely.[58]

There is a decided change of tone in Luther's letters to Spalatin half a year later, however, after his trusted friend had once

[56] *Ibid.,* 51.
[57] *Ibid.,* 264.
[58] *Ibid.*

again renewed his counsel that the Reformer should marry. In the meantime, Katie had made her own hesitant advance and, much to Luther's surprise, his pleased father considered it an excellent opportunity to acquire a grandson. He, too, urged his son to marry.[59] Luther's correspondence with Spalatin at this time indicates that he is at least half-seriously toying with the idea of marriage, although he still refers jokingly to his apparent inability to maintain the affections of even a "harem of nuns."

You write about marrying. You ought not to wonder that I, who am such a famous lover, do not take a wife. It is more wonderful that I, who write so often about matrimony, and thus have so much to do with women [*sic misceor feminis*],[60] have not long since become a woman, to say nothing of marrying one.

But if you wish me to set you an example, you already have one, and a great one. For I had three wives at the same time, and loved them so bravely that I lost two of them, who are about to accept other wooers. The third I am only holding with the left arm, and she, too, perhaps, will soon be snatched away from me. But you are such a laggard in love that you do not venture to become the husband of even one woman. But look out, or I, who have no thought at all of marriage, may sometime get ahead of you prospective bridegrooms. It is God's way to bring to pass the things you do not hope for.[61]

By May, 1525, events began to take another turn, this time for the worse. The Peasants' Revolt was spreading from the south to the north of Germany, becoming more radical as it gained momentum. While fully in sympathy with their demands for social justice,[62] Luther was enraged that the peasants should attempt to make of their cause a Christian revolution.[63] Never could he permit his theology to be improperly employed to confuse the two kingdoms of redemption and creation, the

---

[59] *WA*, Br 3, 890.
[60] The playful tone of this letter and what we know of its writer's character make it necessary to translate these ambiguous words as Smith and Jacobs have done.
[61] *SJ* 2, 305-306.
[62] *WA* 18, 293ff.
[63] *Ibid.*, 299ff.

righteousness of Christ and civil righteousness, the way of the cross and the way of the sword (cf. ch. 4). Luther saw the devil himself at work behind the ravaging and pillages of the party of the *Bundschuh*. Once again deep melancholy descended upon his spirit: surely his end was near, perhaps even the end of the world. In this radical apocalyptic mood, Luther's thoughts returned to Katie. Would not their marriage be a fitting testimony to his faith in a God who would still bring the devil to his knees?

If I ever get home I shall meet my death with God's aid, and await my new masters, the murderers and robbers who tell me that they will harm no one . . . Before I would yield and say what they want, I would lose my head a hundred times, God granting me his grace. If I can do it before I die, I will yet take my Katie to wife to spite the devil, when I hear that they are after me.[64]

A short ten days before his own marriage—apparently still unplanned—Luther was writing to others encouraging them to take the leap. In a letter to John Rühel accompanying his tract on *Why Archbishop Albrecht Should Marry* (1525), Luther anticipates one of the archbishop's counterarguments by citing his own readiness to marry if "my own personal example" would be a helpful influence for the conscience of weaker brothers. Although "I have always feared up to now that I was not fitted for it," Luther discloses that "I have it in mind when commanded by God to marry sometime before I die, even though it will not be much more than an engaged 'Joseph's marriage.' "[65]

Just before his wedding day Luther wrote another letter to Spalatin in which marriage is praised so highly and loudly—from folk proverbs, historical examples, and biblical citations—that we cannot help wondering whether Luther is not trying to persuade himself as much as his bachelor friend. Moreover there is a strong sense of urgency in Luther's rejection of long engagements. "Do not be put off till tomorrow! By delay Hannibal lost Rome. By delay Esau forfeited his birthright. Christ said,

---

[64] *SJ* 2, 310.
[65] *WA*, Br 3, 883.

'Ye shall seek me, and ye shall not find.' Thus Scripture, experience and all creation testify that the gifts of God must be taken on the wing."[66] Luther later recalled that he was not above taking his own advice if he could thereby foil the devil from preventing God's will.

> I advise that the marriage be proclaimed publicly in the church and physically consummated as soon as possible after the engagement. For it is very dangerous to put off the marriage too long since Satan loves to erect obstacles and cause trouble through evil tongues, slanders, and the friends of both parties. This is just what happened at the marriages of Master Philip [Melanchthon] and at Eisleben. For this reason we should help the partners get together with no delay. If I had not married quietly with the knowledge of only a few friends, people would certainly have prevented it.[67]

Providing both the devil and their friends with little opportunity for interference, Martin and Katie were married quickly and quietly on June 13, 1525. The ceremony took place in the evening at the Black Cloister in the company of a small group of close and trusted friends which included Bugenhagen, Apel, Jonas, and the Cranachs.[68] Actually, the officially notarized engagement was arranged and attested to just prior to the wedding service in order to have both ceremonies concluded on the same day. This procedure was perfectly legal in Saxony and quite understandable in light of the unusual circumstances. Luther was confident that "I did the right thing in completing everything in one evening."[69] A long engagement period was hardly to be recommended for an orphaned ex-nun and a condemned ex-monk.

Modern marriage counselors probably would have questioned the marriage itself. It was an open secret in Wittenberg that Martin and Katie did not get along very well because of their clashing temperaments and personalities. Certainly they were not romantically in love, and there is no evidence that any kind of

[66] *Ibid.*, 886.
[67] *WA*, TR 2, 1657.
[68] *SJ* 2, 322.
[69] *WA*, TR 4, 4886.

courtship preceded their marriage. Katie could not have been breathlessly in love with Martin if she could tell one of his best friends that she would also accept him as a substitute for the lover who had jilted her. Martin likewise confessed to his friends afterward that of all the fugitive nuns, he personally found Eva von Schönfeld the most attractive while the proud and haughty Katie alienated him. "I never loved Katie then for I suspected her of being proud (as she is), but God willed me to take pity on the poor abandoned girl."[70] Luther's attitude may not have been uncommon in an age in which romantic love was not considered a prerequisite for marriage. We have no reason at all to doubt Luther's contention that he married primarily as a testimony of faith.

The report is true that I suddenly married Katherine to silence the mouths which are accustomed to bicker at me. I hope to live a short while yet, to gratify my father who asked me to marry and leave him descendants. Moreover, I would confirm what I have taught by my example, for many are still afraid in the present great light of the gospel. God has willed and caused my act, for I neither love my wife nor burn for her but esteem her highly.[71]

Pigtails on the Pillow

Once the leap of faith had been taken, Luther characteristically countered the expected public shock and scorn with two of his strongest weapons: a hearty laugh and a good beer! A joyous public celebration was planned for June 27 to which a large circle of relatives, friends, and acquaintances were invited. His invitations are enlivened with high spirits. In one he writes, "It is my intention to have a little celebration and housewarming to which I beg that you will come and give your blessings. . . . Bring any friends!"[72] And to another:

God has suddenly and unexpectedly caught me in the bond of holy matrimony. I intend to celebrate the day with a wedding breakfast on Tuesday. That my parents and all good friends may be merry, my

[70] *WA*, TR 4, 4786.
[71] *WA*, Br 3, 900.
[72] *SJ* 2, 323.

Lord Katherine and I kindly beg you to send us, at my cost and as quickly as possible, a barrel of the best Torgau beer. . . . I also beg you and your wife not to stay away but happily to appear.[73]

The big day finally arrived and Luther proudly led his bride in the public procession through the streets of Wittenberg. A service in the church, a banquet in the cloister, and a dance in the social room of the town hall rounded out the day's joyful activities. The singing and the laughter of the local celebration were no sooner over, however, than the first public reactions began to reverberate across the land. From old enemies, of course, Luther expected the worst and he was not too surprised when it came. In fact, his marriage was intended to make them "even more foolish and furious,"[74] and he told Spalatin that ". . . it pleases me to have my marriage condemned by those who are ignorant of God."[75]

John Eck, Jerome Emser, and Duke George of Saxony all hurried to get in their barbs by mixing righteous indignation with sneering innuendo. Even that stalwart "Defender of the Faith," Henry VIII of England, felt compelled (and qualified!) to chide Luther on his immoral behavior. Erasmus of Rotterdam looked with condescension upon the "fallen monk" and helped to spread the vicious rumor that Martin was forced to marry Katie because of a child which she allegedly bore him some two weeks after the wedding ceremony. Though he gallantly issued a formal repudiation of the slander some three months afterward (March 13, 1526), the public harm to the Luthers' reputation had already been done.[76]

Probably not even Luther, however, expected that the cruelty would reach the depths to which Lemnius, von der Heyden, and Hasenberg were capable of sinking. Luther's action had undoubtedly lanced a festering sore to the quick and the poison came gushing forth.

[73] *Ibid.*, 328.
[74] *WA*, Br 3, 890.
[75] *Ibid.*, 892.
[76] Cf. Desiderii Erasmi, *Opera Omnia* (Leyden: Vander, 1703-06), III, 900, 913.

How long, most insane and libidinous of apostates, will you abuse the patience, lenity, the tender forgiveness of the most learned men and the most illustrious of princes of Germany, of our most august emperor, of the most holy vicar of Christ—in short of God, most good and great? . . . Luther, leave that seat of pestilence, Wittenberg! You have truly sinned heavily in much, most of all in this, that, as an apostate Monk, almost as lustful as Priapus, you daily and nightly wanton and chamber with a nun, more libidinous, as it were, than Venus, like the horse and mule which have no understanding . . . Obstinate and defiant wretch, abandoned to your own desires, proceed from bad to worse. Fall into the pit of impiety, be snared in the springs of sin, be captured by the net of eternal damnation; be merry until you descend into hell, as you surely will, where, infernal brand! you will burn forever, and be eaten alive by the never-dying worm.[77]

Yet what must have hurt Luther even more than the attacks of his enemies was the disappointment of his friends. Many of them were sorry, first of all, that he had seen fit to marry the unpopular Katie. "All my best friends cried, 'Anyone else but this one!' "[78] Still more distressing was the fact that others questioned the wisdom of Luther's marrying anyone "because of what the world would think." Jerome Schurff reflected the unspoken sentiments of many of the Wittenberg elders when he lamented, "If this monk marries, the whole world will join the devil in laughing at him and immediately bring to naught all that he has accomplished."[79]

Perhaps most distressed and faithless of all was Luther's meek and often priggish co-worker, Philip Melanchthon. Luther loved Philip as a brother and yet was always annoyed by his irenic gentleness which sometimes bordered on compromising weakness when it came to a showdown. When Melanchthon began to vacillate while representing the Lutheran cause at the Diet of Augsburg (1530), for example, Luther chided him harshly "for the greatness of your unbelief."[80] Throughout the Reforma-

[77] *SJ* 2, 452.
[78] *WA*, TR 2, 1657.
[79] Quoted in Heinrich Boehmer, *"Luthers Ehe,"* in *Jahrbuch der Luther-Gesellschaft,* VII (1925), p. 65.
[80] *Ta* 146.

tion struggle, Melanchthon's timidity and qualms over incon-
sequential and often imagined sins compelled Luther to give
him the same hearty advice that he had received from Staupitz
when in the throes of his own *Anfechtungen*. In 1521 he had
written to Philip:

If you are a preacher of grace, then preach a true, not a pretended
grace; and if grace is true you must bear a true, not a pretended, sin.
God does not save pretended sinners. Be a sinner and sin bravely;
but believe more bravely, and rejoice in Christ, who is the victor
over sin, death, and the world. We must sin so long as we are
what we are. This life is not a dwelling-place of righteousness, but
we look, says St. Peter, for new heavens and a new earth in which
righteousness truly dwells . . . Pray mightily, for you are a mighty
sinner.[81]

Perhaps it is understandable, then, why fearful Philip, among
all of Luther's friends, should view the Reformer's marriage
with the most misgivings. Ironically enough, it was Luther who
earlier had helped to prod his shy colleague into his own marriage. Luther had even brought his own parents and sisters with
him to celebrate at Philip's wedding. Melanchthon, however, was
not present at Luther's wedding and was deeply shocked when
he heard about it. Perhaps he was not taken into Luther's confidence because of the growing tension between the two men
over the Reformer's attacks on Philip's fellow humanist, Erasmus. More likely, Luther probably guessed that Philip would
balk and he chose this way to spare him any more qualms of
conscience.

In either case, personal indignation and petty fears strongly
overshadow the remains of an evangelical marriage ethic in a
strange letter of very mixed and upset emotions which Philip
sent (in Greek) to his friend Camerarius a few days after the
wedding service. We quote a particularly unflattering passage
as a quiet reminder of the heroic greatness—and bitter loneli-
ness—which is often demanded of a reformer who feels constrained to make a public testimony to his faith.

[81] *SJ* 2, 50.

You might be amazed that at this unfortunate time, when good and excellent men everywhere are in distress, [Luther] not only does not sympathize with them, but, as it seems, rather waxes wanton and diminishes his reputation, just when Germany has special need of his judgment and authority. . . . These things have occurred, I think, somewhat in this way: The man is certainly pliable, and the nuns have used their arts against him most successfully. Thus probably society with the nuns has softened or even inflamed this noble and high-spirited man. In this way he seems to have fallen into this untimely change of life. The rumor, however, that he had previously dishonored her is manifestly a lie. Now that the deed is done, we must not take it too hard, or reproach him; for I think indeed, that he was compelled by nature to marry. The mode of life, too, while indeed humble, is, nevertheless, holy and more pleasing to God than celibacy . . . Besides this, I have unmistakable evidence of his godliness, so that for me to condemn him is impossible.[82]

Ten days later, fortunately, Melanchthon swallowed his pride and was present along with the rest of Luther's happy but somewhat bewildered and frightened guests at the public wedding festivities. As the month and years passed quickly by, many of these friends were probably pleased (and surprised) at how happy the Luther household turned out to be. Katie soon showed herself to be an efficient, thrifty, and industrious *Hausfrau,* complementing very well her husband's goodhearted but wholly impractical weaknesses when it came to *Gulden* and *Pfennige.* If "Lord Katie" was Martin's favorite nickname for his continually active and energetic wife, it was both by way of gentle teasing and genuine admiration.

The Luther home was richly blessed with three boys and three girls during the first nine years of their married life. The oldest son, Hans, was born in June, 1526, and the youngest daughter, Margaret, entered the family in December, 1534. In addition there was always a host of guests being lodged and fed in the large quarters of the Black Cloister which became the Luthers' permanent home after it had been vacated by the other converted monks. Orphans and widows, relatives and transients,

[82] *SJ* 2, 325.

the sick and the needy, all joined the regular table full of joking and debating theologians, as grateful recipients of the particularly *gemütlich* brand of Luther hospitality. (Luther's old enemy, Karlstadt, was even given refuge during the very first week of their marriage!) Since her home was often transformed into a hospice in good times and a hospital in times of plague, Katie seemed both willing and able to meet the domestic emergencies which an unpredictable age (and husband!) suddenly and continually forced upon her.

It did not take the happy and grateful bridegroom long to realize that God was smiling on their home, for Katie was one of the best things that ever happened to Martin. Certainly she met him more than halfway in their marriage. He knew how difficult it was for people like Katie to try to make him into a fixed star when by nature, he was more like "an irregular planet."[83] Yet the more orderly life which he now experienced was of inestimable benefit to the broken health which had remained with him as a continual reminder of less happy days in the monastery. Katie's tidy housekeeping and loving care undoubtedly added years to Luther's life, for these were simple luxuries which he had not enjoyed for years. "Before I married, the bed was not made up for a whole year and became foul with sweat. But I worked all day and was so tired at night that I fell into bed without knowing that anything was amiss."[84]

Luther began to mellow much more in his later years and although he never set aside the fourth commandment as the divine foundation for his parental authority,[85] he certainly governed his offspring in a far gentler and more humane spirit than anything he had ever known in his own childhood. His genuine love for children is expressed in scores of personal letters and *Table Talk* references. His famous letter to Hans, then four years old, on the wonderful garden for good children (". . . with rosy apples, pears, cherries, and fine ponies with golden bridles

[83] *WA*, TR 5, 5378.
[84] *Sm* 168.
[85] *WA*, TR 5, 6102.

and silver saddles") is only one of many such poignant testimonies of his deep paternal love.[86] It was a very proud father, for instance, who wrote in 1527, "My little Hans sends greetings. He is in the teething months and is beginning to say 'Daddy,' and scold everybody with pleasant little insults. Katie also wishes you everything good, especially to teach you what she declares her little Hans has taught her, namely, the fruit and joy of marriage, of which the pope and all his world was not worthy."[87]

After the day's labors were over, Luther would often gather his family around him to tell stories, play melodies on his lute, and teach them little songs, games, and prayers. It was also around the family hearth that Luther patiently taught his children the fundamentals of the Christian faith out of the *Small Catechism* which he prepared specifically for the religious nurture of the common folk. Evangelical interpretations of the Ten Commandments, Creed, Lord's Prayer, sacraments, and table of duties were given "as the head of the family should teach them in a simple way to his household."[88] For the worship of his little ones, Luther composed the tender Christmas hymn, "From Heaven Above," whose verses include:

> To you this night is born a child
> Of Mary, chosen mother mild;
> This little child, of lowly birth,
> Shall be the joy of all the earth.

> Ah, dearest Jesus, Holy Child,
> Make thee a bed, soft undefiled,
> Within my heart, that it may be
> A quiet chamber kept for thee.

Sadness was mixed with joys in the Luther household, and Martin tasted of the bitter as well as the sweet. No more painful crisis did he and Katie have to face than the untimely death

[86] *WA*, Br 5, 1595.
[87] *SJ* 2, 391.
[88] *WA* 30[I], 243.

of their beloved little Magdalene at the age of thirteen. The intensity of faith and love displayed by this devoted father and child at her deathbed made a deep and lasting impression upon the close friends of the family who shared this hour of grief. When his daughter was very ill [Luther] said: "I love her dearly, but if it be thy will, dear God, to take her, I shall be glad to know that she is with thee." Later, when she was lying in bed, he said to his daughter, "Magdalene, my little daughter, you would gladly remain here with me, your father. Are you also glad to go to your Father who is in heaven?" And the sick girl replied, "Yes, dear father, as God will." The father then cried, "My dear daughter!" ... When his daughter was in the agony of death, he fell upon his knees before the bed and, weeping bitterly, prayed that God might save her if it be his will. Thus she gave up the ghost in the arms of her father. Her mother was in the same room but was farther from the bed on account of her grief.[89]

Probably more than any other single factor, sharing experiences such as this helped to draw Martin and Katie together into a strong and durable bond of mutual fidelity and love. At first it took a lot of patience and understanding for Luther to adjust to such cloister novelties as pigtails on his pillow and female chatter in his ears.

Man has strange thoughts the first year of marriage. While sitting at the table, he suddenly thinks: "Before you were alone, now you are two." Or, in bed, when he awakens, he sees a pair of pigtails lying next to him that he never saw before. In this first year also my Katie used to sit down next to me while I was studying and, not knowing what to say, would begin to ask questions like: "Dear doctor, is the prime minister of Prussia the duke's brother?"[90]

In time, however, as experience was gained, the two became a loving couple deeply attached and devoted to each other. A happy blend of humor and tenderness seems to have permeated their relationship. Martin was especially adept at correcting Katie's shortcomings with a well-timed joke. Idle talk was countered with the suggestion that one should normally pray a little before "preaching a sermon."[91] Criticism of Luther's exces-

[89] *Ta* 50-51.
[90] *WA*, TR 2, 1656. Of interest is the fact that Katie apparently always addressed Luther by his title as a sign of respect.
[91] *Sm* 180.

sive generosity was met simply with the observation that God freely sends men a hundred thousand *Gulden* worth of produce every time he sends down a rain.[92] Constant demands for more orderliness in the house were parried by the "complaint" (in word-play) that he was bound in chains (*Kethen*) upon a death-bed (*auf der Bore*).[93]

Katie's strait-laced propriety was once especially challenged by Luther's playful observation that men seemed gifted naturally for polygamy. As is the eventual fate of most husbands' humor, Katie felt that Martin had reached the point where he was no longer very funny!

Luther: We shall yet see the day when a man will take several wives.
Katie: The devil thinks so.
Luther: The reason, dear Katie, is that a woman can have only one child a year, whereas a man can beget several.
Katie: Paul says, "Let each man have his own wife."
Luther: Aye, his own wife, but not only one; that is not in Paul.
Thus the doctor joked a long time until Katie said: Before I would stand for that I would go back to the convent and leave you and all your children![94]

From his first wedding anniversary onward, Luther's letters and writings have nothing but high praise and loving affection for his "Lord Katie." To Spalatin he wrote in 1526, "I thank you in the Lord for the hearty congratulations which you have sent me. I am a happy husband and may God continue to send me happiness, for from that most gracious woman, my best of wives, I have received, by the blessings of God, a little son, Hans Luther, and by God's wonderful grace, I have become a father."[95] He wrote to Stifel in the same year, "My Katie is in all things so obliging and pleasing to me that I would not exchange my poverty for all the riches of Croesus."[96] He also boasts to his table colleagues in 1531:

[92] *WA*, TR 5, 6238.
[93] *WA*, Br 3, 906.
[94] *Sm* 179-180.
[95] *SJ* 2, 373f.
[96] *WA*, Br 4, 1032.

I would not trade my Katie for France or Venice for three reasons: first, because God gave her to me as a gift and also gave me to her; second, because I often come across other women with far more shortcomings than Katie, and although she has a few weaknesses of her own, they are far outnumbered by her virtues; and third, because faith serves marriage best through its fidelity and honor.[97]

Perhaps only a pastor's wife could appreciate it as a high compliment when her husband calls Paul's Epistle to the Galatians "my Katherine von Bora."[98] But certainly every wife's eyes would sparkle if her husband made her the following declaration of love: "The greatest gift of grace a man can have is a pious, God-fearing, home-loving wife, whom he can trust with all his goods, body, and life itself, as well as having her as the mother of his children. . . . Katie, you have a good man who loves you. Thank God, and let someone else be empress!"[99]

Toward the end of his days, the thought of separation from his beloved wife and children became Luther's saddest fear. Even the most dispassionate reader must marvel at the growth in Luther's feelings of tenderness and love toward the woman whom he married because of pity and theological conviction.

Oh how passionately I yearned for my family as I lay at death's door in Smalkald. I thought that I would never see my wife and little children again. How much pain that distance and separation caused me! I believe that dying people must know the greatest natural love and affection of all, as when a man remembers his wife and a parent thinks of his children. Since, by God's grace, I have recovered, I now love my dear wife and children all the more. No one is so spiritual that he does not feel this natural love and affection; it provides great strength to the bond of fellowship which exists between a man and his wife.[100]

Conclusion

In his last will and testament, Martin left all of his earthly possessions to his "beloved and faithful wife, Katherine," in grati-

[97] *WA,* TR 1, 49.
[98] *Ibid.,* 146.
[99] *WA,* TR 2, 2350a-b.
[100] *WA,* TR 4, 4786.

tude to God for all that their life together had meant to him. The leap of faith which they had taken turned out to be a glorious blessing for them, as it has been since for centuries of other Protestant pastors and their wives, who have followed in their footsteps. Luther knew that the victory of Christ's cross is shared only by those who are also willing to taste of its shame. As he wrote three days after his wedding, "I have made myself so cheap and despised by this marriage that I expect that the angels laugh and the devils weep over it. . . . The world and its wise men have not yet seen how pious and sacred marriage really is."[101]

At the close of his life, however, Luther also knew the deep satisfaction of having inaugurated a social revolution which was rooted firmly in the religious reformation whose personal leadership had been his holy calling from God.

When I was a boy, the wicked and impure practice of celibacy had made marriage so disreputable that I believed that I could not even think about the life of married people without sinning. Everybody was fully persuaded that anyone who intended to lead a holy life acceptable to God could not get married but had to live as a celibate and take the vow of celibacy. Thus many who had been husbands became either monks or priests after their wives had died. Therefore it was a work necessary and useful for the church when men saw to it that through the Word of God marriage again came to be respected and that it received the praises it deserved. As a result, by the grace of God now everyone declares that it is something good and holy to live with one's wife in harmony and peace.[102]

The chapters which follow will be devoted to a careful analysis of those theological and ethical teachings which Luther hoped to confirm by his own personal example.

[101] *SJ* 2, 324.
[102] *LW* 1, 135.

CHAPTER TWO

The Righteousness of God

After the Reformation race had been run—and won—Luther confessed that he often felt as if he had been ridden by God "like a horse with blinkers on."[1] He seldom looked sideways in his single-minded obedience to God's Word. Consequently, he was genuinely surprised when his religious fidelity was rewarded by God with a host of unsought and unexpected domestic gifts. Looking back over two hectic decades, Luther once marveled:

God knows that I never expected to go as far as I did. I thought only of attacking indulgences. Had anyone at Worms told me that in six years I would marry, and then sit at home and father three sons, I would never have believed him.[2]

Just as surprised was Luther at the unforeseen cost of his discipleship. In attacking the indulgence practices of the Roman Catholic church, he was like an operating surgeon who finds himself cutting away far more than he had ever anticipated, to remove a cancerous growth down to its very roots. The struggle over indulgences forced Luther to re-examine the whole Catholic sacramental system of divinely infused grace, which was claimed to empower men to perform meritorious "good works" and "satisfactions" in order to gain salvation (cf. chs. 2, 3).

With the two-edged scalpel of God's Word, Luther carefully followed this religious *moralism* as it worked its way out in two interrelated ethical movements. The first was an arrogant *clericalism* which subjugated civil to ecclesiastical authority at

[1] *WA*, TR 1, 406.
[2] *WA*, TR 2, 1654.

34

the expense of a sound and healthy social order based upon order, justice, and freedom (cf. chs. 4-5). The second was a divisive *monasticism* grounded upon a double-standard morality which depreciated the common life of Christian laymen in order to glorify the uncommon sacrifices of celibate clergymen (cf. chs. 6-7). As will be demonstrated below, all three of these developments within the Roman church had devastating effects upon a truly evangelical marriage ethic. Since their theological destruction was incumbent upon the Reformer, Luther fought against Rome's moralism, clericalism, and monasticism at virtually the same time. For the sake of theological clarity, however, we shall analyze each struggle successively, beginning with the unspectacular origins of the first in the Wittenberg controversies over papal indulgences.

Cheap Grace

The Reformation began with a public testimony of faith. On October 31, 1517, Luther openly challenged all those of the university world in Wittenberg to dispute with him some ninety-five theses on theological issues pertaining to the indulgence-selling campaigns then current. He posted his Latin theses at the customary place for such academic affairs—the door of the Church of All Saints—under the full title: *A Disputation on the Power and Efficacy of Indulgences.* When the time for the proposed debate arrived, however, not a single opponent appeared. Yet a decade later, Luther wrote his stirring hymn, "A Mighty Fortress," in humble gratitude for what God had wrought in the turbulent days and years which followed this inauspicious and disappointing beginning.

It was the spiritual distrust (*Unglaube*) undergirding the sale and purchase of papal indulgences which provoked the sensitive monk to attack. As one of the theological professors at Wittenberg University, Luther was well aware of the religious customs and teachings upon which the sale of papal indulgences was based.[3] For centuries, Christians who had fallen into sin were restored to church fellowship by confessing, professing penitence, and performing certain penitential acts to demonstrate their good faith, such as prayer, fasting, and almsgiving. Once these so-called "satisfactions" had been rendered properly, church and sacramental fellowship was re-effected.

From the sixth century onward, however, particularly in lands governed by Germanic tribal law, the church began to allow 1) paid servants to perform penances by proxy on behalf of their masters, and 2) financial penalties to be substituted for the penitential acts of the believer. This trend culminated in the eleventh and twelfth centuries when the popes encouraged these practices *en masse* in order to stimulate the recruiting of men and funds for the Crusades against the Turks. One could receive either a partial or general ("plenary") remission of the owed satisfaction, an "indulgence," according to the length of military service or the amount of financial support contributed to the papal campaigns.

So popular was the sale of these "Crusade Indulgences" for both buyer (religiously) and seller (financially) that the practice was rechanneled into "Jubilee Indulgences" once the Crusades were over. In designated special years, from 1300 onward, the faithful were granted indulgences for pilgrimages, adoration of relics, worship at certain shrines, sacrifices to celebrated saints, and other religious activities—or their financial equivalents. Moreover, since the decree of Pope Sixtus IV in 1477, the intercessory power of the papacy was extended over purgatory as well as earth, so that indulgences could also be purchased on behalf of deceased loved ones to help effect their release. The Jubilee Indulgence of 1510, for example, was placed on sale in central Germany in 1515 as a plenary indulgence for the benefit of all who would assist in the financial costs involved in Pope

[3] See the historical sketches in Julius Köstlin, *The Theology of Luther,* tr. Charles Hay (Philadelphia: Lutheran Publication Society, 1897), I, 215ff., and in Roland Bainton's *Here I Stand* (New York: Abingdon-Cokesbury, 1950), pp. 71-85.

Leo X's erection of the basilica of St. Peter in Rome. It was the commercial tactics of John Tetzel, the subcommissioner of the indulgence-sales campaign in the Archbishoprics of Magdeburg and Mainz, which precipitated Luther's initial protest.

In the light of these practices, what role did indulgences play in the sixteenth-century theology of the sacrament of penance? In theory, penance was divided into the three acts of confession, contrition, and satisfaction. After the believer had orally confessed all his remembered sins, and professed a truly contrite heart, he was absolved by his confessor of the eternal guilt of his sins. If he was incapable of genuine "contrition" (repentant thirst for forgiveness), he could substitute a mere "attrition" (fear of hell or purgatory) and the sacrament itself would make up the difference. Since the absolution was based upon the imputed merits of Christ as conferred upon the church in the "power of the keys," the doors of hell were closed for this man. Nevertheless, while the eternal guilt for his sins was thereby removed, the gates of heaven were not yet open for him until he had performed the necessary satisfactions to remove the temporal penalties for his sins. In short, Christ's sacrifice saved man only from hell; his own sacrifices were further needed to release him from purgatory.

At this crucial point, indulgences were introduced into the penitential system. While they had no power to remit the eternal guilt of sin (i.e., to replace absolution), indulgences were considered efficacious in limiting or eliminating the temporal penalties (up to millions of years) which would otherwise have to be worked out in purgatory. Hence, while Rome never claimed that a man could "buy his way into heaven," it did encourage men to purchase indulgences to pay their way out of purgatory. In actual practice, then, an unrepentant man with only the fear of purgatory in his heart and the price of an indulgence in his pocket could satisfy the church's demands and be "sure of his salvation" by the mutually profitable "gift of a bishop."[4]

[4] *Sm* 42.

Against this peddling of "cheap grace," Luther's *Ninety-five Theses* proclaim a clear and unequivocal "No!" What is most significant about them for us is that in a groping and yet confident fashion, Luther's theses laid the foundation for a thoroughly evangelical view of Christian piety. He drives right to the religious center by attacking indulgences for discouraging the proper love of God and neighbor. Both religion and ethics are impoverished, cries Luther, when the church of Rome encourages men to buy what is free (the grace of God) at the expense of paying what is owed (the good works of men).

Reserving comment until later on the theses dealing with the relation of the penitent to Christ and his vicar in Rome, we will cull out and combine those which are centrally involved in Luther's contention that indulgences destroy the believer's proper relationship with God and with his neighbors. Then we shall analyze them briefly on the basis of Luther's own theological explanations in the work written a few months afterward entitled *Resolutions or Explanations and Proof of the Theses on the Power of Indulgences* (1518).

When our Lord and Master Jesus Christ said, "Repent" (Matt. 4:17), he willed the entire life of his believers to be one of repentance (1). The pope cannot remit any guilt, except by declaring and showing that it has been remitted by God; or, to be sure, by remitting guilt in cases reserved to his judgment (6). Those who believe that they can be certain of their salvation because they have indulgence letters will be eternally damned, together with their teachers (32). They preach un-Christian doctrine who teach that contrition is not necessary on the part of those who intend to buy souls out of purgatory or to buy confessional privileges (35). Any truly repentant Christian has a right to full remission of penalty and guilt, even without indulgence letters (36). It is very difficult, even for the most learned theologians, at one and the same time to commend to the people the bounty of indulgences and the need of true contrition (39). Christians are to be taught that papal indulgences are useful only if they do not put their trust in them, but very harmful if they lose their fear of God because of them (49). The true treasure of the church is the most holy gospel of the glory and grace of God (62).[5]

[5] *LW* 31, 25ff.

In his preface to the theological *Explanations,* Luther centers his thinking on the all-important first thesis: the Christian's whole life should be one of repentance.[6] He recalls how ". . . no word in all the Bible seemed more bitter to me than 'penitence,' although I zealously simulated it before God and tried to express an assumed or forced love." John von Staupitz, dean of Wittenberg's theological faculty, helped Luther to recover its true meaning: "Penitence is not genuine save when it begins from the love of righteousness and of God, and this by which [The Romans] consider the end and consummation of repentance is rather its commencement."[7]

All hinged on the translation and interpretation of the biblical demand for *metanoia* which means both "penance" and "repentance." Roman theology, depending upon the Vulgate translation of *poenitentiam agite,* stressed the former meaning and enjoined men to "do penance." Staupitz prodded Luther to go behind the faulty Latin interpretation into the original Greek to see that "nothing is more characteristically Pauline" than to translate the expression rather as "repent ye." Paul is not telling men what to do but what to be. Genuine *metanoia* involves the whole man in repentant contrition. Yet it is just this "fundamental change of mind and affection" which Luther believed the sale of indulgences to be discouraging. "They have left us nothing [of contrition] but formal penances and elaborate confession. . . . The doctrine of true repentance was neglected, and only the cheapest part of it, that called penance, was magnified."[8]

Luther's religious concern is immediately evident. While the church certainly represents God on earth, it must always resist the temptation to replace him. God alone remits the guilt of sinful men. Luther reminds the church that the pope and his priests may speak only in God's name. This is not to diminish the "power of the keys" which has been granted to the church.

[6] *SJ* 1, 91f.
[7] *Ibid.*
[8] *WA* 1, 522.

"But it is questionable whether a man is also reconciled to God as soon as he is reconciled to the church. The text certainly says that all things loosed in the church are also loosed in heaven, but it does not seem to follow that therefore absolutely all things are loosed in heaven, but merely those things which are loosed in the church."[9]

The indulgence system is evil in Luther's eyes because it will not let God be the gracious, forgiving Father he is. It is not based upon the love of God but the fear of men. It is high time, says Luther, that we ". . . regard that fabrication and worthless sophistry of the indulgence sellers as an effort to frighten us in the same manner as men desire to frighten little children by the use of masks."[10] If God had really wanted all of these sacrificial "satisfactions" and "indulgences," why did he not say so in Holy Scripture? Are we not doing violence to Scripture's witness of a loving and forgiving Father who is more willing to give than we are to receive, when we incorporate his freely proffered grace into such a cold and calculated commercial transaction? "I do not know whether or not those who speak in such a manner want to make God a usurer or dealer, one who remits nothing to us gratis but who expects us to make a satisfaction as payment for the remission."[11]

Luther insists that a biblical view of the grace of God compels us to confess, ". . . it is not intercession but the favorable hearing of the intercession and the acceptance of it that frees, since souls are set free not by the prayers of the church but by the work of God."[12] God is sovereign and free to act as he will. To try to bribe or cajole his loving action is blasphemy. Hence, "They preach only human doctrines who say that as soon as the money clinks into the money chest, the soul flies out of purgatory."[13] For God's Word is clear: "We have no other hope

[9] *LW* 31, 98.
[10] *Ibid.*, 116.
[11] *Ibid.*, 117.
[12] *Ibid.*, 175.
[13] *Ibid.*

of salvation except in Jesus Christ alone, 'nor is there any other name given under heaven, by which we must be saved.' "[14]

Inseparable from man's religious distrust of God's grace is his ethical disregard of his neighbor's needs. Wrong beliefs cause wrong behavior. Consequently, another important group of Luther's *Ninety-five Theses* is concerned with the disastrous ethical results of the indulgence sales.

A Christian who is truly contrite seeks and loves to pay penalties for his sins; the bounty of indulgences, however, relaxes penalties and causes men to hate them—at least it furnishes occasion for hating them (40). Papal indulgences must be preached with caution, lest people erroneously think that they are preferable to other good works of love (41). Christians are to be taught that the pope does not intend that the buying of indulgences should in any way be compared with the works of mercy (42). Christians are to be taught that he who gives to the poor or lends to the needy does a better deed than he who buys indulgences (43). Because love grows by works of love, man thereby becomes better. Man does not, however, become better by means of indulgences but is merely freed from penalties (44). Christians are to be taught that he who sees a needy man and passes him by, yet gives his money for indulgences, does not buy papal indulgences but God's wrath (45). Christians are to be taught that, unless they have more than they need, they must reserve enough for their family needs and by no means squander it on indulgences (46). Christians are to be taught that the buying of indulgences is a matter of free choice, not commanded (47).[15]

Here Luther moves his argument a significant step forward. Indulgences are not only religiously invalid (regarding sin's guilt); they are also ethically unsound (regarding sin's penalty). Having been freed from sin's eternal guilt by God's gracious forgiveness in absolution, Christians need not fear its temporal punishments and try to avoid them by indulgence purchases. For these punishments are God-pleasing in that they both discipline the believer and serve the neighbor. The substitution of indulgences for acts of mercy works at the cost of both self-improve-

[14] *Ibid.,* 180.
[15] *Ibid.,* 29ff.

ment and neighbor-service. In Luther's view, ". . . canonical penances are imposed only upon those who are sluggards and do not wish to do better or to test the sincerity of their contrition. . . . But the gospel teaches us not to escape the punishment or to relax them but to seek and love them, for it teaches the spirit of freedom and the fear of God to the point of showing contempt for all punishments."[16]

Luther is especially angered by the many clerical peddlers who have taken financial advantage of the poverty-stricken peasants. Feeding on their fear of purgatory, these "ordained parasites" have forced men to purchase indulgences when they were not even able to provide adequately for their own families' needs. Rome is reminded of Paul's warning that a man has "disowned his faith" if he does not provide properly for his family (I Tim. 5:8). "But there are many who have neither bread nor proper clothing and yet, led astray by the din and noise of the preachers of indulgences, rob themselves and bring about their own poverty in order to increase the wealth of the indulgence sellers."[17]

Certainly, ". . . if the pope knew the exactions of the indulgence preachers, he would rather that the basilica of St. Peter were burned to ashes than built up with the skins, flesh, and bones of his sheep."[18] Illustrations are cited where simple folk have been known to sell their clothing or to go out begging in order to procure the necessary indulgence price, often over the protests of their less superstitious and more needy mates. "Therefore I feel that such teaching deserves to be cursed and is contrary to the commands of God. For a wife should live under the authority of her husband and do nothing contrary to his will, even if it were meritorious to do so. Even less should she go begging for indulgences she probably does not need."[19] Already at this early date, Luther grounds man's ethical responsibilities on the firm foundation of the concrete commands of God, however earthy,

[16] *Ibid.*, 197.
[17] *Ibid.*, 204.
[18] *Ibid.*, 206.
[19] *Ibid.*, 207.

ordinary, and unspectacular they might appear to the world. Here, through God's providence, needy neighbors are actually served in realistic social action.

The religious idolatry and ethical irresponsibility inherent in indulgences are also criticized throughout Luther's *Treatise on Indulgences and Grace* (1518). The work is composed of a series of twenty theses at the heart of which the relation of indulgences to grace is presented as a clear "either-or." "My will, my prayer, my advice is that no one buy indulgences any more but leave them for the lazy and sleepy Christians. . . . For [an indulgence] is neither meritorious nor a work of obedience but, on the contrary, a temptation to throw off due obedience. . . . Whether the poor souls can be released from purgatory by means of indulgences I do not know, but I do not believe it."[20]

In his Leipzig debate with John Eck in 1519, Luther confidently went even further and declared indulgences to be a "pious fraud" which belong "to the things which are permitted but not necessary." When his position was condemned by Rome in the papal bull *Exsurge Domine,* Luther let loose with both sarcastic barrels in his *Defense and Explanation of all the Articles Unjustly Condemned* (1521).

But now the holy father pope orders me to recant, and condemns this article. I will be obedient and say, "I confess my error; this article is not true." And this is the reason: The indulgences are not a pious fraud, but an infernal, diabolical, anti-Christian fraud, larceny, and robbery, whereby the Roman Nimrod [Gen. 10:9] and teacher of sin peddles sin and hell to the whole world and sucks and entices away everybody's money as the price of this unspeakable harm. If this recantation is not enough, I will improve on it some other time.[21]

Luther's religious insistence upon the primacy of the grace of God has immediate and far-reaching social-ethical consequences. Illustrated here is the central paradox of Christian discipleship: "Whoever would save his life will lose it, and who-

[20] *WA* 1, 246.
[21] *LW* 32, 64.

ever loses his life for my sake will find it" (Matt. 16:25). If, with the self-love of the piety of Rome, we substitute attrition for contrition and indulgences for good works, we both commercialize our religion and paralyze our ethics. "Away then with all those prophets who say to the people of Christ, 'Peace, peace,' and there is no peace!" (92).[22]

But if, with the self-denial of the piety of Luther, we truly repent of our sin, committing its guilt to God's grace and directing its punishment toward meeting neighbors' needs, God is praised, our neighbors served, and our salvation assured. "Blessed be all those prophets who say to the people of Christ, 'Cross, cross,' and there is no cross!" (93).[23] It is only when "the entire life of believers is one of repentance" (1), that "we may be confident of entering into heaven" (95). The inner unity of Luther's *Ninety-five Theses* attests to the religious-ethical unity of men's life together under God.

In God's Favor

Had Luther's initial protests against Rome been merely ethical or political, social conditions might have been corrected quietly here and there without much further ado. But Luther's concern was essentially religious. He went beyond Tetzel's misuse of indulgences to the indulgences' misuse of God's grace. In so doing, Luther unwittingly called the whole Roman sacramental system into question, for indulgences had become an integral part of the sacrament of penance, which, in turn, was one of the seven "supernatural sails" by which the Roman "ark of salvation" carried its passengers through the sea of life into eternity.

It follows, therefore, by inner necessity, that Luther was forced to divert more and more of his attention from indulgences in particular to sacramental grace in general. At all the chief stations in life, the Roman church was present to infuse the divine power needed for their successful fulfillment: baptism, confirmation,

[22] *LW* 31, 251.
[23] *Ibid.*

the Holy Eucharist, penance, ordination, matrimony, and extreme unction. Since medieval piety was so dependent upon this ecclesiastical "pipeline" of grace, everything which Luther challenged here was bound to have drastic repercussions upon the common life of his people.

God's grace . . . Christ's presence . . . man's faith: in embryonic form, the distinctive elements of Luther's theology of the sacraments emerged early. The *Treatise on the Sacrament of Penance* (1519) clearly points out the widening breach between the sacramental views of Luther and Rome. Properly understood, says Luther, a sacrament offers the total forgiveness of both sin's punishment and its guilt. Despite the fact that the former is "far less important," it has become the center of Rome's teaching and piety. Yet all the indulgences, satisfactions, and merits in the world can gain no more than outer reconciliation with the temporal church. Of infinitely greater importance for salvation is man's inner reconciliation with God himself. To cover the guilt of man's sin, only divine forgiveness or a "heavenly indulgence" can help. "Forgiveness takes away the fear and timidity in a man's heart toward God, making his conscience light and happy, and reconciling him with God. This is what is properly called the forgiveness of sin, whereby man is no longer pained and disquieted by his sin but rather knows with a joyful certainty that it is forgiven by God."[24]

Luther lists the three elements he considers imperative for a sacrament. The first is absolution based upon the divine promise of the power of the keys. The second is grace understood as ". . . forgiveness of sin, the peace and comfort of a good conscience. Therefore it is called a sacrament, a holy sign, in which one outwardly hears words which promise inward spiritual gifts that comfort and pacify the heart."[25] In naming the third constitutive element, Luther confidently ignites the evangelical "dynamite" (*dunamis*) which had long been smouldering within his liberated soul.

[24] *WA* 2, 714.
[25] *Ibid.*, 715.

The third is faith which firmly holds the absolution and the words of the priest to be true in the power of the promise of Christ. It is faith which sees to it that the sacrament works what it is supposed to and which believes that everything which the priest says is true. For as you believe, so it will happen to you. Without such faith, all absolutions and sacraments are worthless, indeed, they do more harm than good. Consequently, there is a saying among the teachers, "It is not the sacrament but the faith that accepts the sacrament, which takes away the sin."[26]

Two consequences are drawn from this position which are of great importance for Luther's view of Christian piety. He maintains, first, that man must ground his faith solely in the gracious promise of God fulfilled in Jesus Christ. In regard to salvation, neither contrition nor works of satisfaction have any trustworthy efficacy whatsoever. "Your contrition and works may deceive you, and the devil will take advantage of them at your death and in times of temptation. But Christ, your God, does not lie to you, and the devil cannot destroy his Word. Therefore, if with a strong faith you build your life upon his Word, you stand upon a rock against which the gates and all the power of hell cannot prevail."[27]

Luther then goes on to say immediately, however, that this repudiation of good works refers *only* to their justifying value before God (*coram Deo*), when man tries vainly to earn the forgiveness of sins. "We cannot deal with God otherwise than through faith in the Word of promise. He does not desire works nor has he need of them."[28] "Good works" are evil—idolatrously evil—if they are performed as a substitute for God's grace; good works are good—faithfully good—if they are performed as the fruits of God's grace. As in the case of Paul himself, Luther's religious ethic of grace was destined to be misunderstood, misrepresented, and misapplied both by activists and quietists throughout the length of his theological career. Yet Luther's greatness in the history of Christian ethics lies in his stubborn

[26] *Ibid.*
[27] *Ibid.*, 716.
[28] *PE* 2, 201.

46

refusal to compromise precisely at this crucial and decisive point.
So that no one will blame me that I forbid good works, I declare
that man should experience earnest contrition and suffering, and
that he should make confession and perform good works. Yet I
must also maintain that the faith of the sacraments is the highest
good and the means by which man receives the grace of God. Thereafter he engages in doing good solely for the glory of God and the
service of his neighbors. Man should not do good in order to trust
in his own works as payment for his sin. For just as God freely
offers his grace to us, we also should serve him freely in return.[29]

In the name of this law-free gospel, Luther attacks "the whole
sea of Roman laws and impossible questions of casuistry" more
sharply than ever before in his *Discussion of Confession* (1520).
Once again, Luther's pastoral concern comes to the fore in the
very first sentence. "In our age, the consciences of almost all
have been led astray by human doctrines into a false trust in
their own righteousness and their own works, and knowledge
about faith and trust in God has almost ceased."[30] Roman sacramental practices are defeating God's purpose. "For the sacrament
of confession was instituted for the quieting, not for the disturb-
ing, of the conscience."[31]

True peace of spirit can never come from trust in our own
confession and satisfactions as we foolishly try to list sins one
by one, and then match each individual transgression with an
appropriate payment of penalty. "God is no merchant!" We
must get behind the individual sins to man the sinful one, and
behind the piecemeal absolutions to God the gracious One.
Luther transcends the moral level and views sin and grace solely
in the light of the fractured religious relationship between man
and God. Man does not simply commit sins; he is a sinner. God
does not merely dispense grace; he is gracious. In a sacrament,
therefore, we do not earn or receive something; we are graciously
received by someone—"God himself."[32]

[29] *WA* 2, 719.
[30] *PE* 1, 81.
[31] *Ibid.*, 92.
[32] *Ibid.*, 83.

I advise, therefore, as John Gerson used to advise, that a man shall now and then go to the altar or to the sacrament "with a scruple of conscience," that is, without confession, even if he has been immoderate in drinking, talking, or sleeping, or has done something else that is wrong, or has not prayed a single one of the Hours. Would you know why this advice is given? Listen! It is in order that a man may learn to trust more in the mercy of God than in his own confession or in his own diligence. For enough cannot be done toward shaking that accursed trust in our own works.[33]

Luther's views on the personal graciousness of God as conveyed by the sacraments of the church reach an early culmination in his vastly influential work entitled *The Babylonian Captivity of the Church* (1520). Culling together all of the growing protests and constructive emphases which we have been tracing, Luther lashes out with the devastating forthrightness of a man who realizes that he has reached the point of no return. Rumors of heresy charges and excommunication have already reached his ears. Therefore, ". . . challenged and attacked, nay, forcibly thrust into the arena, I shall freely speak my mind. Let all the papists laugh or weep together."[34]

It is at the decisive point of sacramental regeneration that the divergence between Luther and Rome on the grace of God comes to the fore.[35] Broadly speaking, classical Roman Catholic theology viewed grace essentially as a supernatural quality or power which God infuses into the souls of men *(habitus infusus)* in order to create a new ethical nature within them capable of doing the good *(gratia creata)*. While God is acknowledged as the "principal cause" of the gift of grace, the sacraments of the church are stressed as the chosen media which contain and convey grace to the recipients. Moreover, these sacraments are effectual simply through their objective administration *(ex opere operato)*, as long as there is no obstacle of mortal sin in the recipient. Their efficacy is in no wise dependent upon the recipient's faith but

[33] *Ibid.*, 95.
[34] *PE* 2, 178.
[35] Cf. Reinhold Seeberg, *Text-Book of the History of Doctrines,* tr. Charles Hay (Grand Rapids: Baker Book House, 1952), Vol. II, ch. 2.

is derived solely from the authority of the indelibly ordained administrator. By Luther's day, this doctrine of infused grace (*gratia infusa*) had become further refined within the Roman sacramental system in order to meet all of the late medieval refinements of sin. As baptism removes original sin, penance destroys mortal sins, and the Eucharist eradicates venial sins.

Against this mechanical and impersonal view, Luther maintains that we must get behind the church-manipulated gifts to the merciful graciousness of the Giver. As he was soon to write, "I accept grace here properly as meaning the favor of God [*favor Dei*], not a quality of the soul as our most recent writers have taught."[36] Properly speaking, then, we must understand by divine grace the personal and loving graciousness of man's sin-forgiving Father: "the Giver of every good and perfect gift." We thereby ground the certainty of our salvation outside ourselves when we distinguish the Giver from his gifts, for the Giver ever remains outside us even while his gifts are at work within us. Hence, what saves man is not what he does—even with divinely infused power—but what God graciously promises to those who faithfully trust in him as the one true God.

Therefore, let us open our eyes and learn to give more heed to the word than to the sign, and to faith than to the work, or the use of the sign, remembering that wherever there is a divine promise there faith is required, and that these two are so necessary to each other that neither can be efficacious apart from the other. For it is not possible to believe unless there be a promise, and the promise is not established unless it be believed. But where these two meet, they give a real and most certain efficacy to the sacraments. Hence, to seek the efficacy of the sacrament apart from the promise and apart from faith, is to labor in vain and to find damnation.[37]

On the strength of this evangelical interpretation of the necessity of man's faithful appropriation of God's grace in terms of merciful favor, Luther proceeds to evaluate the validity of Rome's elaborate sacramental system. Measuring each of the seven Roman sacraments in turn against their biblical require-

[36] *WA* 8, 106.
[37] *PE* 2, 229.

ments, Luther dramatically concludes that only baptism and the Lord's Supper may properly be considered redemptive means of grace ". . . for only in these two do we find both the divinely instituted sign and the promise of forgiveness of sins."[38] It will be of paramount importance for our study that Luther considers marriage to be among the least defensible of the church's sacraments and dismisses it at once from this select category (cf. ch. 6).

Papal Imperialism

Luther did not immediately recognize the inescapable conclusion, that in destroying the theological basis of the indulgence trade and the sacramental system he was also tearing away the foundations from under the feet of the ecclesiastical hierarchy which claimed control over the church's "pipeline" of grace. Yet he rapidly became aware of the basic contradiction between the Roman emphasis on human merit which earns the gifts of the pope as over against the biblical emphasis on the grace of God which freely offers men the gift of salvation for the sake of Christ alone.

Less than a year after the posting of the *Theses,* Luther wrote a personal letter to a close friend in which he entertained for the first time the shocking thought that perhaps the papacy itself was the Antichrist, so evil were its ways.[39] By early 1520, after learning that the Donation of Constantine was a forgery, Luther exclaimed, "I am in such a passion that I hardly doubt that the pope is the Antichrist which the world at large expects, so closely do their lives, acts, sayings, and laws agree."[40] And but a few months later in *The Babylonian Captivity,* he publicly challenged the legitimacy of the papacy on the strength of his repudiation of ordination as a valid sacrament of the church.[41]

In tracing the wellsprings of Luther's protest against the

---

[38] *Ibid.,* 291.
[39] *WA,* Br 121.
[40] *SJ* 1, 291.
[41] *PE* 2, 284.

religious pretentions of the papacy, we must turn first to still another section of the *Ninety-five Theses* to see why Pope Leo X was led to tremble despite the sincere note of subservience in Brother Martin's accompanying letter.[42] The central thrust against the papacy's religious imperialism is contained in the following theses:

The pope neither desires nor is able to remit any penalties except those imposed by his own authority or that of the canons (5). The treasures of the church, out of which the pope distributes indulgences, are not sufficiently discussed or known among the people of Christ (56). That indulgences are not temporal treasures is certainly clear, for many indulgence sellers do not distribute them freely but only gather them (57). Nor are they the merits of Christ and the saints, for, even without the pope, the latter always work grace for the inner man, and the cross, death, and hell for the outer man (58). Without want of consideration we say that the keys of the church, given by the merits of Christ, are that treasure (60). The true treasure of the church is the most holy gospel of the glory and grace of God (62). To say that the cross, emblazoned with the papal coat of arms, and set up by the indulgence preachers, is equal in worth to the cross of Christ is blasphemy (79).[43]

An inevitable consequence of Luther's stress on the free and unearned grace of God is his attack on the church's highly popular "treasury of merits." Luther feels that he has no alternative, since the whole biblical witness to the unique person and work of Christ is seriously weakened by the Roman claim to a kind of reserve fund of accumulated saintly merits. "They say that the saints during this life have contributed many more good works than were required for salvation, that is, works of supererogation, which have not yet been rewarded, but have been deposited in the treasury of the church, by means of which, through indulgences, some fitting compensation takes place."[44]

Luther then addresses himself to these alleged surplus merits of the saints. "No saint has adequately fulfilled God's commandments in this life. Consequently the saints have done absolutely

[42] *PE* 1, 44ff.
[43] *LW* 31, 26ff.
[44] *Ibid.*, 212.

nothing which is superabundant. Therefore they have left nothing to be allocated through indulgences."[45] Here we get the converse of Luther's earlier position: sin-forgiving merit, like sin itself, cannot be treated atomistically. One is first a sinner before he commits sins. Likewise, one must first fulfill the law (in spirit) before one can perform its works (in action). But to fulfill the law of love to God and neighbor is precisely what sinful man is unable and unwilling to do. "Every saint is obligated to love God as much as he can, indeed more than he can, but no one has done or can do that."[46] Since even the best of our good works are sin-tainted and in need of forgiveness, our Lord enjoins all men —saints included—to confess that they are "unworthy servants" who are saved by God's grace alone (Luke 17:10).

If there are no works of supererogation available for the church's disposal, what of the atoning merit of Christ? To maintain the magnanimous character of God's grace, says Luther, a crucial distinction must be made between the "treasury of the church" and the "treasury of indulgences." The two are far from equal since the former is a gift of God and the latter an invention of men. "I argue that this is not the treasury of indulgences; but that it is the treasury of the church only a heretic would deny. For Christ is the Ransom and Redeemer of the world, and thereby most truly and solely the only treasury of the church."[47]

Rome's teaching at this point results in a ". . . wicked deception of the faithful. Such an error arises when we seek to be justified through our own works and righteousness rather than through faith."[48] The basic idolatry of Rome is that it sells to some what is free for all. It encourages men to perform faithless good works instead of accepting God's free gift of grace. It has men busy doing things for God because ultimately it doubts that salvation is possible solely on the basis of accepting what God has done for man in Christ. "What could be more detestable

[45] *Ibid.*, 213.
[46] *Ibid.*
[47] *Ibid.*, 216.
[48] *Ibid.*, 220.

than such a doubt? . . . For if I could obtain one single work, just one-millionth part of the smallest work of Christ, I would be sure of eternal salvation."[49]

Luther has arrived here at the heart of the gospel message that man's salvation depends not upon his own works, but upon "the works of Christ which have been granted to me."[50] It is not because of, but despite, my own righteousness that I am saved when I put my trust solely in the "alien" righteousness of Christ. It is because of Christ, and Christ alone, that God declares me absolved of all my sin. To teach otherwise is to teach heresy, maintains Luther, even if it is done by such illustrious theologians as Thomas, Bonaventura, Alexander of Hales, and all their disciples. Scripture does not support them, for Aristotle has long since replaced Paul as their chief mentor. When authorities conflict, "it is only right to give preference to the truth first, and then to the authority of the pope and the church."[51] There remains but one alternative for the church if it would remain true to its Lord: a Christ-centered "theology of the cross" must replace a pope-centered "theology of glory."

From this you can now see how, ever since the scholastic theology —the deceiving theology (for that is the meaning of the word in Greek)—began, the theology of the cross has been abrogated, and everything has been completely turned upside-down. A theologian of the cross (that is, one who speaks of the crucified and hidden God) teaches that punishments, crosses, and death are the most precious treasures of all and the most sacred relics which the Lord of this theology himself has consecrated and blessed, not alone by the touch of his most holy flesh but also by the embrace of his exceedingly holy and divine will.[52]

A theologian of glory does not recognize, along with the Apostle, the crucified and hidden God alone [I Cor. 2:2]. He sees and speaks of God's glorious manifestation among the heathen, how his invisible nature can be known from the things which are visible [Cf. Rom. 1:20] and how he is present and powerful in all things

[49] *Ibid.*, 221.
[50] *Ibid.*
[51] *Ibid.*, 222.
[52] *Ibid.*, 225.

everywhere. This theologian of glory, however, learns from Aristotle that the object of the will is the good and the good is worthy to be loved, while the evil, on the other hand, is worthy of hate. He learns that God is the highest good and exceedingly lovable. Disagreeing with the theologian of the cross, he defines the treasury of Christ as the removing and remitting of punishments, things which are most evil and worthy of hate. In opposition to this, the theologian of the cross defines the treasury of Christ as impositions and obligations of punishments, things which are best and most worthy of love. Yet the theologian of glory still receives money for his treasury, while the theologian of the cross, on the other hand, offers the merits of Christ freely. Yet people do not consider the theologian of the cross worthy of consideration, but finally even persecute him.[53]

Set over against each other here in stark and vivid contrast are two opposing ways of salvation. On the one hand, we have the suffering love of Christ, the cross, and the inwardness of faith. On the other hand, the ecclesiastical power of the pope, human glory, and the externality of works. Between the two there can be no compromise: "We preach Christ crucified, a stumbling-block to Jews and folly to Gentiles" (I Cor. 1:22). Consequently, Luther concludes with the bold assertion that "the church needs a reformation," but one that only God can effect in his own good time. "Only God who has created time knows the time for this reformation. In the meantime we cannot deny such manifest wrongs. The power of the keys is abused and enslaved to greed and ambition."[54]

Two years elapsed before Luther was prodded into writing his most important doctrinal treatise in this area entitled *The Papacy at Rome* (1520). Taking the opportunity "to explain something of the nature of Christendom [*Christenheit*] for the laity," Luther states the central point of controversy as he sees it. "This then is the question: whether the papacy at Rome, possessing the actual power over all Christendom (as they say), is of divine or human origin."[55] Luther, of course, contends that

[53] *Ibid.*, 227.
[54] *Ibid.*, 250.
[55] *PE* 1, 340.

the power of the pope is human *(de iure humano)* rather than divine *(de iure divino),* and that Christians are to be recognized everywhere by their fidelity to Christ rather than to the pope of Rome.

Unwilling to distinguish between external and temporal realities, Rome's "theology of glory" exalts the latter at the expense of the former. This Luther will not permit. The church is essentially "the body of Christ," an eternal, spiritual, eschatological community of grace which is "in but not of" the world. "This community or assembly consists of all those who live in true faith, hope, and love; so that the essence, life, and nature of the church is not a bodily assembly but an assembly of hearts in one faith, as St. Paul says, 'One baptism, one faith, one Lord.'"[56] Christ himself witnessed to the spiritual nature of the church by telling his disciples that his kingdom is not of this world (John 18:36), and that, therefore, it cannot be localized here or there but is rather alive within the hearts of the faithful (Luke 17: 20-21). Yet is this not precisely what Rome is trying to deny by claiming that the "new Jerusalem" is bound to Rome under a human authority invested with divine right?[57]

On the other hand, if the church is essentially a spiritual community, it follows that ". . . the true church may not and cannot have a head upon earth, and that no one on earth, neither bishop nor pope can rule over it; only Christ in heaven is the head, and he rules alone."[58] This is Luther's primary concern: "The head must give life to the body, and therefore it is clear that on earth there is no other head of the spiritual Christendom but Christ alone."[59] Organizational structure and good order are important and necessary, but they are clearly secondary and dare not obstruct what is of the very essence of the church.

The external marks, whereby one can perceive where this church is on earth, are baptism, the sacrament, and the gospel; and not Rome,

[56] *Ibid.,* 349.
[57] *Ibid.,* 352.
[58] *Ibid.,* 357.
[59] *Ibid.*

or this place, or that. For where baptism and the gospel are, no one may doubt that there are saints, even if it were only the babes in their cradles. But neither Rome nor the papal power is a mark of the church, for that power cannot make Christians, as baptism and the gospel do; and therefore it does not belong to the true church; and is but a human ordinance.[60]

Having quickly overcome the "first two arguments of folly and human reason," Luther turns to Rome's final argument from the Bible. Here they ". . . throw many passages together helter-skelter, whether they fit or not. If this is to be the way, then I can easily prove from the Scriptures that beer is better than wine."[61] The biblical justification for the institution of the papacy ran as follows: "The Old Testament was a type of the New Testament, and because it had a bodily high priest, the New Testament must likewise have one—how else shall this type be fulfilled? For has not Christ himself said, 'Not one jot or tittle of the law shall pass away; it shall all be fulfilled'?"[62]

Luther's primary objection to this Roman interpretation is that it rests upon faulty exegesis. He offers his alternative: "The type is material and external, and the fulfillment of the type is spiritual and internal. What the type reveals to the bodily eye, its fulfillment must reveal to the eye of faith alone, or it is not really a fulfillment.[63] Not only must the fulfillment be spiritual, says Luther, but it must also be attested to in Scripture itself which always clearly ". . . brings the type and the spiritual fulfillment together; otherwise everyone could make of it what he desired."[64] Some biblical examples which meet both requirements are then cited: that the serpent lifted up by Moses signifies Christ is taught by John 3:14; that Adam was a kind of Christ is learned from Romans 5:15; that the rock in the wilderness signifies Christ is from I Corinthians 10:4. But, cries Luther, Rome will not allow any of this because a "theology of glory"

[60] *Ibid.*, 361.
[61] *Ibid.*
[62] *Ibid.*, 363.
[63] *Ibid.*
[64] *Ibid.*, 365.

always prefers temporal fulfillment (by sight) to spiritual fulfillment (by faith).

For Luther, the classical example of this faulty use of Scripture to justify the religious pretensions of the papacy is Rome's interpretation of Matthew 16:18 where the keys of the kingdom are given to Peter. Luther contends that the "rock" *(petra)* on which the church shall be built signifies not the weak and human Peter, but the confessed ". . . Christ and the faith in him, against which no power can ever prevail."[65] As to whether Christ gave the keys to Peter personally, or on behalf of the Christian community, Luther finds scriptural authority for only the latter view.

From these words they have claimed the keys for St. Peter alone; but the same Matthew has barred such erroneous interpretation in the eighteenth chapter (18:18), where Christ says to all in common, "Verily I say unto you, whatsoever ye shall bind on earth shall be bound in heaven, and whatsoever ye shall loose on earth shall be loosed in heaven." It is clear that Christ here interprets his own words, and in the eighteenth chapter explains the sixteenth; namely, that the keys are given to St. Peter in the stead of the whole church, and not for his own person.[66]

But what if the pope insists that the worldly abuses continue uncorrected in the church? "If the pope came to that—which may God forbid!—I would say right out that he is the real Antichrist, of whom all Scriptures speak." Consequently, when word came that a papal bull of condemnation was on its way to him, Luther quickly issued a last-minute warning to Rome entitled *Against the Cursed Bull of the Antichrist* (1520). It declared that any disavowal of the gospel of Christ is satanic, even if it emanates from the so-called vicar of Christ himself. Writing ". . . in virtue of the power which I, like all Christians, have received through baptism . . . and in the name of him whom you persecute," Luther stormed:

Unless you repent and leave off your satanic blasphemies, and that right quickly, know that I, with all who worship Christ, consider the See of Rome to be occupied by Satan and to be the throne of the

[65] *Ibid.,* 380.
[66] *Ibid.,* 373.

Antichrist, and that I will no longer obey nor remain united to him, the chief and deadly enemy of Christ.[67]

Theology of the Cross

It is to Luther's faith in the power of God's Word that we must next turn if we are to appreciate the passionate depths of his protest against the Roman Antichrist who would replace the true Christ, the Son of the living God. For as the struggles over the sacraments served to sharpen Luther's understanding of the nature of God's grace, the abuses of the papacy finally forced him to reject the pope-centered "theology of glory" in Scholasticism for the Christ-centered "theology of the cross" in the Bible.

Luther's conception of the person and work of Christ during this formative period of his thinking may be derived from a detailed analysis of two of his early tracts dedicated to the central biblical theme of righteousness. The first was published late in 1518 under the title *Three Kinds of Righteousness*. Luther's purpose in this work is to distinguish three basic kinds of sin against which he matches three basic kinds of righteousness.

The first level depicts the evil and goodness of natural man.[68] On the one hand, we commit sins according to the external standards of civil law. Today we would call them crimes. Corresponding to these civil crimes is a civil righteousness (*iustitia civilis*) which is motivated by a fear of punishment or hope of reward. Although vitally necessary for the proper ordering of society and the social justice of the community, it is a sub-Christian "righteousness of Jews and Gentiles" based upon the reason and common sense residing (however corrupted) in all of God's human creatures despite their fall into sin (cf. ch. 4).

The second level describes the sinful nature of man as matched by the sinless nature of Christ. This represents the religious dimension of man's existence before God where man stakes his salvation either upon his own self-righteousness (sin) or the alien righteousness of Christ (grace).

[67] *WA* 11, 597.
[68] *WA* 2, 43.

The second sin is essential, inborn, original, alien, of which Psalm 51 says, "Behold, I was shapen in iniquity, and in sin did my mother conceive me." . . .

The righteousness that corresponds to this is in a similar manner inborn, essential, original—which is the righteousness of Christ [*iustitia Christi*]. . . . This is our lot, capital, foundation, rock, and our whole substance wherein we glory forever, as the Apostle says, "Your life is hid with Christ in God" (Col. 3:3) . . . . It becomes your own through faith: "The righteous shall live by faith" (Rom. 1:17). It is that which the gospel properly proclaims. It is not the righteousness of law, but the righteousness of grace . . . . We are condemned on account of alien sin so that we may also be saved by an alien righteousness.[69]

The third level then goes on to spell out the inevitable ethical fruits of both faith and distrust in the everyday lives of men. All that is not born of faith is sin, while all that is born of faith is righteousness.

The third is actual sin, which is the fruit of original sin. These are the sins proper; namely, all the works we do, even the works of righteousness which we accomplish prior to faith.[70]

The righteousness that corresponds to this is the actual righteousness [*iustitia actualis*] flowing out of faith and the essential righteousness . . . . Therefore, whether you sin or not, rely upon Christ and that essential righteousness of grace . . . . And so the works of such faith are most acceptable, even though in regard to you and in themselves they may be unworthy.[71]

In *Two Kinds of Righteousness* (1519) Luther develops even more sharply the organic unity between the second and third levels of sin and righteousness. He points to the intimate relation between the righteousness of God in Christ (religious faith) and its fruit, Christian righteousness (ethical love).

There are two kinds of Christian righteousness, just as man's sin is of two kinds. The first is alien righteousness, that is the righteousness of another, instilled from without. This is the righteousness of Christ [*iustitia Christi*] by which he justifies through faith (I Cor.

---

[69] *Ibid.*, 44.
[70] *Ibid.*, 45.
[71] *Ibid.*, 46.

1:30). . . . This righteousness, then, is given to men in baptism and whenever they are truly repentant. Therefore a man can with confidence boast in Christ and say: "Mine are Christ's living, doing, and speaking, his suffering and dying, mine as much as if I had lived, done, spoken, suffered, and died as he did." Just as a bride-groom possesses all that is his bride's and she all that is his—for the two have all things in common because they are one flesh (Gen. 2:24)—so Christ and the church are one spirit (Eph. 5:29-32) . . . . Through faith in Christ, therefore, Christ's righteousness becomes our righteousness and all that he has becomes ours; rather, he him-self becomes ours . . . . This righteousness is primary; it is the basis, the cause, the source, of our own actual righteousness.[72]

The second kind of righteousness is our proper righteousness, not because we alone work it, but because we work with that first and alien righteousness. This is that manner of life spent profitably in good works, in the first place in slaying the flesh and crucifying the desires with respect to the self . . . . In the second place, this righteousness consists in love to one's neighbor, and in the third place, in meekness and fear toward God . . . . This righteousness is the product of the righteousness of the first type, actually its fruit and consequence . . . . It follows the example of Christ in this respect (I Pet. 2:21) and is transformed into his likeness (II Cor. 3:18).[73]

These two basic works quoted here at length provide us with a classical summary of Luther's picture of the redeeming and sanctifying work of Christ. To be sure, in the later sacramental controversies with other Protestant groups, he was forced to sharpen and expand his views on the person of Christ, the unique relation of his two natures to each other, and the manner of his real presence in Holy Communion. But never once did he modify or compromise this central evangelical core of his posi-tion. He always kept primary the gospel proclamation that "God was in Christ reconciling the world unto himself" in order that all men who trust in him might enjoy eternal life for Christ's sake.

It will not be amiss to point out already the inseparable con-nection which Luther establishes between religion and ethics, even when the primary stress is laid upon religion. Faith and life

[72] *LW* 31, 297-98.
[73] *Ibid.*, 299-300.

are portrayed here as "root and fruit" of the same God-pleasing tree. Luther's only insistence is that we properly distinguish them so that they are neither falsely equated nor falsely separated. *Religiously,* it is always a matter of "either-or." We are either saved by the righteousness of Christ or damned by our own self-righteousness. *Ethically,* it is always a matter of "both-and." We serve others both by reason-obeying civil righteousness and by faith-activated Christian righteousness since the Christian is always at once both sinner and saint (cf. ch. 3).

Regarding man's religious salvation, there is a striking contrast to Rome in the tone and spirit of Luther's "theology of the cross." Where Rome is man-centered, Luther is Christ-centered. Where Rome has man active and Christ passive, Luther has Christ active and man receptive. Where Rome demands commercially, Luther offers graciously. Where Rome calculates quantitatively, Luther bestows qualitatively. Where Rome stresses the outwardness of works, Luther emphasizes the inwardness of faith. Where Rome tries to make man righteous before declaring him so, Luther first declares man righteous and then makes him so. Where Rome encourages the merits and native righteousness of man, Luther glories in the unmerited and alien righteousness of Christ. He summarizes it all succinctly in saying, "It is that which the gospel properly proclaims. It is not the righteousness of the law, but the righteousness of grace."

Closely following Paul, natural man's religious dilemma before God is painted by Luther in the darkest possible colors. All children of Adam are shapen in iniquity and conceived in sin. This sin is "essential, inborn, original, and alien" to man; that is, his whole personality is totally in bondage to evil forces which are opposed to the will of God. Because self-love has replaced God-love, man is a sinner even before he actually sins. His sinful actions are only external reflections and expressions of a corrupted and distorted personality which is unwilling and unable to know and do the good which saves. By uncontrollable inheritance, we are heirs of Adam's sin and guilt; by willful and deliberate rebellion, we personally re-enact Adam's sin and guilt. All humanity shares in the destiny of this fallen state. In God's sight, therefore, no one can act righteously because no one is righteous.

Even the so-called "good" works which man performs are tainted with sin because they are motivated by a heart which is not absolutely faithful and loving. Whatever their social value, then, man's deeds are religiously worthless. "Whatever good is done outside the faith of Christ . . . no more savors of justification than do apples of figs."[74] This is Luther's way of saying, with Augustine, that "pagan virtues are merely splendid vices." God always judges the ethical fruits by the religious roots. As long as man persists in his self-righteousness and unbelief, he is hopelessly damned.

Then in starkly bright and vivid colors, Luther portrays what God has done for us in the vicarious suffering, death, and resurrection of Jesus Christ. Here is God's answer to man's sinful dilemma. It is "that which the gospel properly proclaims"; namely, the righteousness of God's grace. Here there can be no talk of the righteousness of the law, the merits and good deeds of men, or the sacrifices which men make in order to earn salvation. Here, before God, the righteousness of all men and their deeds are as "filthy rags," polluted with pride and distrust. Religiously, man can only be receptive to what Christ has done for him on his behalf. It is for the Savior's sake alone that man is declared and made righteous in God's sight once again.

All the sin to which we fall heir "in Adam" is now overcome by all the righteousness reckoned to those who are "in Christ." Original, alien sin is matched and covered by original, alien righteousness. As the inheritance of sin and guilt is personally undeserved, certainly the declaration of righteousness and new life is just as gratuitous and unmerited. As there was no part of natural man free from the corrupting taint of sin, so there is no part of the Christian's sin which is not covered by the atoning blood of Christ. As our evil deeds were not the roots, but the

[74] SJ 1, 43.

fruits, of our original sin, so too our good deeds do not constitute, but reflect, the gift of original righteousness which is ours solely because of the graciousness of God.

This "all or nothing" quality which dramatically permeates Luther's thinking on Christ's redeeming work is perhaps its most characteristic feature. Men need look nowhere else than to the cross for their salvation. There is no other way to the Father than through the Son. Whoever has been redeemed by Christ has thereby been reconciled to God Almighty. In Christ's life and work we see and hear what God's "glowing furnace of love" is really like.[75] Here in the crucified and risen Savior, as nowhere else, "the mirror of God's fatherly heart" is revealed to his faithful.[76]

The heart of Luther's "theology of the cross" is that man does not become reconciled to God by approaching him in his majesty—"from above"—with human reason and philosophical speculation. One must rather approach him first in his "suffering servant" form—"from below"—in the faithful humility and joyful confidence that "the Word became flesh and dwelt among us" (John 1:14). "For it is the most impious of all temerities when God himself has humbled himself in order that he might be knowable, that a man should seek to climb up in some other way, through his own ingenious devices."[77]

Now just as God hid himself under the rags of Jesus of Nazareth, our life in Christ must likewise be hidden under the sheltering wings of his righteousness. "O it is a great thing to be a Christian and have a hidden life, hidden not in some cell like the hermits, or even in the human heart, which is an unsearchable abyss, but in the invisible God himself. Thus we live in the things of the world, but feed on him who never appears except in the only vehicle of the hearing of the Word."[78] Carrying out this idea further, Luther envisions the whole life

[75] *WA* 10[III], 56.
[76] *WA* 30[1], 192.
[77] *WA* 57, 99.
[78] *Ibid.*, 215.

of the Christian portrayed in the wistful saying of Christ to Jerusalem, "How often would I have gathered your children together as a hen gathers her brood under her wings, and you would not" (Matt. 23:37). As he says in one of the 1522 *Church Postils:*

I know of no lovelier picture or parable in all of Scripture than the one which the Lord draws here of faith and faithful Christians. . . . It is certain that our souls are the chicks, and the devil and evil spirits are the hawks preying in the air, except that we are not wise enough to seek protection under the wings of our hen, Jesus Christ . . . . Faith, when it is genuine, is the way in which the Christian does not depend upon himself or his own faith, but clings fast to Christ and accepts Christ's righteousness as shelter and protection, just as the chick does not trust in its own power and strength, but hides safely under the body and wings of the hen.[79]

With our mind's eye, we can visualize the peasants and their wives nodding in quiet agreement as their preacher wisely illustrates the religious depths of Holy Scripture with the everyday experiences and observations of common life. Everyone can comprehend the graciousness of God's forgiving love when it is represented by the sheltering wings of a hen over her little brood of chicks. But Luther is not satisfied to limit his sermon illustrations to the barnyard. Life in Christ is so intimate a relationship that it must have as personal a referent as humanly possible. Characteristically, Luther often chooses the love between a bride and groom to depict the love between Christ and his church: "For a bridegroom possesses all that is his bride's and she all that is his."

Marriage portrays the union of the divine and human natures of Christ, and the love which he feels for us. This is shown here clearly by the symbol of marriage (Matt. 21:1ff.). For there are many kinds of love, but none is as ardent or as passionate as the love shown by a new bride for her bridegroom. This love does not seek pleasure, or riches, or golden rings, but seeks only the beloved for himself. Even if he has given her everything there is, she would not regard the gifts selfishly, but declare, "I want you for yourself

[79] *WA* 10[I,1], 281.

alone." And even if he has nothing to give her, she will not permit this to weaken her love for him . . . . Now as a bride loves her groom, so Christ loves us and we are to love him, when we are united together by faith.[80]

In true love, then, the beloved is sought for her own sake, for what she is rather than for what she has. Possessions must always be secondary to personality. For whatever the prospective mates bring into their marriage—whether evil or good, sickness or health, wealth or poverty—it is to be shared in common as two become one and the language of "mine" and "thine" is transformed into the marital "our."[81] So too in the marriage of grace and faith between Christ and the Christian, a "royal exchange" takes place in the glorious redemption of man as Christ takes on our sin and we take on his righteousness.[82] And then, to remind us finally that the love of Christ is so creative a power that it overflows all human banks, Luther concludes his sermon with some realistic pastoral counsel: "If you want to do good works, first have faith; if you want to have children, first become a bride—both will follow quickly!"[83]

Conclusion

By 1520, Luther had arrived at the point of irreparable opposition to the theology and practices of the church of Rome. His protest was basically religious. Either the gracious mercy of God or the meritorious works of man is the ground of Christian salvation. Luther held out for the grace of God alone (*sola gratia*) as the bedrock of evangelical worship and piety. No amount of Roman ethical reform could have met Luther's charges at their religious depths before God. Ultimately, it was two different ways of salvation which were set over against each other and men were once again faced with life's most important decision: "Choose this day whom you will serve."

For Luther, "there is no other God" but he who revealed him·

[80] *WA* 10^{III}, 415.
[81] *Ibid.*, 417.
[82] *Ibid.*, 419.
[83] *Ibid.*

self in Jesus Christ. All Christian theology worthy of its name, therefore, must be radically Christ-centered. In the person and work of Christ, God has revealed what his merciful and steadfast love is really like. Men's redemption from Satan and their reconciliation with God are wholly dependent upon what the crucified and risen Christ has done for us. Only when we have faithfully exchanged our sinfulness for his righteousness can we be saved. Consequently, an evangelical "theology of the cross" condemns as idolatrous all human efforts to merit God's grace apart from Christ *(solus Christus).* It must further declare any church which does not acknowledge Christ as its sole head to be the body of the Antichrist. Sinful self-righteousness leads inevitably to religious defeat. "But thanks be to God who gives us the victory through our Lord Jesus Christ."

CHAPTER THREE

The Christian's Righteousness

Luther's sudden decision to enter the Augustinian Order of Hermits in 1505 owed far less to the thunder and lightning of Stotternheim than to the religious storm which was raging within his own soul. To be sure, the fateful vow to St. Anne was taken in a moment of stark terror. He recalled vividly later how ". . . on the road to Stotternheim not far from Erfurt, he was so frightened by a thunderbolt that in terror he shouted, 'Help, dear St. Anne, and I will become a monk!' "[1]

Nevertheless, the deep-seated roots of Luther's panic were essentially religious. The brightly flashing lightning had revealed in the hidden recesses of his soul the guilty fear that a God of wrath was eternally angry with him. Ultimately, it was not the thunderbolt, but the angry God hurling the thunderbolt *at him,* that drove Luther to his knees in such unspeakable fright. " 'O when will you ever become good enough or do enough to obtain a gracious God?' Such thoughts as this drove me into the monastery."[2]

Once safely behind the monastic walls, Luther set about feverishly to "do enough" merits and satisfactions to obtain his "gracious God." But soon he was faced with the unanswerable dilemma of never knowing how much was enough. He piled up "good" deeds endlessly only to end up either wallowing in despair or boasting in pride. His quest for ethical security was always at the expense of his religious certainty.

[1] *WA*, TR 4, 440.
[2] *WA* 37, 661.

I tried to live according to the Rule with all diligence, and I used to be contrite, to confess and number off my sins, and often repeated my confession, and sedulously performed my allotted penance. And yet my conscience could never give me certainty, but I always doubted and said, "You did not perform that correctly. You were not contrite enough. You left something out of your confession; etc." The more I tried to remedy an uncertain, weak, and afflicted conscience with the traditions of men, the more each day found me more uncertain, weaker, and troubled.[3]

It was probably in the spring of 1513 that the breakthrough of God's Word concerning His righteousness finally took place in Luther's heart and mind. Significantly, both heart and mind were transformed, for both personal and theological considerations were involved. Personally, Luther was still trying to find a gracious God by cajoling him with good works. "I firmly believed that I would have to continue to do good works until Christ was rendered gracious to me through them."[4] Theologically, he was troubled by the exegesis of certain verses in the Psalms which he had to treat in class lectures as Professor of Bible at the University of Wittenberg.

It was the feared and hated term "righteousness of God" (*iustitia Dei*) which appears so often in the Psalms and the Pauline epistles which caused him all his anguish. While diligently at work on Holy Scripture in his little room in the tower of the Black Cloister, Luther listened breathlessly as God finally spoke his living and forgiving Word to him.

I was absorbed by a passionate desire to understand Paul in his Epistle to the Romans. Nothing stood in my way but that one expression, "The righteousness of God is revealed in the gospel" (Rom. 1:17). For I hated those words, "the righteousness of God," because I had been taught to understand them in the scholastic sense as the formal or active righteousness whereby God, who is rightous, punishes unrighteous sinners.

I raged in this way with a fierce and disturbed conscience, and yet I kept hammering away at those words of Paul, wishing passionately to know what he meant. After I had pondered the problem

[3] *WA* 40[II], 15.
[4] *WA* 47, 590.

for days and nights, God took pity on me and I saw the inner connection between the two phrases, "The righteousness of God is revealed in the gospel," and "The righteous shall live by faith." Then I began to understand that this "righteousness of God" is the righteousness by which the righteous man lives through the free gift of God, that is to say, "by faith"; and that the righteousness "revealed in the gospel" is the passive righteousness of God by which he takes pity on us and justifies us by our faith, as it is written, "The righteous shall live by faith." Thereupon I felt as if I had been born again and had entered Paradise through wide-open gates![5]

From this decisive moment on, Luther knew himself to be a man with a divine mission ". . . to restore the holy gospel once again." In wrestling with the very heart of biblical theology, Luther heard anew that eternal message of good news which had so fired the spirits of the apostolic church. The gospel was recovered once again as "the power of God for salvation" (Rom. 1:16). Luther proclaimed the unmerited grace of God which offers the unconditional forgiveness of sin—and thereby new life and salvation—to all who have faith in Christ as the Son of God and the Savior of mankind. With this message, the evangelical triumvirate of the grace of God, the cross of Christ, and the faith of man was reunited and restored once again to uncontested sovereignty.

Heaven-storming Reason

If God's mercy is appropriated "by faith alone," intellectual work-righteousness must be regarded as idolatrous. In attacking the religious pretensions of human reason, Luther quickly recognized the baptized philosophy of "that ridiculous and injurious blasphemer, Aristotle," as his chief enemy.[6] Luther's basic complaint against Aristotle was that he had no understanding of the human rebellion against God which Christians call sin. Because of this crucial omission, the Scholastic incorporation of Aristotle into its theological system of salvation always resulted

[5] WA 54, 185.
[6] Sm 26.

in exaggerated stress upon the power and works of man in direct proportion to the diminution of the gracious activity of God in Christ. In this way, the glory of man replaced the cross of Christ as the heart of the Christian faith.

That sinful man is unable by himself either to know or do the saving good in God's sight is the central thrust of the *Heidelberg Disputation* (1518). This may be interpreted as Luther's formal declaration of lifelong independence from Aristotelian metaphysics and ethics. We shall concentrate here on those theses which repudiate the foundation of natural man's glory in his alleged freedom to do the good.

The law of God, the most salutary doctrine of life, cannot advance man on his way to righteousness, but rather hinders him (1). Although the works of man always seem attractive and good, they are nevertheless likely to be mortal sins (3). Free will, after the fall, exists in name only, and as long as it does what it is able to do, it commits a mortal sin (13). The person who believes that he can obtain grace by doing what is in him adds sin to sin so that he becomes doubly guilty (16). Nor does speaking in this manner give cause for despair, but for arousing the desire to humble oneself and seek the grace of Christ (17). The law brings the wrath of God, kills, reviles, accuses, judges, and condemns everything that is not in Christ (23). He is not righteous who does much, but he who, without work, believes much in Christ (25).[7]

Luther insists with Paul that the law is a religious obstacle for natural man's quest for righteousness. In confident dependence upon the Epistle to the Romans, Luther contends that the righteousness of God in Christ is bestowed upon men "without the law" (3:21), for the law serves primarily to "increase sin" (5:20) and to "revive it" (7:9), as it demands what is impossible for the unregenerate. Now if man is incapable of the good even with the "supernatural light" of God's law, how much more morally impotent is he when trying to do the good merely on the strength of his own sinfully corrupted power?

Human works appear attractive outwardly, but within they are filthy,

[7] *LW* 31, 42ff.

as Christ says concerning the Pharisees (Matt. 23:27). For they appear to the doer and others good and beautiful, yet God does not judge according to appearances but searches "the minds and hearts" (Ps. 7:9). For without grace and faith it is impossible to have a pure heart. "He cleansed their hearts by faith" (Acts 15:9).[8]

Clearly, everything man does by the mixed motives of his impure heart will be warped and distorted accordingly. "Whatever does not proceed from faith is sin" (Rom. 14:23). Even when God works through his faithful, their persisting sin leaves its taint upon his work. "This is a comparison. If someone cuts with a rusty and rough hatchet, even though the worker is a skilled craftsman, the hatchet leaves bad, jagged, and ugly gashes. So it is when God works through us."[9]

This is, of course, all the more true of natural man's efforts when unaided by the grace of God. Regarding salvation alone, Luther insists that man has absolutely no free will. That is, his sinful nature in bondage to Satan is incapable of freely willing perfect faith and love to God above all things.[10] No man is religiously neutral: if he is not under God's rule, he is a slave of Satan's. Apart from grace, man is free only to sin. He cannot believe in God by his own reason or strength. For Rome to admonish man to "do what is in him" (facere quod in se est) as a natural foundation for God's supernatural activity, is to try to build grace upon sin, a house upon sand.[11]

For the righteousness of God is not acquired by means of acts frequently repeated, as Aristotle taught, but it is imparted by faith (Rom. 1:17; 10:10). Therefore I wish to have the words "without work" understood in the following manner: Not that the righteous person does nothing, but that his works do not make him righteous, rather that his righteousness creates works. For grace and faith are infused without our works. After they have been imparted the works follow.[12]

The full depth of natural man's hopeless plight before God is depicted in Luther's earlier *Lectures on the Epistle to the*

---

[8] *Ibid.*, 43.
[9] *Ibid.*, 45.
[10] *WA* 56, 355.
[11] *LW* 31, 50-51.
[12] *Ibid.*, 55-56.

Romans (1515-16). Following the fall of Adam in his proud rebellion against God, the righteousness of God and the righteousness of man stand in irreconcilable contradiction to each other. "The chief end of the Apostle in this letter is to destroy all righteousness and wisdom of our own . . . [and to show] that Christ and his righteousness are necessary for their genuine extermination. And he does this until chapter 12, after which he teaches the quantity and quality of the good works we ought to do, on the ground of Christ's own righteousness received."[13]

Luther develops Paul's first chapter on the nature of human sin by tracing man's distorted reactions to the law of God. On the one hand, there are those who disregard it completely, and Luther shares Paul's antipathy toward the wicked actions of those who refuse to acknowledge God's rule over their lives. On the other hand, there are those who are equally guilty before God, but manifest their faithfulness to Satan, paradoxically, by trying to earn their salvation in work-righteousness. In direct opposition to Paul's teaching in Romans 1:17, these men seek justification through the works of the law and not by grace through faith alone.

This sinful arrogance leads men to self-deception, for the God of holy love sees beneath the sham performances to their cold and selfish hearts. They do not love to do what they ought to do. It is not enough for men to obey the letter of the law outwardly ". . . unless they do it with a cheerful and pure will."[14] But the unregenerate ". . . do good works wholly from fear or from love of reward and not with a cheerful will."[15] This is why an evangelical ethic always gives priority to the gracious love of God before it treats the faithful response of man. "For grace is to be sought in order that a man, changed in spirit, may desire and perform all things with a cheerful and willing heart, not from servile fear or puerile cupidity, but with a free and virile mind. This the Spirit alone works."[16]

[13] *WA* 56, 3.
[14] *WA* 56, 278.
[15] *Ibid.*, 235.
[16] *Ibid.*, 337.

With relentless logic, Luther then traces man's sins back to a corrupted will, which, in turn, is in bondage to evil forces which control his whole personality as an unrepentant sinner.[17] In this connection Luther employs the term "concupiscence" (*concupiscentia*) to describe the whole "fleshly" character of man's original sin against God. Although the term certainly includes man's sensual and sexual disobedience against God's will, it refers more properly, in its totality, to man's sinful self-centeredness as over against God-centeredness, his proud disobedience of the first commandment of God's law. Luther can allude to the same basic reality by describing natural man as being so centripetally orientated that everything in life is sucked to destruction in the whirlpool of his own ego.

For Scriptures describe man as curved in upon himself [*incurvatus in se*] so that not only bodily goods, but spiritual goods also he turns to himself, and seeks himself in all things . . . For man makes himself the final and ultimate object and idol . . . This crookedness and depravity and iniquity is described many times in Scripture under the name of fornication and idolatry [whoring after false gods] . . . and is in the hidden depths of our nature, nay, rather it is our nature itself, wounded and in ferment through the whole so that not only is it impossible to remedy without grace, but it is impossible fully to recognize it.[18]

Hence, for Luther, there can be only two religious alternatives in life: either God-worship or self-worship, God-love or self-love, the righteousness of grace through faith or the righteousness of law through works. Before God, man must either be covered by the alien righteousness of Christ or stand naked in the guilt and shame of his own sin. "For the judgment of God is infinite in subtlety. And there is nothing so refined, but it is gross in his presence, nothing so righteous that it is not unrighteous, nothing so true that it is not found a lie, nothing so pure and holy that it is not polluted and profane in his presence."[19]

[17] *Ibid.*, 312.
[18] *Ibid.*, 356-61.
[19] *Ibid.*, 246.

Against this background, we can understand more readily the cause for Luther's lifelong polemic against any attempt to substitute reason for faith, or to combine reason with faith, in man's religious relations with God *(coram Deo)*. Luther had high praise for man's use of reason socially and politically (cf. ch. 4). He regarded its use in matters of faith, however, as an expression of human distrust in the all-sufficiency of God's gracious self-revelation in the life and work of Christ. Regarding salvation, ". . . it is impossible to harmonize faith and reason. . . . You must abandon your reason, know nothing of it, annihilate it completely, or you will never enter heaven."[20]

It is precisely the "heaven-storming" presumption of reason which Luther attacked so bitterly because of the serious inroads that it had made in the Scholasticism of Rome. The following passages are characteristic: "Virtually the entire *Ethics* of Aristotle is the worst enemy of grace. . . . Briefly, the whole Aristotle is to theology as darkness is to light."[21] Or again, "Aristotle is a shameless slanderer, a comedian, the most artful corrupter of minds. If he had not lived in flesh and bones, I should not scruple to take him for a devil."[22]

As for Thomas Aquinas, ". . . he never understood a chapter of the gospel or of Aristotle," if he really thought that he could reconcile revelation and reason, the Word of God and the words of men.[23] The venerated position of Thomas in Roman Catholic theology had little influence on Luther once he was armed with God's Word. "I think that this great man is to be pitied, not only for drawing his opinions in matters of faith from Aristotle, but for attempting to base them on him without understanding his meaning—an unfortunate superstructure upon an unfortunate foundation."[24]

In such "matters of faith," man's sinful reason is corrupted by

[20] *EA* 44, 156-57.
[21] *LW* 31, 12.
[22] *WA*, Br 1, 34.
[23] *WA*, Br 1, 301.
[24] *PE* 2, 188.

74

" . . . a great, destructive, and dangerous blindness."[25] It refuses arrogantly to limit its exercise to its acknowledged competence in temporal matters, ". . . but rather wants man to be clever in divine matters, such as how we can achieve God's grace, how we can become free from sin, how we can get a good conscience, and how we can become reconciled with God."[26] In fact, "Frau Hulda, the devil's whore," remained Luther's favorite epithet for all beguiling human reason which would seduce man away from the true God in order to worship his own man-made idols.

Usury, drunkenness, adultery, and murder can all be detected and understood by the world as sinful. But when the devil's bride, reason, the pretty prostitute, enters into the picture and wishes to be clever, what she says is accepted at once by people as if she were the voice of the Holy Ghost . . . . She is surely the devil's chief whore.[27]

Luther could picture no kind of compromise with any theology which depended as much on man's finite and sinful reason as on Holy Scripture. "I simply believe that it is impossible to reform the church unless the canon law, scholastic theology, philosophy, and logic as they are now taught, are thoroughly rooted out . . . that the pure study of the Bible and the church fathers may be restored."[28] Once again, then, we are thrown back to the scriptural message of "salvation by grace through faith alone" as the foundation of evangelical worship and piety. "This Word of God is the beginning, the foundation, the rock, upon which all works, words, and thoughts of man must build. . . . This trust and faith is the beginning, middle, and end of all works and righteousness."[29]

God's Living Word

Luther so confidently attacked the various elements which comprised the power-structure of Rome because he was certain that his teachings were grounded solidly in the Christian's only

[25] *EA* 47, 129.
[26] *Ibid.*, 128.
[27] *EA* 16, 142.
[28] *SJ* 1, 83f.
[29] *PE* 1, 297.

ultimate authority: the living Word of God. He successively examined indulgences, the sacramental system, the papacy, Scholastic metaphysics, sacrificial good works, and fearlessly declared them all to be wanting when measured against the absolute Word of God in Holy Scripture.

When he was finally called to recant his position at the Imperial Diet of Worms in April, 1521, Luther gave a ringing testimony to the scriptural foundations of his evangelical faith.

Since then your serene majesty and your lordships seek a simple answer, I will give it in this manner, neither horned nor toothed: Unless I am convinced by the testimony of the Scriptures or by clear reason (for I do not trust either in the pope or in councils alone, since it is well known that they have often erred and contradicted themselves), I am bound by the Scriptures I have quoted and my conscience is captive to the Word of God. I cannot and will not retract anything, since it is neither safe nor right to go against conscience. I cannot do otherwise, here I stand, may God help me, Amen.[30]

All too often this truly heroic scene has been so romanticized that we fail to do justice to the central paradox of Christian freedom exhibited here. Luther proves himself master of Rome only as he confesses himself to be "captive to the Word of God." Moreover, in an illuminating letter to Emperor Charles V written a few days after he left Worms, Luther reiterates his sincere belief that this is the "very crux of the controversy" between Rome and himself. He insists ". . . that the Word of God to me should remain free and unfettered. . . . And in no circumstances is it left to human choice whether to belittle and jeopardize the Word of God, no matter how far men may excel in eminence, numbers, doctrine, and sanctity."[31]

Having examined Luther's "tower-experience" at the outset of this chapter, we know the truth of his claim here that his ". . . prejudice in favor of the Word of God was born in me by what the Scriptures preached." Again, the personal address— "the living Word of God to me"—is of the utmost significance

[30] *LW* 32, 112-13.
[31] *WA*, Br 2, 401.

for Luther. He is bearing public witness to that decisive moment when he believed the living God spoke his living Word *to him* through the gospel declaration of Romans 1:17. In that personal encounter, the words of Scripture became "transparent" to the loving self-revelation of God. Luther acknowledged God as his own sin-forgiving Father when the Bible conveyed God's gracious Word to him under the power of the inner testimony of the Holy Spirit. In fidelity to the One who came not to teach truths but to declare, "I am the Truth," Luther could state boldly that ". . . the New Testament should really be only a living Word and not a written word; that is why Christ wrote nothing."[32]

Hence, Word and Scripture were neither identified nor separated by Luther despite the demands of human reason. Faith testifies rather to a self-disclosing God hidden under the "servant rags" of the testimony of believers to his mighty acts in history. Luther does not pretend to understand or explain this mystery of divine revelation. In the simplicity of faith which gratefully accepts all the precious gifts of God as miracles, Luther characteristically treasures the Old and New Testaments as ". . . the swaddling clothes and manger in which Christ was wrapped and laid."[33] The manger is not itself the baby, but one must first go to the manger if the baby is to be found: so too with Holy Scripture and the Word of God.

Since it is the gospel alone which is "the power of God for men's salvation," Luther boldly sets forth this gospel—the good news of God's redeeming act in Christ—as the "true test by which to judge" the apostolic value of the Scriptures.[34] "Whether they deal with Christ or not" is the evangelical touchstone set forth in Luther's *Prefaces to the Books of the New Testament* (1522). In the "manger" of Scripture, we must learn to distinguish the inseparable swaddling clothes from the Christ-child himself, the words of men from the Word of God.

From this you can now judge all the books and decide among them

[32] *WA* 10[1,2], 34.
[33] *WA* 10[1,1], 576.
[34] *PE* 6, 478.

which are best. John's Gospel and St. Paul's Epistles, especially that to the Romans, and St. Peter's first Epistle are the true kernel and marrow of all the books . . . . But St. James' Epistle is really an epistle of straw, compared to them, for it has nothing of the nature of the gospel about it . . . . Hebrews does not lay the foundation of faith, which is the work of an apostle. Nevertheless he does build finely thereon gold, silver, and precious stones . . . even though wood, straw, and hay be mixed in with them.[35]

In the light of this background, it comes as no surprise to find that Luther's enforced exile at the Wartburg was dedicated to his first and last great love—the translation and exposition of Holy Scripture for the saving benefit of his fellow Germans, for so many of whom the Latin Bible was largely a sealed and unknown treasure. This unexpected sojourn gave Luther a glorious opportunity to dedicate to the Bible the consecrated study which he had long accused Rome of neglecting in its preoccupation with philosophical theology. We recall Luther's earlier complaint that ". . . when the attempt is made to reprove them out of the Scriptures, they raise the objection that the interpretation of the Scriptures belongs to no one except the pope."[36] This papal imperialism cannot be tolerated by Luther.

If we are all priests and all have one faith, one gospel, one sacrament, why should we not also have the power to test and judge what is correct and incorrect in matters of faith? . . . All these and many other texts make us bold and free, and we should not allow the Spirit of liberty, as Paul calls him, to be frightened off by the fabrications of the popes. But we ought to go boldly forward to test all that they do or leave undone according to our interpretation of the Scriptures, which rests on faith, and compel them to follow not their own interpretation, but the one that is better.[37]

This passage is also important as a corrective to some prevailing misinterpretations of Luther's view which would suggest that every Christian may interpret the Bible as he sees fit. Luther would be the first to damn any kind of biblical *laissez faire* grounded on the alleged "right of private judgment." No man

[35] *Ibid.,* 443-44, 477.
[36] *PE* 2, 65.
[37] *Ibid.,* 75-76.

who confesses himself to be "captive to the Word of God" could ever advocate the sanctity of everyone's private judgment regarding Scripture. Luther maintains here that "our interpretation of Scripture" is "the one that is better" because "it rests on faith." That is to say, it is not Luther's personal interpretation of Scripture, but Scripture's interpretation of itself, which is decisive. Luther's own understanding of the "righteousness of God" in the Psalms, for example, came to him only after he studied the phrase more diligently in a new and clearer context in Romans. He is always willing to have his interpretation of Scripture corrected—but only by Scripture itself.

Luther also maintains that we cannot speak about Scripture until we have first encountered the living Christ who is himself "the king and lord of Scripture."[38] All our human interpretations of the Bible must become captive to the Word under the power of the Holy Spirit. "In like manner, St. Paul rebukes St. Peter as a man in error. Therefore it behooves every Christian to espouse the cause of faith, to understand and defend it, and to rebuke all errors."[39] It is clear that Luther's intention is not to substitute personal anarchy for institutional tyranny in the area of biblical interpretation. His primary concern is that everyone permit Scripture—or better, God through Scripture—to speak for itself.

This is made abundantly clear in Luther's constant insistence that his teaching is no novel personal discovery, but is rather the recovery of a truth which is as old—and as reliable—as the cross of Christ itself. He feared his own overnight popularity and notoriety more than anyone. "I had hoped that people would henceforth pay more attention to the Holy Scriptures themselves, and let my books go, now that they have served their purpose and led men's hearts into and up to the Scriptures, which was my reason for writing my books. What is the use of reading many books, and yet always staying away from the chief

[38] *WA* 40[1], 420.
[39] *PE* 2, 76.

book? Drink rather from the fountain itself than from the rill that has led you to the fountain."[40]

In a similar humble spirit, Luther is vexed that his enemies have begun to identify his teachings and followers as "Lutheran" rather than as "Christian." As his books bow to Holy Scripture, Luther personally abases himself in the presence of his own Lord and Savior. "Who is this Luther? My teaching is not my own, and I have not been crucified for the sake of anyone. . . . Why should it happen to me, miserable stinking bag of worms that I am, that the children of Christ should be called by my insignificant name? . . . I am and will be nobody's master. With the one church I have in common the teachings of Christ who alone is our Master."[41]

Hence it was Luther's appeal to Holy Scripture—and Scripture alone—as the rule and standard for all Christian faith and life, which provided his followers with such comforting assurance and his opponents with such frenzied dismay. He scornfully dismissed the attacks of the theological faculty of Paris, for instance, because, as biblically groundless, they were not even worthy of his consideration. "Who has ever heard or read of such audacity to match that of the asses of Paris who compare themselves to the apostles and councils, and unashamedly write that they will speak and judge without scriptural authority because the apostles also did so?"[42] And the same against Thomas Murner: "You never quote Scripture at all, but merely write what fancy dictates. . . . For this reason I want Scripture. Scripture, Murner; Murner, Scripture! Or else seek another combatant; I have other things to do than to attend to your Scripture-less chatter."[43]

These words are a thinly veiled witness to what Luther had experienced himself in his dramatic recovery of the Christian gospel in his study of Scripture. For it was Romans 1:17 which

[40] SJ 2, 189.
[41] PE 3, 218-19.
[42] WA 8, 291.
[43] PE 3, 394.

provided the evangelical key to the mystery of the "righteousness of God." Here Luther learned clearly for the first time that God's Word addresses men both as law and as gospel, and that Christians can understand God's will for their lives only when they distinguish "what God demands of us" (law) from "what he promises to us" (gospel). It was only when Luther was enlightened by the Holy Spirit to see that God's righteousness is a free gift promised to all who believe, that he broke through from the work-righteousness of Rome to the righteousness of faith in the New Testament.

Hitherto I lacked only a proper distinction between the law and the gospel. I considered both to be the same, and Christ to differ from Moses only in time and perfection. It was when I discovered the difference between the law and the gospel, that they are two separate things, that I broke through.[44]

By the time of the *Explanations,* Luther could already employ the dialectic of law and gospel with incisive precision to describe the twofold rule of God as the Creator and Redeemer of a fallen humanity. It had rapidly become an essential feature of his "theology of the cross."

When God begins to justify a man, he first of all condemns him; him whom he wishes to raise up, he destroys; him whom he wishes to heal, he smites; and the one to whom he wishes to give life, he kills.[45]

According to the Apostle in Romans 1:3-6, the gospel is a preaching of the incarnate Son of God, given to us without any merit on our part for salvation and peace. It is a word of salvation, a word of grace, a word of comfort, a word of joy, a voice of the bridegroom and the bride, a good word, a word of peace.[46]

But the law is a word of destruction, a word of wrath, a word of sadness, a word of grief, a voice of the judge and the defendant, a word of restlessness, a word of curse. For according to the Apostle, "The law is the power of sin" (I Cor. 15:56), and "the law brings wrath" (Rom. 4:15); it is the law of death (Rom. 7:5, 13). Through the law we have nothing except an evil conscience, a restless heart, a troubled breast because of our sins, which the law

---

[44] *WA,* TR 5, 5553.
[45] *LW* 31, 99.
[46] *Ibid.,* 231.

points out but does not take away. And we ourselves cannot take it away. Therefore for those of us who are held captive, who are overwhelmed by sadness and in dire despair, the light of the gospel comes and says . . . . "Behold the Lamb of God, who takes away the sin of the world" (John 1:29).[47]

This quotation is a particularly vivid representative of literally thousands of other like passages which can be found in virtually all of Luther's sermons, expositions, and treatises. He felt it his peculiar God-given task to restore the proper distinction between the law and the gospel to the church. Although he deemed the ability to make this crucial distinction in both religion and ethics as "the mark of a true theologian," Luther honestly felt that ". . . no book has been written since Scripture—not even by the church fathers—in which these two words or sermons of God have been properly handled and distinguished."[48]

Even if the sweeping breadth of this assertion owes something to his fervor for the living Word of God, it can still confidently be asserted that Luther's dialectical treatment of the "proper" (gospel) and "strange" (law) expressions of God's loving rule of mankind has had no peer in Christian theology. It was Luther's greatness that he refused to modify or compromise one iota of the tension-filled opposition between the law and the gospel as antithetical ways of salvation.

There is a stark, dramatic quality to this kind of proclamation which elicits only two possible responses: the leap of faith or total offense. There is no attempt to explain, to bargain, to pacify, or even to popularize in a "theology of the cross." The stakes are too high for that. As every man must die for himself, so too must he believe for himself.[49] "Historical faith says, 'I hear that Christ has suffered and died.' . . . True faith, however, says 'I believe that Christ has suffered death *for me.*"[50] It is "your neck," your eternal blessedness which is dependent upon the

[47] *Ibid.*
[48] *WA* 10[1,2], 155.
[49] *PE* 2, 391.
[50] *WA* 44, 720.

trusting commitment of all that you have and are to Jesus Christ. Faith is a living, daring confidence in God's grace, so sure and certain that a man would stake his life on it a thousand times. This confidence in God's grace and knowledge of it makes men glad and bold and happy in dealing with God and with all his creatures; and this is the work of the Holy Spirit in faith. Hence a man is ready and glad, without compulsion, to serve everyone, to suffer everything, in love and praise of God, who has shown him this grace.[51]

Faith is a divine work in us. It changes us and makes us to be born anew of God (John 1:13). It kills the old Adam and makes altogether new men, in heart, and spirit, and mind, and powers, and brings with it the Holy Ghost. O it is a living, busy, active, mighty thing, this faith; and so it is impossible for it not to do good works incessantly. It does not ask whether there are good works to do, but before the question rises, it has already done them, and is always at the doing of them. He who does not do these works is a faithless man.[52]

The Divine Indicative

As these last dynamic words indicate, Luther's protest against Rome was essentially religious but inevitably ethical as well. It is immediately self-evident from the once-for-all sacrifice of Christ for man, that man is not to sacrifice to God. In an evangelical "theology of the cross," man lives by faith in what God has done; all that man can do is to accept God's incomparable gifts in the spirit of "prayer, praise, and thanksgiving." Since God has taken care of man's salvation, Luther concludes that man is free to dedicate his sacrifices to the well-being of his neighbor who is really in need of them. If our love for each other is to reflect God's love for us, then "our neighbor is every man, especially he who needs our help."[53]

The shape of Luther's social ethic, therefore, is at once Christ-centered and neighbor-directed. Since Christ died *for us,* we are free from the bondage of self-righteousness. But since Christ also lives *in us,* we are free for the service of Christian righteous-

[51] *PE* 6, 452.
[52] *Ibid.,* 451.
[53] *WA* 40[II], 73.

ness. No longer God's enemy, the Christian is free to become the voluntary channel of God's serving love to all mankind. Luther's ethic is grounded solidly on the biblical promise that once God has declared man righteous by grace through faith (justification), he makes him righteous by grace through hope and love (sanctification).

It is startling to hear the same Luther who is so pessimistic about the morals of natural man become so enthusiastic over the ethics of the Christian. The decisive difference, of course, lies in the power-filled intervention of the Holy Spirit in and through the activities of the Christian. It is this stress on the surging, ongoing, overflowing action of the indwelling Spirit of God which is the most characteristic feature of Luther's view of the Christian life.

An ethic of grace always places the "divine imperative" of God's demands subservient to the "divine indicative" of God's deeds. Men learn to do God's will once they are enlisted into his service against the forces of evil in this world. Conformed, in faith, to the "mind of Christ," Christians can best determine what they should be doing by first learning what God is doing. In contrast to the Roman separation between what God has done and what man must do, Luther gives God all the glory and distinguishes only between 1) what he has once done for us and for our religious salvation in Christ, and 2) what he continues to do in and through us for our ethical service in the Holy Spirit. Empowered by the grace of God, the true disciple becomes "the organ or instrument of Christ," since "Whoever acts out of faith knows from the outset that such works are not his but God's."[54]

It is one of the central paradoxes of the Reformation—as it is of the New Testament—that ethical activity is generated most powerfully in those who practice religious receptivity. Certainly this was true of Luther. Like the prophets of old, he always felt "more acted upon than acting" whenever the living Word of God

[54] *LW* 31, 56.

overpowered him and enlisted him in Christ's service. His bold confidence that "God does not lie" provided Luther with a divine source of peace and power which amazed his followers. They were continually reminded by him that they must look ultimately to God's leadership in the Reformation.

Good Heavens! Spalatin, how excited you are! More than I or anyone else. I wrote you before not to assume that this affair was begun or is carried on by your judgment or mine or that of any other man. If it is of God, it will be completed contrary to, outside of, above and below, either your or my understanding . . . . Let God see to it, for he acts through me, since I am certain that none of these things have been sought by me, but that they were drawn from me, one and all, by a fury not my own.[55]

All I have done is to further, preach, and teach God's Word; otherwise I have done nothing. So it happened that while I slept or while I had a glass of Wittenberg beer with my friend Philip [Melanchthon] and with Amsdorf, the papacy was so weakened as it never was before by the action of any prince or emperor. I have done nothing; the Word has done and accomplished everything . . . . I let the Word do its work.[56]

This living, active God at work in faithful men is the divine source of power generating the Christian's deeds of serving love. It is only because God first loves us that we are capable of transmitting that same love to others (I John 4:10-11). When Paul says, "I, yet not I, but Christ in me," he is witnessing to himself as a righteous channel of loving service. He gives God the glory for the good which he—yet not he, but Christ in him—is able to do for others. This is not, as in the ethics of Rome, a question of grace merely completing that which nature has already begun. Here it is rather a case of radical repentance and conversion where nature has to die unto self in order to be reborn and live unto Christ and others. In the miracle of faith, man remains man and yet becomes God's. His will is to do God's will, and in God's service he finds perfect freedom. His sinful independence is replaced by a faithful dependence upon God and a loving interdependence with his fellow men.

[55] *SJ* 1, 286.
[56] *WA* 10[III], 18f.

Luther's treatise on *The Freedom of a Christian* (1520) provides us with a helpful starting point to review his rapidly growing insistence that a true faith must issue in good works. To employ one of his own favorite figures, "It is quite as impossible to separate works from faith as to separate heat and light from fire."[57] Whereas most of Luther's early writings against Rome referred specifically to man's religious position before God (*coram Deo*), Luther expands his horizon in this work to include man's relations with his fellow men as well (*coram hominibus*). Purposely including ethics as well as religion, Luther intends this work to encompass "the whole of Christian life in a brief form."[58]

How the demands of religion ("the inner man") and ethics ("the outer man") seem to "contradict each other" but actually "fit together beautifully" is described by Luther in two classical theses:

A Christian is a perfectly free lord of all, subject to none. A Christian is a perfectly dutiful servant of all, subject to all.[59]

This paradox is grounded in the person and work of the Christian's humble Lord. "So Christ, although he was Lord of all, was 'born of woman, born under the law' (Gal. 4:4); and therefore was at the same time a free man and a servant, 'in the form of God' and 'of a servant'" (Phil. 2:6-7).[60] As Christ has both a human and a divine nature, "man has a twofold nature, a spiritual and a bodily one. According to the spiritual nature, which men refer to as the soul, he is called a spiritual, inner, or new man. According to the bodily nature, which men refer to as flesh, he is called a carnal, outer, or old man (II Cor. 4:16). Because of this diversity of nature, the Scriptures assert contradictory things concerning the same man, since these two men in the same man contradict each other" (Gal. 5:17).[61]

---

[57] *PE* 6, 452.
[58] *LW* 31, 343.
[59] *Ibid.*, 344.
[60] *Ibid.*
[61] *Ibid.* In trying "to make the way easier for the unlearned," Luther loosely correlates "old and new" with "inner and outer" here. If followed strictly,

Luther describes first the "inner man" as one who has been justified by grace through faith for Christ's sake, and thereby needs nothing more for his eternal life and blessedness. "One thing, and only one thing, is necessary for Christian life, righteousness, and freedom. That one thing is the most holy Word of God, the gospel of Christ."[62] This gracious act of God in Christ provides the groundwork for the spiritual freedom of the Christian man. As faith apprehends the forgiveness and new life which God offers, it accepts the gospel, fulfills the law, and unites the soul with Christ.[63] Especially significant is the way in which Luther again develops Paul's analogy of the marital union.

> The third incomparable benefit of faith is that it unites the soul with Christ as a bride is united with her bridegroom. By this mystery, as the Apostle teaches, Christ and the soul become one flesh (Eph. 5:31-32). And if they are one flesh and there is between them a true marriage—indeed the most perfect of all marriages, since human marriages are but poor examples of this one true marriage—it follows that everything they have they hold in common, the good as well as the evil. Accordingly the believing soul can boast of and glory in whatever Christ has as though it were its own, and whatever the soul has Christ claims as his own. Let us compare these and we shall see inestimable benefits. Christ is full of grace, life, and salvation. The soul is full of sins, death, and damnation. Now let faith come between them and sins, death, and damnation will be Christ's, while grace, life, and salvation will be the soul's.[64]

By this glorious "royal marriage" sealed with the "wedding ring of faith," the Christian shares in the royal prerogatives of Christ himself. This is the basis for the first paradoxical assertion that "A Christian is a perfectly free lord of all, subject to none." It is imperative to note that Luther limits this freedom and lord-

however, such a formulation would lead to the very Platonic body-soul dualism which the Reformer denies so vehemently elsewhere. Biblically speaking, man's creatureliness provides the occasion but not the cause of his sinfulness. Since the dimensions of creation and redemption are always distinguishable, however inseparable, we dare never equate religion ("inner") with rebirth ("new"), or ethics ("outer") with sin ("old"). See *WA* 2, 167 for a more characteristic example of Luther's dialectical approach to Scripture in the "old man's" sinful perversion of the "outer man's" sexual life.

[62] *LW* 31, 345.
[63] *Ibid.*, 349ff.
[64] *Ibid.*, 351.

ship of the Christian to the spiritual or religious dimension of man's existence. "Here, however, we are not inquiring what works and what kind of works are done, but who it is that does them, who glorifies God and brings forth the works. This is done by faith which dwells in the heart and is the source and sub-stance of all our righteousness."[65] In Christ, then, before God, the Christian is free from all those forces of evil which would prevent his justification by faith: sin, death, the devil, God's wrath and his law.

But having said all this, Luther maintains that we have de-scribed only the first half—albeit the primary half—of the para-doxical shape of the Christian life. Until now we have been speaking of the religious commitment of the actor; now we turn to his ethical actions. When it is this "outer man" of whom we speak, then the second of the theses applies: "A Christian is a perfectly dutiful servant of all, subject to all." Luther contends that the peculiar mark of the righteousness of faith as over against the righteousness of works is that the self gives way to the neighbor as the center of ethical concern.[66] It is his need in his situation that the Christian is called to meet. Neighbor-love is predicated not upon the extension but the replacement of self-love, as the Christian "lives only for others and not for himself."[67]

This is a truly Christian life. Here faith is truly active in love (Gal. 5:6), that is, it finds expression in works of the freest service, cheer-fully and lovingly done, with which a man willingly serves another without hope of reward; and for himself he is satisfied with the fulness and wealth of his faith.[68]

We are now in a position to appreciate Luther's opening state-ment that the paradoxical form of the Christian—free in faith while bound in love—is grounded in the "suffering servant" form voluntarily assumed by the Son of God. It is the inescapable ethical expression of a "theology of the cross" which worships a

[65] Ibid., 353.
[66] Ibid., 364.
[67] Ibid.
[68] Ibid., 365.

God who humbles himself, finding strength in his "weakness" and wisdom in his "foolishness." After Christ has first become the Lord of our faith, he serves also as the Prototype of our love. In a fragmentary and anticipatory way, Christians are to show the same kind of selfless love to their neighbors as God in Christ has shown toward them. In the miracle of faith, Christians become nothing less than "little Christs" to their neighbors!

A Christian ought to think: "Although I am an unworthy and condemned man, my God has given me in Christ all the riches of righteousness and salvation without any merit on my part out of pure, free mercy, so that from now on I need nothing except faith which believes that this is true. . . . I will therefore give myself as a Christ to my neighbor, just as Christ offered himself to me; I will do nothing in this life except what I see is necessary, profitable, and salutary to my neighbor, since through faith I have an abundance of all good things in Christ."[69]
We conclude, therefore, that a Christian lives not in himself, but in Christ and in his neighbor. Otherwise he is not a Christian. He lives in Christ through faith, in his neighbor through love. By faith he is caught up beyond himself into God. By love he descends beneath himself into his neighbor.[70]

In eloquence seldom equalled and never excelled in Christian theology, Luther provides his followers here with a clear and unequivocal mandate for a faith-activated life of social-ethical service to men everywhere. As certain as the rising of the sun is the flow of good works from a life truly committed to a Lord who came "not to be served, but to serve" (Mark 10:45). Luther warns only that we dare not mix our freedom in faith with our bondage in love, and try, like Rome, to free what is bound (love), and bind what is free (faith).

These two sayings, therefore, are true: "Good works do not make a good man, but a good man does good works; evil works do not make a wicked man, but a wicked man does evil works." . . . We do not, therefore, reject good works; on the contrary, we cherish and teach them as much as possible. We do not condemn them for their

[69] *Ibid.,* 367.
[70] *Ibid.,* 371.

own sake but on account of this godless addition to them and the perverse idea that righteousness is to be sought through them.[71]

For the rest of his public career, Luther tried to show and teach how "the Christian must take the middle course" between what we would today call legalism and license. On the right hand were the "proud and haughty" legalists who sought salvation by faithless activism. On the left hand were the "lazy and slovenly" libertarians who frustrated salvation by loveless passivism. "The first misuse their forgiveness, the others their regeneration; both refuse to be subjects to the glory and majesty of God."[72]

Free to Serve

If Luther was adamant that the Christian is free from the law in faith, he was equally insistent that the believer is bound to the law in love. Christ frees man from having to sacrifice good works toward God, allowing him in love and gratitude to re-direct them toward his neighbors. God does not need his service, but his neighbors do. This "suffering servant" form which is re-enacted in faithful love by all of Christ's disciples, is developed more fully by Luther in his classical formulation of the universal priesthood of believers.

As early as 1519, Luther's *Treatise on the Sacrament of Penance* contained a passage which was to work like yeast in his later theology. He is attacking the Roman teaching that the right of declaring forgiveness resides only in the ordained clergy by virtue of the power of the keys which has been passed on to them by Christ via Peter. Luther contends that the keys were given to Peter (Matt. 16) on behalf of the whole church (Matt. 18), and that, consequently, whenever God's Word and man's faith are operative, the clergy have no exclusive monopoly on the declaration of absolution. God alone forgives sin, and in God's name any Christian may declare the forgiveness of sins to the penitent.

The priests, bishops, and pope are only the servants of the Word of

[71] *Ibid.*, 361, 363.
[72] *WA* 15, 729.

Christ. It is in Christ's Word alone that you should trust, as a sure rock, for the forgiveness of your sins. . . . It follows that in the forgiveness of penance, nothing more is done by a pope or a bishop than could be done by any ordinary priest, or, for that matter, by any Christian layman. Every Christian, even a woman or child, can declare in God's name that "God forgives you of your sin," and you may be faithfully certain that your sin has as surely been absolved as if God himself spoke to you.[73]

This thought is further developed in the 1520 work entitled *Treatise on the New Testament that is the Holy Mass.* Luther concludes from his study of the inner nature of the Sacrament of the Altar that ". . . we do not offer Christ as a sacrifice, but that Christ offers us."[74] The only sacrifice which Luther permits as legitimate for a Christian is the Spirit-worked response of "prayer, praise, thanksgiving, and of ourselves," in gratitude for God's redeeming act in the death and resurrection of Christ. "Therefore all Christians are priests; the men, priests, the women, priestesses, be they young or old, masters or servants, mistresses or maids, learned or unlearned. Here there is no difference unless faith be unequal."[75]

It is significant that the doctrine of the priesthood of all believers finds a decisive expression in each of the great Reformation treatises of 1520. It has clearly become an essential component of Luther's understanding of the Christian life. It may be noted, parenthetically, that there is not the slightest hint here of any of the typical American Protestant "rugged individualism" in religious and ethical affairs. Luther is not saying that every man is his own pastor and that he therefore does not need the church because of his own "private pipeline" to God. Every Christian is described rather as *his neighbor's priest,* mediating to him—in church and society—the manifold gifts of God. We recall at once Luther's powerful summary of *The Freedom of a Christian:* "I will therefore give myself as a Christ to my neighbor, just as Christ offered himself to me."

[73] *WA* 2, 716.
[74] *PE* 1, 314.
[75] *Ibid.,* 316.

Luther introduces the same biblical insight again in connection with his repudiation of ordination as a valid sacrament in *The Babylonian Captivity of the Church*. He sees the glorification of the Roman priesthood as an evidence of clerical imperialism which does violence to the true nature of the church as a communion of saints. "Here, indeed, are the roots of that detestable tyranny of the clergy over the laity."[76]

If they were forced to grant that as many of us as have been baptized are all priests without distinction, as indeed we are, and that to them was committed the ministry only, yet with our consent, they would presently learn that they have no right to rule over us except in so far as we freely concede it (I Pet. 2:9). Therefore we are all priests, as many of us as are Christians. But the priests, as we call them, are ministers chosen from among us, who do all that they do in our name (I Cor. 4:1).[77]

It is also an important, but often overlooked, fact that Luther's contention that every Christian is his neighbor's priest constitutes a crucial part of the theological foundation of his *Open Letter to the Christian Nobility of the German Nation*. The "first wall" which has to be torn down if the church is ever to be reformed, insists Luther, is the ecclesiastical myth that "the spiritual is above the temporal power." Luther sets out to destroy this myth with his biblical counterproposal of the priesthood of all believers. In this instance, Luther appeals to the nobility primarily as the leading lay priests of the German church ". . . since the clergy, to whom this task [of correcting abuses] more properly belongs, have grown quite indifferent."[78]

Luther insists that the sharp Roman cleavage between the clergy and the laity has no biblical justification. "Through baptism all of us are consecrated to the priesthood . . . and there is no difference at all but that of office."[79] The ordained ministry is merely one among many other functional offices of Christian service. It is not, as claims Rome, a separate order of men in-

[76] *PE* 2, 278.
[77] *Ibid.*, 279.
[78] *Ibid.*, 61.
[79] *Ibid.*, 66.

vested with an "indelible character" (*character indelebilis*), whose unique service is "religious" while that of the laity is only "temporal."[80] This means very simply that all of life is God's, and that all neighbor-serving work is equally God-pleasing.

Therefore, just as those who are now called "spiritual"—priests, bishops, or popes—are neither different from other Christians nor superior to them, except that they are charged with the administration of the Word of God and the sacraments, which is their work or office, so it is with the temporal authorities,—they bear sword and rod with which to punish the evil and protect the good. A cobbler, a smith, a farmer, each has the work and office of his trade, and yet they are all alike consecrated priests and bishops, and every one by means of his own work or office must benefit and serve each other, that in this way many kinds of work may be done for the bodily and spiritual welfare of the community, even as all the members of the body serve one other.[81]

Along with his other great studies of 1520, Luther's *Treatise on Good Works* also helped to set the course for the Reformation in the vital area of social ethics. Well aware that ". . . when I exalt faith and reject those works done without faith, they accuse me of forbidding good works," Luther takes the Ten Commandments of the Old Testament and recasts them in the light of the New Testament in such a way as to avoid the twin dangers of moralism and quietism (cf. ch. 4). Luther's non-legalistic interpretation of the law of God centers man's whole life—religious and ethical—in the faithful and loving fulfillment of the first commandment. To have "no other gods" is not merely one-tenth of God's will for man; it comprises all of it. Ultimately, there is only one absolute commandment with nine appended illustrations of how a life committed to God in faith expresses itself in love while meeting the everyday challenges of life. The refrain, "We should so fear and love God that we . . . ," always introduces an ethic of grace in Luther's explanation of each of the last nine commandments in the *Small Cathechism*.

All the commandments of the law are summed up in the law of

---

[80] *Ibid.*, 66-68.
[81] *Ibid.*, 69.

love; that is, if they are not performed in love, they are against God and worthless. You must act accordingly. No matter what the work, your eyes should always remain centered on love. Laws may even be broken, if necessary, in order to alleviate a neighbor's troubles and suffering. For our deeds should exhibit the kind of love Christ assigns to our lives. . . . This love of neighbor is like unto the first commandment of the love of God.[82]

When the service of our fellow men is incorporated into the service of God, we have such an intimate union of faith and love that an evangelical "ethic of the first commandment" can call faith itself the best of all good works, even when it is clearly recognized that "faith is a divine work in us." Luther writes, "The first and highest, the most precious of all good works is faith in Christ . . . for in this work all good works must be done and receive from it the inflow of their goodness, like a loan."[83] This living faith is what makes all priestly deeds good and equal in God's sight, since they are performed with a reverent disposition and motivation—for the glory of God and the benefit of the neighbor.

If you ask [Rome] whether they count it a good work when they work at their trade, walk, stand, eat, drink, sleep, and do all kinds of work for the nourishment of the body and the common welfare, and whether they believe that God takes pleasure in them because of such works, you will find that they say, "No." They define good works so narrowly that they are made to consist only of praying in church, fasting, and almsgiving. Other works they consider to be in vain, and think that God cares nothing for them. So through their damnable unbelief, they curtail and lessen the service of God, who is served by all things that are done, spoken, or thought in faith . . . even if it were so small a thing as picking up a straw.[84]

Luther's description of the priesthood of all believers in terms of faithful and loving service to one's neighbors has been developed at length here because it remained *normative* in his ethics for the rest of his life. To be sure, further tensions and

[82] *WA* 10[III], 343.
[83] *PE* 1, 187.
[84] *Ibid.,* 188.

qualifications are introduced when we are continually reminded that faith is always at war with distrust, and love is ever at odds with justice in the religious and ethical dimensions of every Christian's daily life. This is a very real part of the Christian's suffering in a "theology of the cross." Nevertheless, the norm remains constant and is repeated tirelessly in tract after tract and sermon after sermon: "The whole gospel teaches nothing more than faith in God and love of neighbor."[85]

When you accept Christ as a divine gift and do not doubt him, then you are a Christian. And once you have Christ as the Ground of your salvation, then follows the second step. Accept him also as your Exemplar [Archtypum] giving of yourself for your neighbors as he gave himself for you. This puts both faith and love into operation and God's commandments are fulfilled by man's joyful willingness to suffer all things.[86]

All Christian faith and life can be summarized simply in terms of faith and love, through which a man is placed between God and his neighbors as a medium which receives from above and transmits again through below. Like a vessel or pipe, man should act as a channel through which the fountain of God's gifts flows uninterruptedly to nourish others. See, these are truly God-conformed men who receive everything they have from God in Christ, and then testify to their faith in God-like generosity to their neighbors. Through faith we become God's children . . . through love we become gods ourselves.[87]

Righteous and Sinful

In order to integrate Luther's teaching on faith active in love with his constant insistence upon the need for suffering and self-mortification in Christian daily life, we must now introduce his conviction that sin persists in the life of the redeemed. For Luther, as for Paul, the Christian is at once both righteous and sinful *(simul iustus et peccator)*. In himself, he is "sinful in fact" *(in re)*; in Christ, he is "righteous in hope" *(in spe)*.[88]

This means that in the Christian life there is a tension be-

[85] *WA* 8, 15. See, e.g., *WA* 8, 355; 9, 672; 10^{III}, 174; 12, 420.
[86] *WA* 10^{I,1}, 12.
[87] *Ibid.*, 100.
[88] *WA* 56, 272.

tween faith and distrust which qualifies and conditions every-thing which has been said thus far. There is both continuity and discontinuity between the old and the new, the flesh and the Spirit, the law and the gospel, the old man in Adam and the new man in Christ. Up to now the discontinuity has been stressed in the radical rebirth, the total transformation of personality and joyful service to others which is inherent in man's accept-ance of the good news of God's mighty act in Christ. Now we must briefly examine the other side of the paradox: the historical continuity which accompanies the eschatological discontinuity as the unbelief of the natural man wars constantly against the faith of the believer.

Men must always move between fear and hope as between two mill-stones. At no time dare they deviate either to the left or to the right, for this leads inevitably to the godless extremes of security or arrogance. Through their security, men deviate to the left and disregard the fear of God. . . . Through their arrogance, men de-viate to the right and believe that all their efforts are pleasing to God even if they do not fear him. Since they do not acknowledge themselves to be sinners, it follows necessarily that they do not fear God.[89]

The second article of Luther's *Defense and Explanation* fol-lowing the Leipzig Debate with Eck is concerned with the biblical teaching that sin remains in every Christian, even after baptism. Luther finds particularly in the epistles of Paul the indisputable documentation for his position that a Christian liv-ing by faith is simultaneously justified and sinful as both saint and sinner.

Luther's description of the self-contradiction within the Chris-tian man consists not in the Greek dualism of body and soul, but in the biblical struggle between "flesh" and "Spirit"; that is, between sinful self-centeredness and faithful God-centered-ness. Man's dilemma is not grounded in his finitude as a creature but in his rebellion as a sinner. And yet his finitude is intimately involved in this struggle, for it is precisely man's unwillingness

[89] *St. L.* 4, 416.

to recognize his limitations as a creature of God which provides the occasion for his sin. The Christian believes, but not completely; he loves, but not wholly; he hopes, but not totally. "I believe; help thou my unbelief," is the cry of a man in whom God has inaugurated a saving work which is not yet completed. The whole Christian life after baptism is nothing more than waiting for the revelation of salvation which man already has.[90]

It is evident that sin remains in the baptized and the saints as long as they are flesh and blood and live on earth and that the condemnation of this article in the bull is most un-Christian. But let us add further evidence. St. Paul says in Romans 7:22, "I delight in the law of God, in my inmost flesh, but I see in my members another law at war with the law of my mind and making me captive to the law of sin which dwells in my members." St. Paul confesses here that he finds a good law and will in his spirit, and also an evil law and will in his members. How is it then possible to deny that sin remains in a holy baptized man?[91]

Moreover, St. Paul adds even more plainly in the same passage, "I myself serve the law of God with my Spirit, but with my flesh I serve the law of sin." Does not that make it abundantly clear that one and the same man finds in himself two things? Through the Spirit, he wills the good and serves the law of God and is godly. . . . But with the rebellious flesh, he wills evil, and takes pleasure and delight in the service of evil. . . . Because of the Spirit, this man is godly; because of the flesh he is a sinner.[92]

When Luther is forced to present his views in concentrated form in his *Preface to Romans,* he again pictures the Christian life in terms of a dramatic struggle between self-rule (flesh) and God-rule (Spirit). This penetrating insight into the genuinely biblical meanings of "flesh" and "Spirit" is of great significance for Luther's teachings on sex life. It is obvious at once how antithetical are the views of the Bible and the world. "Flesh does not refer to unchastity, but to all sins, above all to unbelief, which is the most spiritual of vices. On the other hand, [Paul] calls him a spiritual man who is occupied with the most

[90] *WA* $10^{1,1}$, 108.
[91] *LW* 32, 20.
[92] *Ibid.*, 21.

external of works, as Christ, when he washed the disciples' feet, and Peter, when he steered his boat and fished. Thus 'the flesh' is a man who lives and works, inwardly and outwardly, in the service of the flesh's profit and in this temporal life; 'the Spirit' is the man who lives and works, inwardly and outwardly, in the service of the Spirit and the future life."[93]

This distinctively biblical view of the whole man (*totus homo*) as being both of the flesh and of the Spirit, is vital for Luther's understanding of the Christian life. There is absolutely no possibility here of some kind of spiritual "inwardness" as a Christian alternative to carnal "outwardness." The lines are drawn horizontally, so to speak, rather than vertically: that is, both flesh and Spirit have both inner and outer expressions since it is the whole man—both religiously and ethically—for which God and Satan are contending.

Luther's characteristic descriptions of the dynamic quality of Christian life are so true to the paradoxical witness of Scripture that it defies any final codification or systematizing by the theologian. "For I do not do the good I want, but the evil I do not want is what I do" (Rom. 7:19). Like Paul, Luther ends by viewing Christian existence entirely in terms of daily death and rebirth. "Baptism signifies two things—death and resurrection; that is, full and complete justification. The minister's immersing the child in the water signifies death; his drawing it forth again signifies life (Rom. 6:4). . . . You have thus been baptized once in the sacrament, but you must be constantly baptized again through faith; you must constantly die, you must constantly live again."[94]

This same existential tone permeates the tracts and sermons in which Luther describes the action-packed life of the Christian between Satan and God in terms of continual struggle and strife. A believer's whole life consists, paradoxically, in "waiting for the holiness he already has."[95] As saint and sinner at once,

[93] *PE* 6, 453.
[94] *PE* 2, 230.
[95] *WA* 10^{I,1}, 108.

he is always "on the way" in his earthly pilgrimage. "For this life is always a moving forward from faith in faith, from love in love, from patience in patience, and from cross in cross."[96]

This life, therefore, is not righteousness but growth in righteousness, not health but healing, not being but becoming, not rest but exercise. We are not yet what we shall be, but we are growing toward it. The process is not yet finished, but it is going on. This is not the end, but it is the road. All does not yet gleam with glory, but all is being purified.[97]

In the daring trust of this life-committing faith, Luther concludes his defense of the view that sin continues as an enemy throughout the Christian life. We can now understand, therefore, why he considers it right and proper that a good part of the Christian's ethical life should consist in the performance of good works and the endurance of suffering. They are as necessary for his own purging as for his neighbor's service.

Insofar as he is righteous (*iustus*), the Christian's social action is the joyful and voluntary expression of his faith active in "spontaneous love in obedience to God."[98] But insofar as he is still sinful (*peccator*), the Christian's social action is the cross which he is forced to bear in order ". . . to reduce the body to subjection and purify it of its evil lusts."[99] As liberated by the gospel, he serves others voluntarily; as goaded by the law, he serves others begrudgingly and unwillingly. In either case, however, God sees to it that man's pride is checked and his neighbors served, as good works contribute to the general welfare of the community no matter what the motive of the actor.

Conclusion

For Luther, the biblical message of salvation is a tension-filled unity which can be viewed from the perspective of any one of its constitutive elements. He can speak of "grace alone," "Christ alone," "Scripture alone," or "faith alone" and mean thereby

[96] *WA* 15, 502.
[97] *PE* 3, 131.
[98] *PE* 2, 329.
[99] *Ibid.*

the same saving event as seen from its eternal source, historical expression, apostolic witness, or personal appropriation. In fidelity to this Christ-centered faith, Luther roundly condemned the moral and rational work-righteousness inherent in the philosophical theology of Rome. Before God, reason must submit to Scripture and works must bow to faith. In an evangelical "theology of the cross," men confess that "the righteous shall live by faith."

With their salvation thus assured in the atonement of Christ, grateful Christians are free to redirect their reason and good works toward contributing to their neighbors' welfare. Luther grounds his ethic in the paradoxical nature of Christian freedom which accepts liberation from satanic bondage as the divine invitation for human service. All men act as their brother's keeper: willingly in faith, begrudgingly in rebellion. As the Christian is at once both saint and sinner, his enforced service aids his self-discipline while his voluntary service meets his neighbor's needs. Against the presumption of Roman clericalism, Luther insists that all Christians be permitted the beneficial exercise of their God-given priesthood in service to their God-given neighbors.

In opposition to all unevangelical ethics of principles, "blue laws," ideals, or rules and regulations, Luther portrays the biblical pattern of a life of faith active in love. A Christian ethic based upon the "divine indicative" of God's grace preserves the freedom of the believer under the guidance of the Holy Spirit through the Bible, the church, and prayer, to discover anew in each concrete situation what the will of God permits or requires of him then and there. "Live as free men, yet without using your freedom as a pretext for evil; but live as servants of God."

As we turn now for some of this direction in the theology of society which complements Luther's theology of service, we do so confidently in the knowledge of the basic "Why" of Christian social ethics. In depicting the growing communal thrust of Luther's theology, we have traced his recovery of this central biblical affirmation: Man is saved by God's grace, for Christ's sake, through faith alone; thereby freeing him to serve his neighbors with all the good works that a God of love empowers. "We love because he first loved us."

CHAPTER FOUR

Righteousness and Social Justice

Faith and life were inseparable for Luther since he confessed Christ as the living Lord of both. How a man lives is the ethical reflection of what he believes and whom he worships. Faith in Christ frees man for service to his neighbors: a loveless faith is as un-Christian as a faithless love.

Yet Luther also insisted that we are not to identify the realms of faith and of life. Unless we clearly make the proper biblical distinctions between them—without separating them—we will never be able to do justice to the twofold way in which God rules his fallen and sinful world. God is one; yet he governs men differently as Creator and as Redeemer. God's Word is one; yet it confronts men differently as law and as gospel. God's kingdom is one; yet it incorporates men differently into its temporal and eternal dimensions. Now it would be much easier to explain God's rule over men if we were able to separate them into saints and sinners (like Rome), and then describe how he governs each. But the biblical witness is clear that this is impossible short of the Last Judgment.

Luther concluded from Scripture that God does not rule two different groups of people in two different ways, but rather that he governs all men in a twofold way: his "proper" way of giving (via the gospel) and his "strange" way of demanding (via the law). Fidelity to God and his Word means that we neither separate nor equate the law and the gospel, for their equation leads to clericalism as surely as their separation leads to secularism. Luther held that it is fatal both to our religion and to our ethics if we do not properly distinguish the realm of faith (under the gospel) from the realm of life (under the law).

In maintaining this crucial distinction, however, he never relinquished his primary assertion of the fundamental unity of law and gospel—worship and service—in the eternal strategy of God and in the daily lives of men. Only by asserting both their provisional diversity (*vs.* clericalism) and their ultimate unity (*vs.* secularism) could Luther arrive at an evangelical theology of society which freely renders what is due to God and Caesar. His doctrine of the "two kingdoms" exposed the prevailing clericalism of Rome and provided Evangelicals with the theological foundations for a just and responsible society under God.

God's Twofold Rule

Luther's organic view of Christian faith and life made his ethical protest against the temporal imperialism of Rome inevitable. At stake for him ultimately was not whether German homes and communities would be ruled by priests or by princes, but whether or not they would be ruled by God—to be sure, *through* priests and princes—in keeping with the double-edged sword of his Word: preservation of creatures via the law and salvation of sinners via the gospel. What really determined Luther's thought and action in this crucial area of domestic life was neither German patriotism nor medieval patriarchalism, important as both these factors were in conditioning and coloring the concrete forms which his views took. Ultimate alone for Luther was his fidelity to the teaching of Scripture on the nature of God's twofold rule of church and society, and the important role which the priesthood of all believers plays in each.

Church-ruled homes and towns were an abomination in Luther's eyes. He characterized the Roman teaching that "the spiritual is above the temporal power" as "the very first wall to be torn down" in the many reform proposals contained in his *Open Letter to the Christian Nobility.* Moreover, in his treatise on *The Papacy at Rome,* Luther described the papacy as a human administrative arrangement rather than a divine ordinance. One of Rome's arguments was its exegesis of Christ's charge to Peter, "Feed my sheep" (John 21:15). Instead of conferring upon Peter and his personal successors an authority above all others, this verse, in Luther's eyes, shows up Rome's disposition to feed upon the sheep of God instead of nourishing them with the Bread of Life.

"Feeding," in the Roman sense, means to burden Christendom with many human and hurtful laws, to sell the bishoprics at the highest possible price, to extract the annates from all benefices, to usurp authority over all foundations, to force into servitude all the bishops with terrible oaths, to sell indulgences, to rob the whole world by means of letters, bulls, seals and wax, to prohibit the preaching of the gospel, to appoint knaves from Rome to all places, to bring all litigation to Rome, to increase quarrels and disputes—in short, to allow no one to come freely to the truth and to have peace.[1]

It is because of this worldliness within the See of Rome that ". . . the pope and the Romanists cannot bear any questioning and investigating of the foundation of papal power, and everyone is accused of doing a scandalous, presumptuous, and heretical thing, who is not satisfied with their mere assertions, but seeks for its real basis."[2] Luther insists, however, that the context makes it clear that Peter's "feeding" of the sheep is dependent upon his prior love of God.[3] Unlike civil authorities, whose jurisdiction persists even when they are personally unrighteous, Luther holds that ecclesiastical authority may be judged in terms of its faithfulness to its divine commission.

Perhaps you might reply, that a subject can be obedient to temporal authority even if that authority were not righteous; why should one not be obedient to the pope's authority? . . . Answer: The Scriptures do not call temporal authority "feeding," and in the New Testament there is no instance where God publicly appointed anyone to temporal power, although no such power arises without his secret ordering. For this reason, St. Peter calls such powers "ordinances of men" (I Pet. 2:13), because they rule not by God's Word, but

[1] *PE* 1, 383.
[2] *Ibid.*, 390.
[3] *Ibid.*, 387.

by God's governance, and it is not needful, therefore, that such rulers should be righteous. But inasmuch as we here have God's Word, "Feed my sheep," neither the shepherd nor the sheep can fulfill this Word except by obedience to God and righteousness of life.[4]

Luther's concern is that the church exercise its power responsibly under God for the benefit of those under its authority. One of the prime requisites for good rule is a judicious recognition of God-given boundaries, and it is here that Luther considers Roman clericalism to be most guilty. In its zeal to "Christianize" society, Rome has virtually deified an institution at the expense of its living Lord. That all of life must be ruled by God does not at all mean that it must be governed by the church.

Against the Roman attempt to divide Christendom into two different classes of society—clergy and laity—Luther protests in the name of the universal priesthood of believers. On the other hand, against the Roman attempt to centralize all earthly power in the hands of a pope as the vicar of Christ, Luther insists equally strongly that God has instituted civil authority to carry out the non-redemptive dimensions of his reign over mankind. Both these elements—the oneness of God's people and the twofold means of God's rule over them—are kept in dialectical tension in Luther's *Open Letter to the Christian Nobility*.

There is really no difference between laymen and priests, princes and bishops, "spirituals" and "temporals," as they call them, except that of office and work, but not of "estate"; for they are all of the same estate—true priests, bishops and popes—though they are not all engaged in the same work.[5]

I say then, since the temporal power is ordained of God to punish evildoers and to protect them that do well, it should therefore be left free to perform its office without hindrance through the whole body of Christendom without respect of persons, whether it affect pope, bishops, priests, monks, nuns, or anybody else.[6]

In keeping with this diversity of function under the over-

[4] *Ibid.*, 386.
[5] *PE* 2, 69.
[6] *Ibid.*, 70.

arching unity of God's rule, Luther proceeds to list a total of thirty-one prevailing "works of the Antichrist" from which the common people are forced to suffer because of the arrogance or incompetence of their ecclesiastical and civil rulers. That the first twenty-six are directed against the clergy of Rome indicates where Luther felt the greater danger to lie in 1520. Unlike our own day, it was church clericalism and not state secularism which was the chief thorn in Luther's flesh. The very first abuse condemned in the *Open Letter* is the shameful worldliness of the Roman pontiff.

It is a horrible and frightful thing that the ruler of Christendom, who boasts himself vicar of Christ and successor of St. Peter, lives in such worldly splendor that in this regard no king or emperor can equal or approach him, and that he who claims the title of "most holy" and "most spiritual" is more worldly than the world itself. . . . These indeed are the very works of the very Antichrist.[7]

Following a long and detailed treatment of the concrete clerical abuses which emanated from Rome, Luther addresses himself only briefly to a few "failings of the temporal estate" since ". . . of what the temporal powers of the nobility ought to do, I think I have said enough in the little book, *On Good Works*. There is room for improvement in their lives and in their rule, and yet the abuses of the temporal power are not to be compared with those of the spiritual power, as I have there shown."[8] Consequently, in this writing of 1520, Luther simply asserts his conviction that "it is the duty of the authorities to seek the highest good of the subjects," and that appropriate social and economic reforms are necessary in such matters as "extravagance and excess in dress," "the spice traffic," "the traffic in annuities," "the abuse of eating and drinking," and "the maintenance among us of open and common houses of prostitution."[9]

A far different situation prevailed three years later which precipitated Luther's writing of *Secular Authority: To What*

---

[7] *Ibid.*, 80.
[8] *Ibid.*, 163.
[9] *Ibid.*, 158ff.

Extent It Should Be Obeyed (1523). On first glance, its title might suggest that Luther found it necessary to protest against the godless inroads of a secular state so soon after he had challenged the clericalism of an overzealous church. Actually, the very opposite comes closer to the truth. *Weltlich* meant civil, temporal, non-ecclesiastical authority for Luther and his medieval contemporaries, and if we translate this today as "secular," we should carefully disavow as anachronistic any of the irreligious and antireligious associations which the term currently suggests to us.

In reality, it was not the state's lack of religion, but Rome's employment of the civil sword precisely for the propagation of its clericalism, which elicited from the Reformer this very significant work. In his letter of dedication to Duke John of Saxony, Luther recalls what a thorny problem the relation of civil to religious authority has been for the Christian church throughout its turbulent history. More concretely, the apparent contradiction between religious perfection and ethical responsibility—both of which are enjoined upon Christians in Scripture—seems virtually irreconcilable.

For example, Matthew 5–7 and Romans 12–15 seem to talk two different languages to two different worlds. Yet to sever the two does violence to the unity of God's people. Such a tactic leads inevitably to the double-standard morality of Rome in which the inferior laity need be obedient only to the minimal demands of social responsibility ("precepts"), while the superior clergy is obligated to obey the more rigorous commands of religious perfection ("counsels"). Luther soundly condemned this ethical dualism within the one church. Religiously, it encourages hypocrisy; politically, it stimulates priestcraft; socially, it breeds division. Moreover, it has absolutely no biblical foundation: "They who believe and love the most are the perfect ones, whether outwardly they be male or female, prince or peasant, monk or layman."[10]

[10] *PE* 3, 233.

Essentially, Luther's task was to re-establish the theological co-ordination of civil and religious authority which had been advocated in Augustine's *City of God* prior to the late medieval church's program of subordinating the civil to the religious sphere. The uniqueness of Luther's formulation, however, lies in its implicit rejection of any kind of biblical-philosophical synthesis (as with Plato in Augustine or with Aristotle in Thomas), and his explicit correlation of the totality of human experience with the strictly biblical categories of God's rule of mankind by law and by gospel as the two-edged sword of his Word. Ultimately, Luther's doctrine of the "two kingdoms" is grounded firmly in the New Testament eschatology of the two ages (aeons) in Adam and in Christ.

Luther devotes the first part of *Secular Authority* to an emphasis on the divine character of the establishment and maintenance of civil authority. He does so in conscious opposition to the views of both the Romans and the sectarian radicals *(Schwärmer)* who alike depreciate the civil realm as religiously inferior and contaminating to a truly Christian life. While Luther believes that "if all the world were composed of real Christians, that is, true believers, no prince, king, lord, sword, or law would be needed," his biblical realism convinces him that "Christians, however, are few and far between," and that even he who confesses Christ as Lord remains sinful while "on the way" to becoming a true Christian.[11] As a remedy against the sin of the world, therefore, God has ordained secular authority "for the punishment of the wicked and the protection of the upright."[12]

We must firmly establish secular law and the sword, that no one may doubt that it is in the world by God's will and ordinance. The passages which establish this are the following: "Let every soul be subject to power and authority, for there is no power but from God. The power that is everywhere is ordained of God. He then who resists the power resists God's ordinance. But he who resists God's

[11] *Ibid.,* 234, 237.
[12] *Ibid.,* 233.

ordinance shall bring himself under condemnation" (Rom. 13:1ff.).
Likewise, "Be subject to every kind of human ordinance, whether
to the king as supreme, or to the governors, as to those sent of him
for the punishing of the evil and for the reward of the good" (I Pet.
2:13).[13]

It would be difficult for us to overemphasize the decisive influence which these biblical passages played in the formative
stages of Luther's social ethics. The more Rome neglected them,
the more Luther stressed them, often forcing both into rigid
positions which did not always take the totality of the biblical
witness (e.g. Rev. 13) into balanced consideration. Nevertheless,
Luther could present an impressive array of biblical citations
to document his contention that "this penal law existed from
the beginning of the world."

Actually, and more accurately, none of Luther's sources refer
to God's institution of secular authority in creation itself before
the fall of Adam. As he himself was later to insist, "There was
no need of civil government, since nature was unimpaired and
without sin."[14] The remedial character of the state is traced
back to Cain's fear of the sword of civil punishment, which he
would not have known ". . . if he had not seen and heard from
Adam that murderers should be slain." Its validity is then continually reaffirmed throughout biblical history, says Luther, by
God (Gen. 9:6), the law of Moses (Exod. 21), John the Baptist
(Luke 3:14), and Christ himself (Matt. 26:52).[15]

Yet parallel with all these affirmations, Luther recognizes that
some passages like Matthew 5-7 and Romans 12 ". . . would make
it appear as though in the New Testament there should be no
secular sword among Christians."[16] Luther's classical reconciliation of this abiding Christian dilemma is grounded in his master-
ful delineation of the "two kingdoms" in which man's living
God reigns as both Creator-Preserver and Redeemer-Sanctifier.
Luther boldly drives the mystery of the tension between the "two

[13] *Ibid.*, 231.
[14] *LW* 1, 115.
[15] *PE* 3, 231-32.
[16] *Ibid.*, 233.

ages" of Scripture back into the diversified activities of the Triune God. Since the Christian lives on earth by faith and not sight, Luther's doctrine is intended as a confession of faith in the lordship of God over all of his creation, rather than as either a political program or a metaphysical system. It views mankind from the perspective of eternity, seeking out the handiwork of a God whose mighty acts in history—through human instruments —are perceptible only to the eyes of faith.

Luther charges that it is blasphemous for man to designate some realm of God's creation as "secular" or "profane," if we thereby judge it to be unworthy of his divine activity or self-sufficient in its own autonomy. God rules everyone and everywhere. It is he alone in whom "we live, and move, and have our being." And yet, because not all of God's creatures acknowledge his lordship, he rules men differently as their Creator and as their Redeemer.

We must divide all the children of Adam into two classes; the first belong to the kingdom of God, the second to the kingdom of the world. Those belonging to the kingdom of God are all true believers in Christ and are subject to Christ . . . and the gospel of the kingdom. . . . All who are not Christians belong to the kingdom of the world and are under the law. Since few believe and still fewer live a Christian life, do not resist evil, and themselves do no evil, God has provided for non-Christians a different government outside the Christian estate and God's kingdom, and has subjected them to the sword. . . . For this reason the two kingdoms must be sharply distinguished, and both permitted to remain; the one to produce piety, the other to bring about external peace and prevent evil deeds; neither is sufficient in the world without the other.[17]

The key points in Luther's position are these: 1) God is the Lord of *both* kingdoms, although he rules by different means (law and gospel) for different ends (peace and piety) in each; 2) every Christian lives in *both* kingdoms simultaneously—in the kingdom of God insofar as he is righteous, and in the kingdom of the world insofar as he is sinful; 3) the two kingdoms are to be sharply *distinguished* from one another, which means that

[17] *Ibid.,* 234-37.

the realms of law and gospel are to be neither separated (in secularism) nor equated (in clericalism) but permitted to co-exist in harmonious interaction and co-ordination as complementary expressions of God's creative and redemptive activity among men.

Against this broad background, let us turn first to Luther's description of the "kingdom of God." Here he lays chief emphasis upon faith and love, i.e., the righteousness of God in Christ and its fruit, Christian righteousness, as the constitutive elements in the realm of God's redemptive work. It is the graciousness of God and his law-free gospel which is essential both for man's eternal salvation (by faith alone) and for the temporal service of his neighbors (by faith active in love). "Christ is not a legislator but the fulfiller of the law."[18] When led by the Holy Spirit of the living God, the Christian—as righteous—knows no law but the faithful transmission of divine love (I Tim. 1:19).

A good tree does not need any teaching or law to bear good fruit; its nature causes it to bear according to its kind without any law or teaching. A man would be a fool to make a book of laws and statutes telling an apple tree to bear apples and not thorns, when it is able by its own nature to do this better than man with all his books can define and direct. Just so, by the Spirit and by faith, all Christians are thoroughly inclined to do well and keep the law, much more than anyone can teach them with all the laws, and need, so far as they are concerned, no commandments or law.[19]

It is on the strength of this combination of faith and love that Luther is able to repudiate the Roman separation of "general precepts" for the laity and "counsels of perfection" for the clergy. The divorce inherent in this double-standard morality is un-biblical and therefore illegitimate for Christian ethics. All the Bible is addressed to all men, but most of humanity rejects it. This, then, is the key distinction for Luther: not Christian clergymen *vs.* Christian laymen, but all Christians *vs.* all non-Christians. Scripture does not make divisions among Christians, but it

[18] *WA* 2, 494.
[19] *PE* 3, 235.

does distinguish them clearly from non-believers. On the one hand, "There is neither Jew or Greek, there is neither slave nor free, there is neither male nor female; for you are all one in Christ Jesus" (Gal. 3:28). On the other hand, "For I tell you, unless your righteousness exceeds that of the scribes and the Pharisees, you will never enter the kingdom of heaven" (Matt. 5:20).

In concrete terms, this means for Luther that the ethic of the Ten Commandments is enjoined upon all of God's creatures, while the ethic of the Sermon on the Mount is addressed exclusively to committed Christians.[20] It goes without saying, of course, that insofar as Christians remain sinful, they fall with all men under the "Thou shalt nots" of the Ten Commandments. It is of the greatest importance for our understanding of the totality of Luther's social ethics that we clearly distinguish this twofold righteousness of man which corresponds to the twofold rule of God in the two kingdoms of redemption and creation:

1) *Christian righteousness* is the piety generated by the Holy Spirit in the hearts of Christians in the form of faith active in love;

2) *civil righteousness* is the morality of which all rational creatures are capable—Christians included—in the form of law-abiding social justice.

Required of the Christian, therefore, is both a calculating love which takes the form of justice ("wise as serpents") and a sacrificial love which "exceeds" the demands of the law ("gentle as doves").

Luther's primary concern in *Secular Authority* is with the Christian righteousness which believers exercise for their neighbor's benefit in the realm of civil and temporal affairs. It is not as though they were to perform different functions or to engage in different activities from those of their non-believing fellow

[20] *Ibid.*, 238.

men. The decisive difference between the "stations" or "offices" (*Stände*) which all men hold, and the "callings" or "vocations" (*Berufe*) which only Christians have, is that of inner motivation. It is not what we do or where we do it, but rather why and how it is done, that pleases God. Once again, the ethical fruits are judged by the religious roots.

There is no great difference between a Christian and a civil honest man [*hominem civiliter bonum*]. For the works of a Christian in outward show are base and simple. He does his duty according to his vocation, he governs the commonweal, he guides his family, he tills the ground, he gives counsel, he aids and succors his neighbor. These works the carnal man does not much esteem, but thinks them to be common and worth nothing, being such things as the laity and the heathen also do. . . . Yet they are good works indeed, and accepted of God, because they are done in faith, with a cheerful heart, and with obedience and thankfulness toward God.[21]

Applied concretely to the issues at hand, this means for Luther that Christians are voluntarily to submit themselves to the authority and demands of civil officers and rulers for the sake of the general welfare of the community. Believers and non-believers alike are all children of God whom Christians are to look upon as "neighbors" in need of personal love and social justice.[22] The question of bearing arms on behalf of the civil community—in the light of the non-resistance demands of the Sermon on the Mount—is thereby settled in terms of the two kingdoms. Personally, no man may take up the sword on his own behalf as one Christian acting among other Christians (under the gospel). But socially, he may bear arms as a Christian citizen acting on behalf of others in the larger community of non-Christians (under the law). In a fallen and sinful world, Christian love will often have to do some strange and dirty work (*opus alienum*) in order to protect the good and punish the wicked.

Therefore, should you see that there is a lack of hangmen, beadles, judges, lords, or princes, and find that you are qualified, you should offer your services and seek the place, that necessary government

[21] *WA* 40[I], 573.
[22] *PE* 3, 239.

may by no means be despised and become inefficient or perish. For the world cannot and dare not dispense with it.[23]

Luther's biblical realism has forced him to come forward with a stirring cry for men to assume their Christian social responsibility. Since civil occupations serve God's creating and preserving rule among his children, all Christians are to become involved in social affairs for the sake of the commonweal. The absolutes of the Sermon on the Mount relate to man only in his personal relationships with his fellow believers. They cannot prescribe ethical conduct for a sinful society at large. Nor should the refusal of Christ and his apostles to take up the sword discourage us from our own responsible citizenship.[24] Their calling was the unique one of establishing the kingdom of God, yet never once did they forbid, but always strongly encouraged, the active participation of their followers in the exercise of love to their fellow men. Neighborly service does not endanger salvation by grace; it is its responsible by-product.

In this manner, Luther believed that his social ethic fulfilled the dialectical requirements of Holy Scripture, while at the same time maintaining the crucial distinction between the law and the gospel, the kingdom of the world and the kingdom of God. At heart, Luther's whole presentation is a brilliant expansion (in social terms) of his earlier description of the paradoxical role of the Christian man who is free in faith to serve in love. "In this way, then, things are well balanced, and you satisfy at the same time God's kingdom inwardly and the kingdom of the world outwardly; at the same time suffer evil and injustice and yet punish evil and injustice; at the same time do not resist evil and yet resist it. For in one case you consider yourself and what is yours, in the other you consider your neighbor and what is his."[25]

Civil Righteousness

We have already given great emphasis to the religious dimension

[23] *Ibid.*, 241.
[24] *Ibid.*, 246.
[25] *Ibid.*, 241.

of man's existence under the rule of God's gospel. This realm Luther describes variously as "the kingdom of God," "the kingdom on the right hand," "the kingdom of Christ and the gospel," and "man before God." What is of special interest for us now, however, is the way in which all of this is related by Luther to the second of the two kingdoms: "the kingdom of the world," "the kingdom on the left hand," "the kingdom of Caesar and the law," and "man in community life." Luther asserts with Paul that the ethical dimensions of man's existence is properly under the reign of God's law whose religious function of damning sin *(usus theologicus)* is always coupled with its ethical function of preventing crime *(usus politicus).*

To put it as briefly as possible here, Paul says that the law is given for the sake of the unrighteous, that is, that those who are not Christians may through the law be externally restrained from evil deeds. Since, however, no one is by nature Christian or pious, but every one sinful and evil, God places the restraints of the law upon them all, so that they may not dare give rein to their desires and commit outward, wicked deeds.[26]

The indispensable key to Luther's understanding of the "kingdom of the world" is his conviction that God has ordained civil authorities ". . . to restrain the un-Christian and wicked so that they must keep the peace outwardly, even against their will."[27] This means that God in his loving providence has so structured daily life in the civil community that all men—"even against their will"—are constrained to live in conformity with at least a minimal standard of social morality if only out of the fear of punishment or hope of reward.

In comparison with Christian righteousness, of course, this so-called civil righteousness *(iustitia civilis)* comes off a very poor second. Whereas Christian righteousness springs forth from faith, and is therefore joyful and willing, civil righteousness is forced out of unbelief, and is consequently "murmuring" and involuntary. Since "all that does not proceed from faith is sin" (Rom.

[26] *Ibid.*, 235.
[27] *Ibid.*, 236.

14:23), civil righteousness has absolutely no justifying value—
no matter how enlightened its self-interest might be. It is "inherently vicious" at the core, however attractive its surface.[28]
Luther remains unequivocal in his religious condemnation of all
social-ethical behavior which is not fired by the loving heart of
one who has confessed Christ as his Lord and Savior. "Where
there is only secular rule or law, there, of necessity, is sheer
hypocrisy, though the commandments be God's very own. Without the Holy Spirit in the heart, no one becomes really pious, he
may do as fine works as he will."[29]

Yet parallel with the many statements which condemn all
civil righteousness as sinful in the sight of God, there are other
writings of Luther which consider the moral efforts of unregenerate men to be relatively "righteous" in the realm of creation, even when they remain wholly unacceptable in the realm
of redemption. For instance: although hating and killing might
be considered equally sinful in heaven, it is clearly the lesser
of two evils if society can at least compel a man to control his
murderous actions even if not his hateful thoughts. In a fallen
and sinful world, ethics must often be satisfied with the imperfect
second-best. Consequently, God punishes sin with sin and employs sinful individuals and institutions as imperfect dikes against
even more demonic expressions of man's unfaithful rebellion
against his Maker. "God is himself the founder, lord, master,
demander, and rewarder of both spiritual and civil righteousness.
There is no human order or power which is not a godly thing."[30]
Works of civil righteousness, therefore, fall on the boundary
line between the two kingdoms as ultimately evil, but provision-
ally good; they are products of sin which are at once remedies
against it.

Learn here to speak of the law as contemptuously as you can in
matters of justification [*in causa iustificationis*] . . . but apart from
justification [*extra locum iustificationis*], we ought with Paul to

[28] *WA* 40[II], 526.
[29] *PE* 3, 237.
[30] *WA* 19, 629.

think reverently of the law, to commend it highly, to call it holy, righteous, good, spiritual, and divine.[31]

Perhaps the most cogent illustration of Luther's ambivalent attitude toward civil righteousness is the unexpected way in which he lauds the social expressions of goodness which natural man's reason and common sense can effect—apart from the gospel—for a just and peaceful society. Luther was convinced that all God's rational creatures—despite sin—are still capable of a high degree of civil righteousness by virtue of the divine law which God has written "with his own finger" into their hearts at creation.[32] Even the most cursory reading of Luther's writings reveal a surprising number of references to the distinction between God's twofold rule by law and gospel in the two kingdoms, and the admirably high position afforded man's reason when it is employed in the service of neighbors and limited to managing the technical affairs of everyday life.[33]

Here you must separate God from man, eternal matters from temporal matters. Involving other people, man is rational enough to act properly and needs no other light than reason. Consequently, God does not bother to teach men how they are to build houses, or make clothes, or marry, or make war, or sail a boat. For all such matters, man's natural light is sufficient. But in divine matters, such as man's relation to God and how God's will is fulfilled for our eternal salvation, here man's nature is completely stone-blind.[34]

In marked consistency with his earlier teachings is Luther's systematic portrayal of the proper exercise of reason and force to achieve social order and civil justice in his *Sermons on Exodus* (1524-1527). In the first place, there must be a clear distinction between the realms of creation and redemption, the kingdom of men and the kingdom of God.

You have often heard of the differences between religious and civil authority. In the spiritual realm men are ruled by God through Christ as the head of all believers, although neither Christ nor the believers are ever openly seen. In the civil realm Christ does not

---

[31] *WA* 40[I], 558.
[32] *WA* 10[III], 373.
[33] See e.g., *WA* 10[III], 380; 16, 251, 353.
[34] *WA* 10[I,1], 531.

exercise his rule directly, for he has delegated his powers to human rulers who are to govern their citizens in moderation, justice, and equity.[35]

In the second place, the non-redemptive rule of the sword in the kingdom of men is aimed at the establishment of a just and orderly society in which men may live in peace and the gospel might be proclaimed unto the ends of the earth.

Here we have described for us how the people of Israel were united together under a civil government and how that government was organized. [Moses] attends first to the civil authority before ordering the religious authority . . . . This is because the civil sword must first be exercised to secure peace and order on earth before anyone can preach with the necessary time, place, and tranquillity. When men are compelled to take up spears, guns, and swords in time of strife, there is little opportunity to preach God's Word.[36]

In the third place, the non-redemptive rule and maintenance of the civil realm should be governed by a judicious use of reason and common sense which is implanted by God into every human being. In public office, personal piety is no substitute for political prudence. As he was to insist so often later, "Better a wise Turk than a foolish Christian," when it comes to running the state for the social welfare of all.

God has placed man's civil life under the dominion of natural reason which has ability enough to rule physical things. Reason and experience together teach man how to govern his wife and family, how to care for his livestock, and how to do everything else that belongs to sustaining a life here on earth. These powers have been graciously bestowed by God upon man's reason, and we need not look to Scripture for advice in such temporal matters. God has seen to it that even the heathen is blessed with the gift of reason to help him live his daily life.[37]

Finally, Christians should be vigilant and not mix the two kingdoms by demanding of pagans in the kingdom of the world what is possible only among Christians in the kingdom of God. Centuries before the repeal of the ill-fated Eighteenth Amend-

[35] *WA* 16, 352.
[36] *Ibid.*
[37] *Ibid.*, 353.

ment, Luther insisted that "the world cannot be run by the gospel . . . . The sheep, to be sure, would keep the peace and would allow themselves to be fed and governed in peace, but they would not live very long."[38] Rather than attempt any naive and fruitless "Christianization" of the fallen social structures in the community, Christ's followers should dedicate their consecrated brains to learn even from pagans how best to live their daily lives so as to achieve the most equitable society possible under human reason, justice, law, and order.

Pagans have been found to be much wiser than Christians. They have been able to order the things of this world in a far more capable and lasting way than have the saints of God. As Christ said, "The children of this world are wiser in their own generation than the children of light." They know how to rule external affairs better than St. Paul or the other saints. It is because of this that the ancient Romans had such glorious laws and ordinances . . . without any counsel or guidance from Holy Scripture or the apostles.[39]

Consequently, without at all weakening the distinction between the two kingdoms, Luther can gratefully view all the provisional victories of dedicated men over hunger, sickness, crime, and social evils in general, as "signs" and foretastes of the coming kingdom of God when the rule of Christ will be all in all. Political peace and social justice remain qualitatively inferior to the peace of God and his righteousness, but—like the long finger of John the Baptist in Grünewald's "Crucifixion"—they point to the coming kingdom even while not a part of it. Many a critic of Luther's alleged "cultural quietism" would do well to read Luther himself to challenge their unexamined prejudices.

Just as the spiritual government or office should instruct people how to act in relation to God concerning their eternal salvation, so too the civil government should rule people so as to insure that man's body, goods, wife, children, household, and all his possessions remain in peace and safety for his earthly happiness. For God would have civil government become a prefiguration [Vorbild] of the true blessedness of his heavenly kingdom.[40]

[38] PE 3, 236.
[39] WA 16, 354.
[40] WA 51, 241.

The Law of Nature

Just as Luther was able to subsume all the Christian righteousness of the kingdom of God under the loose heading of "the law of Christ," he often included everything that we have described heretofore as civil righteousness within the kingdom of men under the general rubric of "the law of nature." This ambiguous designation has caused untold grief in Luther research ever since, for it is at once obvious from the theological foundations of his ethics that Luther could not possibly have meant by this term what it had traditionally stood for in the Aristotelian categories of Roman Catholic moral theology.

Perhaps most helpful today is Gustaf Aulén's recent suggestion that we first incorporate the material to which this tradition-laden term refers into Luther's overarching doctrine of the two kingdoms. If we then interpret it in terms of "the law of creation," we readily divest it of any non-Christian metaphysical coloration and relate it directly to the ongoing creative activity of God in his temporal rule of the kingdom of the world. This certainly preserves the religious intention behind Luther's usage of a term whose meaning has become radically secularized for us since the godless philosophical inroads of the eighteenth century.[41]

In general, we may safely say that Luther conceived of the relation between "natural law" and "the law of Christ" in dialectical terms of radical correction and fulfillment. They reflect precisely the same provisional opposition and ultimate unity as between law and gospel, justice and love, reason and revelation, creation and redemption. In short, they are but another expression

---

[41] Cf. Gustaf Aulén, *The Faith of the Christian Church*, tr. Eric H. Wahlstrom and G. Everett Arden (Philadelphia:Muhlenberg, 1948), p. 189. "The idea *lex naturae* has often appeared as a substitute for the *lex creationis*, or *lex creatoris*, of Christian faith. *Lex naturae*, the law of nature, could be described as a rationalized and secularized variety of *lex creationis*. The foundation of both is a universal law. The difference between them can be defined in this way, that *lex naturae* is a metaphysical conception, while *lex creationis* is a religious concept, originating in the relation to God and inseparably connected with faith in God as Creator."

of the twofold way in which the Triune God governs his children as both their Creator and their Redeemer.

Luther's doctrine of the bondage of man's will and reason to the forces of evil, precluded any possibility of anyone living a righteous life apart from Christ. Yet, as we have seen, even the sinner remains a creature of God who bears within his heart—in however distorted and corrupted a form—a knowledge of the law of his Creator. Man in rebellion no longer possesses a saving knowledge of God, but he still has a conscience which witnesses to the contradiction between right and wrong. And he still is rationally cognizant of the "law of nature" which tells him that "man should do good and avoid evil," that good is rewarded and evil punished, and that he must do good to others if he wants to be treated well in return.[42] For Luther, the ethic of natural law is the morality of the "Golden Rule."

It is unrighteous in God's sight for me to refuse to serve my neighbor in need for I am then unjustly depriving him of what the Lord has provided for his benefit. I am obligated to treat him according to the natural law, "Do unto others as you would have them do unto you" (Matt. 7:12). And as Christ said, "Give to him who begs from you" (Matt. 5:42).[43]

These words introduce us concretely to the ambiguity in Luther's view of civil righteousness or natural law morality. In some instances he clearly subordinates natural law to Christian love while in others he couples the two so closely together as almost to equate them. For Luther, it would seem that social justice is the necessary form which Christian love takes in a given situation while yet falling short of the disinterested quality of sacrificial love (agape) which God revealed in Christ. The following quotation, for instance, illustrates the one side of his position; namely, that justice is a sub-Christian, pagan virtue. Here it is emphasized that to love each other as we would like to be loved in return (Matt. 7:12), is qualitatively inferior to loving each other as Christ has loved us (John 13:34-35).

[42] *WA* 10[I,1], 203.
[43] *WA* 10[III], 291.

The lepers here teach us faith while Christ teaches us love. Love does for the neighbor as it has seen Christ do for us. As he said, "For I have given you an example, that you also should do to others as I have done to you. . . . By this all men will know that you are my disciples, if you have love for one another" (John 13:15, 35). . . . Love does not fight or dispute; it is there only to do good. For this reason love always does more than it is obligated to do, going beyond the demands of the law. Consequently, St. Paul says that among Christians there should be no need for recourse in the civil law courts since love does not seek or stress its own rights, but desires only to do good to others (I Cor. 6:1).[44]

On the other hand, there are many important passages in Luther which lend great weight to the view that civil justice is the social expression of Christian love. Just as the "Golden Rule" is itself incorporated by Christ into the Sermon on the Mount, so too the Christian life in the temporal kingdom should be governed by the natural law of equity and moderation. Here followers of Christ join their non-believing neighbors in doing good to all men—though their motivation is radically different. One of Luther's 1522 sermons on Philippians 4:4-7 gives us a striking example of this "Christianized" natural law ("equity") which should govern Christians in their temporal pursuits.

The word the Apostle uses here *(epieikeia, equitas, clementia, commoditas)* is perhaps best rendered as "leniency." This is a virtue by which man is guided to treat others with fairness and equity, and through whose practice man avoids setting himself up as the final rule and judge. Leniency permits men to distinguish between strict and merciful law, and to moderate that which is too strict: this is *equitas.*[45]

Luther is referring here to the classical medieval distinction between positive law *(iustum)* and natural law *(aequum),* in which the spirit of the law softens and qualifies the rigid application of the letter of the law, when its strict enforcement would do more harm than good in a concrete case. Natural law is the source and norm under which all human laws are to be held accountable. It is ". . . the heart and the empress of all laws, the

---

[44] *WA* 8, 364.
[45] *WA* 10[1,2], 174.

fountain from which all laws flow forth."[46] And yet at other times, meaning apparently the very same thing, Luther can call love ". . . the judge of all laws and their sound understanding";[47] it is the "queen and mistress" which should ". . . govern all external civil laws in the world."[48]

When pressed for a more specific description, however, Luther will go no further than seeing deeply imbedded within natural law an abiding concern for the welfare of the neighbor.[49] "There should be a moderation in life which mitigates, adapts, and guides our capacities and behavior so that we feel constrained to be good, follow, shun, do, leave, and suffer in keeping with our neighbor's needs, even if it is at the cost of goods, honor, or personal comfort."[50] And then, after citing several examples of such "equity" in the lives of Christ, Peter, and Paul, Luther concludes: ". . . nothing else is necessary for a Christian but faith and love, with love determining what is to be done or not done according to its contribution to society."[51]

Since Luther himself complained that "we invent many fables about natural law,"[52] we shall perhaps have to conclude that at different times and places Luther was treating various dimensions of this central ethical paradox: As two parallel lines meet only at infinity, the forces of love and law meet only in eternity. In terms of our presentation, the morality of natural law may be viewed as part of the "strange work" of God's non-redemptive activity under the law. Underneath the distorted mask of Aristotle's "law of nature," there is concealed the loving Creator of all mankind whose will is that all men should love one another. "The law of nature lives in us as heat and fire in flint. Its use is

[46] *WA*, TR 6, 6955.
[47] *BA, Er* 1, 368.
[48] *WA* 17^{II}, 92.
[49] As a faithful biblical theologian, Luther has Paul to thank for his dilemma. It is the same Paul who damns all non-Christian behavior in Romans 1 who is here lauding the pre-Christian moral virtues of the Greeks in Philippians 4!
[50] *WA* 10^{I,2}, 174.
[51] *Ibid.*, 176.
[52] *WA* 56, 355.

like that of a mirror, for it cannot be separated from the law of God." [53]

How deftly Luther was able to handle this dialectical relationship between natural law and the law of Christ is well expressed in his analysis of the place of the Ten Commandments in the ethical life of the Christian. He addressed himself to this controversial issue in his work *Against the Heavenly Prophets* (1525) to repudiate the radical sectarian attempts to re-establish an Old Testament theocracy in sixteenth-century Germany. In a letter to Spalatin contemporary with the treatise, he objected vigorously to the program of the *Schwärmer*.

Those men who brag about the laws of Moses are to be despised. We have our civil law under which we live . . . . The laws of Moses were binding only upon the Jewish people in that place which he had chosen; now they are a matter of liberty. If these laws are to be kept there is no reason why we should not be circumcised too, and observe the whole ceremonial law.[45]

Probably most Christians would agree with Luther's contention that the civil and ceremonial laws of the Jews were limited in their jurisdiction to the theocratic conditions of ancient Israel. Certainly this is the view of Paul in his controversy with the Galatians. Though this initial decision has some important social-ethical consequences (e.g., on church-state relations, sabbath regulations and "blue laws," etc.), an even more basic question concerns the moral law of the children of Israel as transmitted to them by Moses in the form of the Ten Commandments. What is the status of this Decalogue in Christian ethical life? In a very significant formal opinion which Luther (together with John Bugenhagen and Philip Melanchthon) sent to Wolf von Salhausen on the authority of the law for the Christian, the reply is given as follows:

This is what should be preached in this case: First, the law should be preached in order to expose and punish sin. As Christ says, "Repentance and forgiveness of sins should be preached in Christ's

[53] *WA*, TR 2, 2243.
[54] *SJ* 2, 223.

name" (Luke 24:47) ; and Paul's words, "The law is our custodian" (Gal. 3:24) . . . . Further, God also desires that the law should be preached for the sake of social peace and order against those godless and crude men who live immoral lives. As Paul says, "The law is not laid down for the righteous" (I Tim. 1:9).[55]

The problem then arises: If the twofold purpose of the law is to expose sin *(usus theologicus)* and to prevent crime *(usus politicus)*, this covers the Christian as a citizen and insofar as he remains sinful. But what is the role of the law for a Christian insofar as he is righteous?[56] More concretely, are the "Thou shalt nots" of the Ten Commandments binding upon the Christian? Luther's startling response is typically dialectical: as Mosaic law—no; as natural law—yes!

This very profound view is developed most cogently in a decisive section of the work *Against the Heavenly Prophets.* Luther has just concluded a defense of the Christian freedom of Evangelicals either to keep or to destroy former Roman church images, depending upon their state of faith and the state of local conditions. To answer Andrew Karlstadt's charge that this liberty violates the letter of the Mosaic law, Luther replies vigorously that this does not concern him because Christians who are under the dispensation of the New Testament gospel are not bound by the Old Testament dispensation of the Mosaic law. Christ has liberated us from the law—all the law—from the minutest ceremonial nicety to the Decalogue itself. "For Moses is given to the Jewish people alone, and does not concern us

---

[55] *WA* 15, 229.

[56] Despite most American Lutheran catechisms to the contrary, recent Luther research has proved conclusively that Luther taught no third use of the law *(usus didacticus)* in the Calvinistic-Melanchthonian sense of a "guiding rule of life for the regenerate." For Luther, the Christian—as righteous—knows no law but love. "So then a Christian is divided into two times. Inasmuch as he is flesh, he is under the law; inasmuch as he is Spirit, he is under grace . . . . The time of the law therefore is not perpetual, but has its end, which end is Jesus Christ" *(WA* 40[I], 525). Moreover, the *Formula of Concord* (VI) should not be misinterpreted on this issue to sanction an unevangelical and pietistic conception of regeneration. Its so-called "third use of the law" is merely the specific application of the universal first use *(usus theologicus)* to the Christian insofar as he remains sinful, in keeping with Luther's teaching that the Christian is at once both sinful and righteous. Cf., e.g., Werner Elert, *The Christian Ethos* (Philadelphia: Muhlenberg, 1957), § 46.

Gentiles and Christians. We have our gospel and the New Testament."[57]

If the sectarians reply that the Scripture cited by Luther (I Tim. 1:9; Acts 15:10; Galatians and Corinthians) abrogates the Mosaic civil and ceremonial law but refers in no way to the moral law of the Decalogue, Luther insists that the *whole* law of Moses is of one piece. Rationalistic subdivisions of the law are an unbiblical invention of men. Viewed religiously, the law is a way of salvation which must be completely obeyed or completely rejected. Christians who are saved by God's grace through faith alone have no other alternative but to disavow all ways of salvation which do not center in the cross of Christ. This includes the sub-Christian orientation of the Mosaic law in which God shows his steadfast love only to the "thousands of those who love me and keep my commandments" (Exod. 20:6).

I know very well that this is an old and common distinction [between civil, ceremonial, and moral laws], but it is not an intelligent one. For out of the Ten Commandments flow and depend all the other commandments and the whole of Moses. Because he would be God alone and have no other gods, etc., he has instituted so many different ceremonies or acts of worship. Through these he has interpreted the first commandment and taught how it is to be kept. To promote obedience to parents, and unwilling to tolerate adultery, murder, stealing, or false witness, he has given the judicial law or external government so that such commandments will be understood and carried out. Thus it is not true that there is no ceremonial or judicial law in the Ten Commandments. Such laws are in the Decalogue, depend on it, and belong there.[58]

This daring position becomes crucial, of course, when one views the first commandment in this law-free setting. Does Luther's position mean that the believer in Christ is also free from belief in the one true God, beside whom there is no other? Of course not, cries Luther, but it is not necessary that man derive the knowledge of God from the Mosaic law. That there is a God is known by everyone from the law written on men's

[57] *LW* 40, 92.
[58] *Ibid.*, 93.

hearts (Rom. 1:19-20). What kind of loving God he is we know from the gospel of his self-revelation in Jesus Christ (John 3:16). In neither case is Moses necessary, "For to have a God is not only a Mosaic law, but also a natural law."[59]

From here Luther moves on to the extremely significant affirmation that there is a basic identity between the law of God in the hearts of men and the law of God in the Mosaic Decalogue.[60] At bottom, they are elaborations of the Matthew 7:12 "Golden Rule," which is itself a natural law summary of the Old Testament message of the law and the prophets. And since God the Creator and God the Redeemer are essentially one, the content and aim of all this law can be said to be love, as Paul himself maintains in Romans 13:9. It is this covenanted law of love (*Gebot*)—long predating the Mosaic law (*Gesetz*) which "four hundred and thirty years afterward . . . was added because of transgressions" (Gal. 3:17-19)—that Christ did not abrogate but radically corrected and fulfilled (Matt. 5:17). "However, the devil so blinds and possesses hearts, that men do not always feel this law. Therefore, one must preach the law and impress it on the minds of people till God assists and enlightens them, so that they feel in their hearts what the Word says."[61]

Luther concludes that insofar as the Ten Commandments provide us with a concise statement of the natural law governing all of sinful mankind ("to honor parents, not to kill, not to commit adultery, to serve God, etc."), they are carefully to be obeyed. But insofar as they include special matters above and beyond the natural law which are peculiar to the Jewish theocracy ("legislation about images and the sabbath, etc."), they may be regarded as time-bound statutes of the Jewish law code which are not binding upon Christians.

It is as when an emperor or a king makes special laws and ordinances in his territory, as the law code of Saxony [*Sachsenspiegel*], and yet common natural laws such as to honor parents, not to kill, not to

[59] *Ibid.*, 96.
[60] *Ibid.*
[61] *Ibid.*, 97.

commit adultery, to serve God, etc., prevail and remain in all lands. Therefore one is to let Moses be the *Sachsenspiegel* of the Jews and not to confuse us Gentiles with it, just as the *Sachsenspiegel* is not observed in France, though the natural law there is in agreement with it.[62]

The church instructs its members in the Ten Commandments, therefore, because ". . . the natural laws were never so orderly and well written as by Moses."[63] In no instance should this practice be used to justify the reintroduction of any legalism in Christian daily living. Insofar as the Christian remains sinful, he is bound only to that part of the Decalogue which coincides with natural law (civil righteousness). Insofar as he is righteous, however, he is free from all law—Mosaic and natural alike—in the liberating power of God's grace (Christian righteousness). Consequently, righteous Christians will find it continually necessary ". . . to make new Decalogues as did Christ, St. Peter, and St. Paul," in responding faithfully to the Holy Spirit of the living God.[64] This whole evangelical orientation toward the law of God is of the utmost importance for the Christian's domestic stewardship in terms of his obedience to the Lord of the fourth and sixth commandments in keeping with the spirit of Christ.

It is hoped that the somewhat subtle nuances of Luther's thought as described in this chapter might help to refute the mistaken notion (particularly common in Anglo-Saxin Calvinism) that Luther was an "immoral antinomian." Along with what we have written, even the most casual examination of his heated polemics against the antinomian, John Agricola, should convince any impartial reader that this simply was not true—any more than it was true of his theological master, St. Paul.[65] An antinomian is one opposed to all law *(anti-Nomos)* in the Christian life. Paul and Luther, however, taught that the Christian is 1) free from the law as a way of salvation, but 2) bound

[62] *Ibid.,* 98.
[63] *Ibid.*
[64] *WA* 39[1], 47.
[65] See *WA* 39[1], 359-584 for Luther's extensive *Disputations Against the Antinomians.*

to the law both religiously in so far as he acts sinfully, and ethically in so far as he acts civilly.

The essentially negative coloration with which Luther always invests the law, therefore, is due primarily to his profound insight into the absolutely unselfish quality of God's forgiving and life-giving love *(agape)*. When measured against this love of God in Christ, man's love and goodness always fall short. "The commandments teach a man to know his illness, so that he feels and sees what he can do and what he cannot do, what he can and what he cannot leave undone, and thus knows himself to be a sinner and a wicked man."[66] Hence, while good and holy in and of itself, the law of God always confronts man as an enemy which accuses him of his persisting self-righteousness. "Thou shalt not" both exposes and presupposes our sin before God and our crimes among men. Luther knows the Bible too well to be seduced by any philosophical idealism or moralistic perfectionism.

Realistically, therefore, despite all the proximate hopes which the Christian may have within this world—and have them he must if he is to remain faithful to Christ's lordship—he nevertheless remembers that his ultimate hope is beyond history in a trans-historical kingdom which is not of this world (John 18:36). In the present sinful age in which the dethroned powers of evil are not yet completely annihilated, true self-giving love is destined always to be crucified. The imperfect love of the Christian shares the tragic triumph of the perfect love of God in Christ. It is put to death, as was Jesus, by the best which men have to offer in their government, and the highest they have to offer in their religion. Sin is so all-pervasive a power at the core of humanity that God's love for men in Christ's action, as well as his love through men in Christian action, is all destined historically to be "lost and unrequited." The man of faith goes on loving and serving because of the love of Christ and despite the hate of the world.[67]

[66] *PE* 2, 354.
[67] *WA* 36, 435.

The Christian dares never forget that it is only by faith that he lives in the power of the risen Lord. His "growth in grace," then, is not a steady, unambiguous, quantitatively measurable succession of steps upward on the ladder of moral perfection. It is rather man's ever-growing willingness "to progress by beginning anew."[68] Grace is God's and not man's; to grow in grace is to grow out of self into God. In short, what really grows in grace is not man's own native goodness, but rather his faith in the goodness of God. Indeed, "the more progress a man has made, the less does he count himself to have progressed."[69] His newness of life manifests itself in the growing mastery of himself as God-ruled "Spirit" over himself as self-ruled "flesh" in the ongoing struggle of "becoming a Christian." The first word of the Reformation remains the last word for the regenerate: "The entire life of believers should be one of repentance."[70]

This ambiguity in the religious status of the individual Christian inevitably renders extremely precarious the entire Christian social-ethical endeavor. Even as dethroned by Christ, "the old bitter foe" continues to remain so powerful a force in the world —"on earth is not his equal"—that social evil is ultimately beyond the province of effective human action. We may partially check it or tentatively channel it, but we can never completely control it. The kingdom of God, therefore, is not ours to build but God's to give. To pray, "Thy kingdom come," means to confess in humility that "The kingdom of God comes indeed of itself," and then to ask in trusting hope "that it may come unto us also."[71] Discounting the growing apocalyptic coloration of his views in later years, Luther's biblical eschatology provided him with the realistic limits to Christian social action in a fallen world.

Knowing that the kingdom is safely "in God's hands," the Christian is free to witness to its coming with joyful confidence.

[68] *WA* 4, 350.
[69] *WA* 9, 107.
[70] *LW* 31, 25.
[71] *WA* 30^{1}, 251.

A true eschatology does not invite apathy but routs anxiety. For "the love of Christ constrains us" to do whatever we can for our needy neighbors in personal love and social justice. Scripture assures us that our social-ethical "holding action"— within the divinely created ordinances—is absolutely indispensable for God's battle strategy against Satan until Christ returns in glory to consummate the victory he has already won on the cross. Though we cannot add "one cubit" to our religious stature in God's sight by performing such good works, we can and should do all in our power to work toward the kind of just and peaceful society which truly "prefigures" the kingdom of God.

Conclusion

With this challenge we draw to a close our explanation of Luther's doctrine of the two kingdoms. Against the clericalism of Rome so prevalent in his day, Luther proclaimed the liberating message that society need not be run by the church in order to be ruled by God. In the kingdom of God, the Redeemer rules all believers religiously via Christ, the gospel, and personal faith. In the kingdom of men, the Creator rules all sinful creatures ethically via Caesar, the law and civil obedience. As both Creator and Redeemer, God is the Lord of both kingdoms; as both righteous and sinful, the Christian is a subject of both kingdoms. Hence, for a biblical theology of society, the two kingdoms must always be properly distinguished, but never separated in secularism or equated in clericalism.

In this dialectical fashion, Luther dramatically reaffirmed the sacredness of all of God's creation by stressing the ordinary tasks of the common life as those which best serve our neighbors' needs. Whether empowered by Christ in faith-activated love (Christian righteousness) or compelled by Caesar in law-abiding reason (civil righteousness), the Christian lives not for himself but for the benefit of others. And nowhere is this more apparent —and important—than in the God-ordained fortress of our common life, the Christian household.

CHAPTER FIVE

The Common Life

Luther's understanding of God's Word convinced him too that "No man is an island, entire of itself." Man is so created that he is always in relation to his Creator and his fellow creatures. It follows that life in community is not man's choice; it is his destiny. "Man lives not only alone in his own body but also among other people while he is on earth. It is not possible for him to be without continual contact with his neighbors both in words and in deeds."[1]

The greatness of Luther's ethical realism lies in his incorporation of this myriad of social interaction into the never-ceasing rule of God. This means that God ordains life so that every man is born as someone's son, educated as someone's pupil, governed as someone's subject, supplied as someone's customer, married as someone's husband, nurtured as someone's parishioner, and finally blessed as someone's father, only to begin this common human cycle for another socially conditioned child of God. Indeed, to spin this web of human interdependence even more intricately, man participates in most of these complementary relationships simultaneously, and is as actively engaged in shaping the lives of others as they are in affecting his. Whether willingly or not, therefore, all men are regularly engaged in mutual service for the general welfare of the community.

We find many people who declare that they would like nothing better than to lead a godly life. . . . For this reason God has ordained various estates *(Stände)* in which men learn how to live and suffer for others. Whether in the estates of marriage, spiritual rule,

[1] *WA* 7, 34.

or civil rule, all men are commanded by God to dedicate themselves in toil and labor to mortifying their flesh and dying unto self.[2]

It is characteristic of Luther's social ethic that he views the common life of everyday affairs as the theater of God's creative activity.[3] It is precisely here—in the market place, behind the plow, in front of the stove—that Luther portrays God at work. Here it is that God's mighty battles against Satan are being fought. Here it is that unrighteous men are forced by God's law to serve others for their self-mortification. Here it is also that righteous men are empowered by God's love to serve their neighbors freely and gladly. Christians dare never forget while in the thick of a busy day ". . . that God is within them, working and ruling; namely, the Holy Ghost himself."[4]

In his description of the priesthood of all believers, the Reformer asserted his conviction that the practice of Christian faith dare not be limited to ordained professionals. The Roman divorce between sacred and secular labor was judged to be an unbiblical denial of the responsibility of every Christian to serve his neighbors as a faithful steward of those gifts which God had entrusted to him. It was Luther's belief that every believer engaged in socially productive work was in full-time Christian service. God's service can no more be limited to the pulpit and altar than he himself could. After all, ". . . it is not God, but our neighbors, who need our good works."[5]

Perhaps nowhere is this concern more poignantly illustrated in Luther's works than in the picturesque Christmas sermon of 1522 in which he tries to show how "faith and love always do more than is necessary, for both are living, creative, active, and overflowing."[6] As a striking example of this God-pleasing service in our common life, Luther reminds us that the shepherds returned not to a monastery, but to their sheep, after they had seen the Christ-child in the manger! Coming to know and love

[2] WA 2, 734.
[3] WA 8, 32.
[4] Ibid., 35.
[5] WA 10^III, 222.
[6] WA 10^{I,1}, 136.

Christ does not necessarily change what we do, but rather how, why, and for whom we do it. This is Christian freedom for service. Faith transforms our occupations into Christian vocations.

Christian freedom is not bound to any particular work, for all works which come along are of equal worth to a Christian. The shepherds did not run off to the desert, don cowls, shave their heads, or change any of their external practices in clothing, time, food, or drink. They returned instead to serve God by caring for their flocks. For Christian faith does not consist in external activities which man has to change, but in an inward transformation by which he receives a new heart, spirit, will, and disposition. He does exactly the same external works as his neighbor who has no faith. A Christian knows that everything depends upon faith alone, and he is free to go, stay, eat, drink, work, or live as other men in public offices and estates without anyone ever knowing of his Christianity.[7]

Occupations as Vocations

It is historically significant that the impressive foregoing quotation is dated 1522. It was only after four long and painful years of antimonastic polemic that Luther began to see clearly that the biblical doctrine of vocation, or calling, was the only adequate corrective for the Roman notion that the true Christian life demanded severance from the normal and natural communal responsibilities of everyday life. However, once Luther arrived at the insight that the good life is the ordinary one—lived in an extraordinary way—it became an integral and permanent part of his social ethics.

On St. John's Day of 1522, Luther preached a very important sermon in which he positively related for the first time man's eternal calling as a Christian and his temporal calling as a citizen.[8] Here we are shown one of the very concrete ways in which the interaction of God's twofold rule of man by law and gospel takes on practical ethical significance. For Luther insists that when God calls a man he calls all of him: religiously and ethically, from here to eternity.

[7] *Ibid.,* 137.
[8] *Ibid.,* 305ff.

The boundary line between the two kingdoms is drawn squarely through the heart of every single Christian. Insofar as he remains sinful, the occupations and offices which man holds serve the negative purpose of religious self-discipline (the *mortificatio* of civil righteousness). But insofar as he is righteous, man's occupations and offices are transformed by faith and love into divine vocations of neighborly service (the *vivificatio* of Christian righteousness). Only by faith can man hear God's call for eternal life "hidden" in the humble form of Jesus of Nazareth. In like fashion, only by faith can man hear God's call for temporal service "hidden" under the mundane forms of blood, sweat, and tears in everyday life. In short, when we love to do what we ought to do and have to do, then we have answered Christ's call: "Take up your cross and follow me."

The revolutionary import of what Luther is saying in this sermon is immediately apparent. His text is taken from John 21, in which Christ commands Peter to follow him after he has been commissioned to feed Christ's sheep. The whole medieval ethos was dependent upon the notion that those who were truly called to "feed Christ's sheep" must follow him by way of obedience to a rigidly stereotyped imitation of his public ministry (*imitatio Christi*). In other words, to be called by Christ meant to leave your secular pursuits behind, and to assume some kind of "religious" life with its accompanying disciplines and rules.

But Luther points out that in this passage Christ does not demand the same of John as he does of Peter. To the questioning Peter, Christ replied, "If it is my will that he remain until I come, what is that to you? Follow me!" (John 21:22). Luther sees in Christ's words a clear indication that a diversity of services dependent upon the God-given diversity of gifts is the biblically enjoined pattern for Christian community life. "Christ fulfilled his own office and vocation, but thereby did not reject any other."[9] To try to imitate Christ or the saints in some static and legalistic manner in no way takes account of what God's

[9] *PE* 3, 246.

will is for your life with its very different gifts and neighbors.

Disregarding all the lives and examples of the saints, a Christian should wait and see what is specifically commanded of him and then remain true to his calling. O this is a necessary, wholesome teaching today! It is practically a universal custom in our day to try to imitate the works of the saints, believing this to be pleasing to God. . . . Yet Christ speaks clearly against this in the passage at hand: "Do not think that I want the same from you as I want from him. Wait until I command your responsibilities; you will find out soon enough what they are. I desire many different servants and they will not all have the same work to do."[10]

Luther then goes on to make a point which remained crucial for his understanding of the Christian life: Works can only be called "good" when they have been commanded by God and not when they have been invented by men, especially churchmen. God has not left himself without a witness. The inner testimony of the Holy Spirit in the Bible provides us with a clear account of the self-revelation of God's loving will. It is here that we are to listen when we want to know what the Lord requires of us. To invent one's own good works—especially when they contradict and prevent the fulfillment of those works which God has actually commanded—is ultimately idolatry, for it substitutes self-will for God-will.

There are many people who are busy doing everything but that which is commanded of them. They hear, for instance, that some saints went on pilgrimages for which they have been highly praised by the church. The fools then proceed to abandon the wives and children which God has commanded for them, and run off to St. James' or somewhere, without seeing at all that their callings are totally different from those commanded by God for the saints which they are following blindly. The same kind of thinking motivates all the foundations, fastings, dress, celebrations, priestcraft, monkery, and nunnery. It is all nothing but human vanity and the avoiding of God's command and call for true discipleship.[11]

Christians are therefore to beware of self-invented behavior

[10] *WA* 10[1,1], 306.
[11] *Ibid.*, 307.

which mechanically copies what may once have been God's calling for someone else at the expense of what the living God now commands man to be doing in his own unique situation. But suppose man asks what he should do if he first avoids copying the examples of others but is then not called himself. This provides Luther with the opportunity to make his chief point: *Every* Christian is called by God to obey his commands in keeping with what and whom he has been given. Talents and neighbors are given by God, not chosen by man. Christian obedience demands that we bring the two together in a spirit of loving service. Where you are with what you have is the place and manner in which you are to live your faith. "What is God's will for me?" is answered realistically by the discovery of "What are my neighbor's needs of me?"

How is it possible that you are not called? Are you not either a husband or a wife, a son or a daughter, a servant or a maid? Take, for example, the most humble of estates. As a married man, do you not have enough to do in governing your wife, child, household, and property so that everything is done justly and in obedience to God's will? In fact, if you had four heads and ten hands, it would not be enough to meet all of your responsibilities without having time to run off to pilgrimages or to perform other "holy" works. . . . Instead we spend our time counting rosary beads and doing other such things which do not serve our callings in the least.[12]

The close association of God's "command" and man's "calling" in these passages provides us with the key to Luther's understanding of community life under the law of the Creator in the kingdom on earth. "For God to command is for God to create," since God creates by divine fiat.[13] The whole of God's creation, therefore, is ruled through this vast nexus of social relationships, each of which embodies in institutional form and structure a particular command of God. All offices and stations of life—domestic, social, economic, political, ecclesiastical, etc.—are included in the kingdom of men as God's divinely ordained

[12] *Ibid.*, 308.
[13] *WA* 12, 328.

bulwarks in his continuing warfare against Satan. God is at work in and through all of them "working order out of chaos and good out of evil."[14] We will now examine how this actually takes place in the home as the nucleus of Christian life in community.

The Christian Household

"Thou shalt honor thy father and thy mother" was regarded by Luther as the undisputed backbone of all civil authority and social welfare in the kingdom of men on earth. Following the traditional Augustinian enumeration, he divided the Decalogue into two tables of three and seven commandments each, with parental honor in the chief position at the head of the second table.[15] As the first commandment determines man's religious life under the first table of the law, it was asserted that the fourth commandment determined his ethical life under the second. For Luther this crucial commandment is grounded firmly in God's delegating all "dominion" over the earthly kingdom to Adam and Eve as the first parents of mankind (Gen. 1:28). Consequently, after he had successfully challenged the temporal sovereignty of the church of Rome, Luther's evangelical theology of society compelled him quite naturally to rebuild the walls of the social order upon the solid biblical foundation of the family and home under God.

Luther's earliest treatments of the Ten Commandments in general—and the fourth commandment in particular—were in connection with the late medieval custom of providing penitents with religious handbooks in which specific sins and virtues were carefully catalogued in order to aid them with their confessions. Luther soon deviated from the Roman norm, however, by listing only such sins and virtues as were connected with the

[14] *WA* 40[1], 174.
[15] Luther's numbering of the Ten Commandments follows the practice of the Roman Catholic church, and is different from that of other Christians and also of the Jews. In Lutheran practice, the first two commandments are combined as one, and the tenth is divided into the ninth and tenth.

Decalogue itself, thereby omitting the many non-biblical moral standards common in such manuals elsewhere.

A concrete illustration of Luther's early method may be seen in *A Brief Explanation of the Ten Commandments, the Creed, and the Lord's Prayer*. Although not actually published until 1520, the material on the commandments is a reproduction of an earlier work of Luther's which condensed a series of sermons preached shortly before the posting of the *Theses* in 1517. We will list here first the sins forbidden and then the virtues enjoined for family life under the fourth commandment.

Against the fourth: he who is ashamed of his parents because of their poverty, their failings, or their lowly position; he who does not provide them with food and clothing in their need; much more, he who curses them, speaks evil of them, hates them, and disobeys them; he who does not from the heart esteem them highly because of God's commandment; he who does not honor them, even though they do wrong and violence; . . . he who does not help men to keep this commandment and resist those who break it; here belong all forms of pride and disobedience.[16]

Fulfillment of the fourth: willing obedience, humility, submission to all authority because it is God's pleasure, as the Apostle St. Peter says, without retort, complaint, or murmuring (I Pet. 2:18). Here belongs all that is written of obedience, humility, submissiveness, and reverence.[17]

Luther's radical reduction of the usually extensive number of atomistically listed sins and virtues is an early portent of future developments. His genius for evangelical simplicity is already coming to the fore, however, parallel to the traditional listings. "From all this it follows that the commandments command nothing but love and forbid nothing but love; nothing but love fulfills the commandments and nothing but love breaks them."[18] Soul-searching repentance can hardly provide the proper occasion for exhibiting one's proficiency in the niceties and nuances of a legalistic canon law which obscures both the gra-

[16] *PE* 2, 360.
[17] *Ibid.*, 365.
[18] *Ibid.*, 364.

ciousness of God and sinfulness of man. As he was soon to complain:

By thus getting down to the thing itself, the penitent, of whom I have so often spoken, does away entirely with that riot of distinction; to wit, whether he has committed sin by fear humbling him to evil, or by inflaming him to evil; what sins he has committed against the three cardinal virtues of faith, hope, and charity; what sins against the four cardinal virtues; what sins by the five senses, what of the seven mortal sins, what against the seven sacraments, what against the seven gifts of the Holy Spirit, what against the eight beatitudes, what of the nine *peccata aliena,* what against the twelve Articles of Faith, what of the silent sins, what of the sins crying to heaven; or whether he has sinned by or against anything else. That hateful and wearisome catalogue of distinction is altogether useless, nay, it is altogether harmful.[19]

The ties with the Roman tradition became even more strained in Luther's 1519 work entitled *A Short Instruction on Penance.* Emphasis shifts sharply here from individual sins to the whole man as a sinner. It is not what a man does but what a man is which makes him do what he does that now receives prominence. Though a brief listing of transgressions is still appended to each commandment, Luther stresses the need for a more qualitative approach than has been prevalent heretofore in Roman Catholicism. "If a man desires to confess all of his mortal sins, he should do so as follows: 'My whole life and everything that I do, say, and think is sinful and damnable.' For the worst mortal sin of all is to believe that you are not really guilty of any."[20]

The evangelical breakthrough with regard to Christian family and home life occurs dramatically in the *Treatise on Good Works* (1520).[21] No longer does Luther try to pinpoint sins and virtues under each commandment in casuistic fashion. Nor does he treat the Ten Commandments any longer as a static, timeless, immutable moral code whose duties are incumbent upon all good

[19] *PE* 1, 90-91.
[20] *WA* 2, 60.
[21] *PE* 1, 173ff.

church members. Instead, with the liberating spirit of freedom which permeates the whole treatise, Luther shows how faith in the God of the first commandment works itself out through love and justice into every dimension of man's life. The following nine commandments are treated simply as "paradigms of love," illustrations of the transforming power of the grace of God when it is confidently appropriated by the man of faith.

There is only one law for Christians: the "Great Commandment" of love for God and neighbor. The last nine commandments could just as well be numbered at nineteen or at twentynine, depending upon how concretely one wished to depict Paul's teaching: "The commandments . . . and any other commandment are summed up in the sentence, 'You shall love your neighbor as yourself' . . . for love is the fulfilling of the law" (Rom. 13:9-10). In short, when Luther views the Ten Commandments ("the law of nature") from the perspective of faith and love ("the law of Christ"), he shows how all community life is transformed once the righteous live by faith.

Christian faith is such a free thing that it is not bound to any special estate, but is active in, over, and throughout all estates. It is therefore not necessary for man either to leave or to enter a special estate in order to be saved. No matter in which estate the gospel and faith find you, there you may remain and still be assured of your salvation.[22]

This is nowhere more true than in the family. When Luther turns to the second table of the law, he sees a God-pleasing priority in the order of the last seven commandments. The honor we owe to our parents at home is analogous to the reverence we owe to God in worship. "From this commandment we learn that after the excellent works of the first three commandments there are no better works than to obey and serve all those who are set over us as superiors."[23] Indeed, parents rule over their children "in God's stead," and they are consequently to be "honored"; that is, treated with a respect which transcends

[22] WA 12, 126.
[23] PE 1, 250.

141

love and approaches reverence.[24] Parents are thus invested with an authority which is prior and superior to all other earthly authority—kings and popes included![25]

Luther sees a basic human need met by the requirements of this commandment. "For every one must be ruled and be subject to other men. Wherefore we see again here how many good works are taught in this commandment since in it all our life is made subject to other men."[26] Life is so structured by its divine Creator and Preserver that no man can live as a law unto himself. Man's quest for such independent autonomy ("You will be like God." . . . "Am I my brother's keeper?") is precisely his sin. For his necessary self-discipline and self-mortification, then, every person is made answerable to someone above him in respect and authority. Power is a fundamental and necessary fact of life in a fallen world. Luther's main concern here is to show how faith can so transform the facts of life that, in this instance, power can be exercised and obeyed in a spirit of loving responsibility to God.

It is recognized at once, however, that this is no easy task since both parents and children fall sinfully short of their divine callings. On the one hand, strict parents are disobeyed by their children who resent parental authority and discipline as an unwarranted curb on their own self-assertive desires. On the other hand, there is the even more common failing of indulgent parents who weakly renounce their parental responsibilities for the proper rearing of their children and look not to God's service but the world's pleasures as their highest goal. Luther condemns such parental delinquency as approaching idolatry. "What else is it but to sacrifice one's own child to an idol and to burn it, when parents train their children more in the way of the world than in the way of God?"[27]

24 *Ibid.*, 251.
25 *WA* 16, 354.
26 *PE* 1, 252.
27 *Ibid.*, 253.

Luther asserts that for the foundation of a strong home, parents must ". . . make known God's commandments to their children that the generations to come might know them and declare them to their children's children" (Ps. 78:5). The strategic location of the home in the rule of God makes it imperative that it act effectively as a crucial link between a child's religious relation to God and his ethical relations with his fellow men. "For, truly, the knowledge and fulfillment of the first three and last six commandments depends altogether upon this fourth commandment, since parents are commanded to teach them to their children."[28]

Moreover, this parental responsibility is not a blank check to be exercised promiscuously by anyone who happens to be sexually potent. Irresponsible exploitation of parental power "after the fashion of the world" justifies the children's legitimate disobedience ". . . for God, according to the first three commandments, is to be more highly regarded than the parents."[29] Nor is it only temporal disobedience which unfaithful parents can expect. God is not mocked. His stewards are accountable to him for all the gifts which he has so generously bestowed upon them, not the least of which are their children. Theirs is a sacred trust which dare not be abused. "Parents cannot earn eternal punishment in any way more easily than by neglecting their own children in their own home, and not teaching them the things which we have spoken of above."[30]

Conversely, however, there is no good work more pleasing in God's sight than the domestic piety which results from a family's cheerful obedience to this crucial commandment. Faith and love, of course, constitute the decisive difference between just another house and a truly Christian home.[31] Where God is faithfully and lovingly acknowledged as Lord of the home by both parents and children, there can be a mutual recognition

[28] *Ibid.*
[29] *Ibid.*, 254.
[30] *Ibid.*, 256.
[31] *Ibid.*, 257.

of the responsibilities and privileges inherent in the God-given callings of each. When children are reared and parents are obeyed "in confidence of divine favor," the biological facts of life are transfigured into a pious household in which God's blessings overflow for the common good of all.[32]

When Christian faith is operative in love, there are no bounds to the good works and services possible in the parent's physical and spiritual nurture of their children. For the physical care of her loved ones, God empowers a mother to administer a miniature hospital on their behalf. For their spiritual nurture, the Holy Spirit calls a father to be a minister in their own little chapel. That the father is also to sit as judge at the head of the table is taken for granted by Luther. And when his God-given authority is disobediently challenged by his children, they should be soundly punished, but in such a way that "rod and apple sit side by side."[33]

On a small scale, then, the home has all the problems and all the opportunities of the community at large. For its closely knit members, it is a society in embryo: a combination church, state, court, hospital, schoolroom, and playground all in one. It provides the young with a safe place for moulding character and gaining experience. Here they can learn to love and be loved, to trust and be trusted, to obey and be obeyed, to forgive and be forgiven. Consequently, although it dare never end there, the home is truly the right place for Christian charity to begin.

Thus it is true, as men say, that parents, although they had nothing else to do, could attain salvation by training their own children. If they rightly train them to God's service, they will indeed have both hands full of good works to do. For what else are the hungry, thirsty, naked, imprisoned, sick, strangers, than the souls of your own children? With them God makes of your house a hospital, and sets you over them as chief nurse, to wait on them, to give them good words and works as meat and drink, that they may learn to trust, believe, and fear God. . . . O what a blessed marriage and home

[32] *Ibid.*
[33] *WA* TR 3, 3566b.

were that where such parents were to be found! Truly it would be a real church, a chosen cloister, yea, a paradise.[34]

The sacredness of the common life and its God-given tasks is clearly reaffirmed here as one of the indispensable pillars of Luther's theology of society under God. It is in meeting the ordinary, everyday needs of my neighbors—here under the same roof—that I am to act as "God's co-worker" (I Cor. 3:9). In the obedience of faith, I become the willing instrument of God himself as he is constantly engaged in preserving his theater of creation from satanic decay and destruction. "All creatures are masks of God [larvae dei] which he permits to co-operate and help him with his work. He can and does act without our help, but he wants us to be totally dependent upon his Word."[35]

And yet it is the very "ordinariness" of the Christian ethic which makes it such a scandal to the world. Mammon loves the glamorous and the spectacular. To plow a field or bake some bread seems far too "common" to have any real ethical significance. Such tasks are every bit as humble and unspectacular as the man Jesus, of whom the faithless of his day also asked, "What good thing can come from Nazareth?" Is Christian faith deluded in confessing a God who works "hidden" beneath the very "masks" of his own creation? Despite all the stress on pompous externality in medieval Roman piety, Luther maintained throughout his life that if man's heart is right then his deeds are good, no matter what the world thinks or sees. "For God's eyes look not upon the work but the obedience empowering the work."[36]

In believing that "All things are pure to the pure in heart," Luther's faith was simple enough to trust that after a conscientious day's labor, a Christian father could come home and eat his sausage, drink his beer, play his flute, sing with his children, and make love to his wife—all to the glory of God!

For God has commanded women to keep children well-disciplined,

---

[34] PE 1, 255.
[35] WA 17[II], 192.
[36] WA 10[I,i], 310.

and properly clothed and bathed. However humble these tasks may be, they are good works in God's sight. A man also does good works when he runs his household well. Even if he did a hundred small tasks a day, they would all be considered good if done in faith. Cutting wood or heating a room is just as holy for him as praying a rosary is for a monk, for all works of a pious man are good because of the Holy Spirit and his faith.[37]

Although Luther never relaxes the biblical admonition that wives are to "be subject" to their husbands in principle, it is surprising to note how flexibly (for medieval times) this is to be administered in actual practice.[38] Once again it is a case of reasonableness *(epieikeia)* mollifying the strict demands of the law of nature *(lex naturae)*. As the rod and the apple must co-exist in relations between parents and children, so too the final word and the reconciling kiss are both necessary in the relations between parents with different and yet complementary functions. Like his children, a man's wife is also to be ruled gently but firmly.

This distinction is made in nature and in God's creation also, where no women (still less children and fools!) can or ought to exercise rule, as experience tells us, and as Moses says, "Thou shalt be in subjection to thy husband" (Gen. 3:16). The gospel does not abolish this natural law, but confirms it as the ordinance and creation of God.[39]

If the wise husband often "looks through his fingers"—within limits!—in overlooking his mate's shortcomings, it can usually be attributed to his recognition of the honored position which she holds as a mother within the household. As one whose thinking was strongly influenced by the Jewish spirit of the Old Testament in this regard, Luther characteristically paid far more

---

[37] *WA* 10[III], 376.

[38] The elevated status and eventual emancipation of women on Protestant soil came about only much later as an unsought secular by-product of the Reformation's repudiation of celibacy as the highest Christian calling. Implicit in the doctrine of the priesthood of all believers is the recognition that a woman's calling may transcend the traditional German boundaries of "children, kitchen, and the church" *(Kinder, Küche, Kirche)*.

[39] *PE* 5, 276.

respect to women as mothers than as wives. Insofar as a woman shares in the blessings of God's creation by the bearing of children, she is to be given the honor due all parents under the fourth commandment.

Even though woman is a weak vessel and instrument, she holds the highest honor of motherhood. For all people are conceived, born, nursed, and nourished by women; from mothers come all the babies living and their descendents. Their glory as mothers, therefore, should cover and hide all of their weaknesses as women. A pious, God-fearing mate should think, "I have received so much good; why should I not also suffer a little evil?"[40]

In daily experience, Luther afforded the normal, ongoing administration of the household *(oeconomia)* to the mother. Here she plays an indispensable role whose importance for the maintenance of a healthy society cannot be underestimated. For Luther there is no higher calling on earth than that of the Christian homemaker. "Without women the household and everything else that belongs to it would quickly fall apart. The collapse of the civil government, the towns, and the police would soon follow. In short, the world could not do without women even if men were capable of bearing children themselves."[41]

It is no accident that ". . . a woman can do more with a child with one little finger than a man can with both fists."[42] Luther firmly believed that part of God's order in creation was for mothers to remain at home to care for their needy broods. In a jesting observation owing more to Saxon wit than biblical exegesis, Luther could even detect a divine purpose in the contours of the female anatomy! "Men have broad chests and narrow hips. This means that they have more understanding than do women with their smaller chests and broader hips and buttocks. Women should therefore sit quietly at home, keeping house and bearing and rearing their children."[43]

---

[40] *WA*, TR 4, 4138.
[41] *WA*, TR 2, 1658.
[42] *WA* 20, 149.
[43] *WA*, TR 1, 55.

Perhaps most illustrative of the high regard which Luther held for the services of pious mothers is his characteristic employment of maternal analogies when he wishes to point to the kind of love God himself exhibits toward his children. Christ, for instance, is said to show mercy on his disciples' pride and anger with the patient devotion displayed by a mother "as she washes the swaddling clothes of her beloved."[44] Or again, Luther can compare the righteousness of God as it embraces men with the overabundance of "love, kisses, and affection" with which a good mother is sure to envelop her little loved ones.[45] For as most of mankind will testify—the celibate priests notwithstanding—"The way a mother cherishes her baby has no earthly equal."[46]

Turning now to the paternal side, Luther's *Exposition of the 127th Psalm* (1524) provides us with a helpful summary of his views on the father's responsibilities to his family and home life. Central to his position is the conviction that while the work of the home is to be free from the control of the church, it still remains accountable to God. Thus it is neither clericalized nor secularized. Concretely, this means that the home is liberated from the legislation of Roman canon law and is free to be governed by man's own reason and common sense (civil righteousness). And yet, like all other institutional structures in the realm of creation, the family is one of the most strategic places where civil offices can be transformed into religious callings through the exercise of man's faith active in love (Christian righteousness). Employing the imagery of Psalm 127, Luther presents the biblical picture of a pious, well-integrated household in which all its members are engaged in mutual service and loving care to the greater glory of God.

At the outset, Luther contrasts the building of a house with the making of a home. True homemaking demands far more than the exercise of human reason, important as this is within its

[44] *WA* 10[III], 239.
[45] *WA* 10[I,1] 296.
[46] *Ibid.*

own dominion. Faith must also humbly acknowledge that "Unless the Lord builds the house, those who build it labor in vain" (Ps. 127:1).

We must first realize that "to build a house" in this context means far more than fashioning wood and stone into walls and roof, rooms and chambers. Beyond all this, it refers essentially to what belongs inside a house, to what we Germans mean by being a householder in the realm of what Aristotle called *"oeconomia."* It encompasses the whole household of parents, children, servants, livestock, and property (Exod. 1:20ff.) . . . . For Solomon is trying to describe a Christian marriage and home here in order to instruct man how to become a Christian husband, father, and head of a household.[47]

Everyday experience teaches us that man is not sovereign over the destiny of his household. No mere human reason can guarantee the health and wealth of a family, the extent of its success, or the number of its children. Misfortune, sickness, impotence, and natural catastrophes are ever-present dangers which transcend man's rational control.[48] The biblical answer to such innumerable problems connected with home life is not "to remain outside in unchastity," but rather to lay all one's domestic troubles in prayer upon the broad shoulders of God.

The head of a family and household will have many problems and worries for they always accompany a house. But God is bigger than any house. If he can govern the heavens and the earth, he can also take care of a little house . . . . We see, therefore, that true stewardship must always be practiced in faith. Man must first confess that the welfare of the house depends not upon his own ability and activity, but ultimately upon the blessings and support of God himself.[49]

Luther is quick to warn that this does not mean that man is neither to work hard nor to plan carefully for his family's temporal welfare. God will provide—but through man's work. Unlike his redemptive activity which is done alone, God's creating and preserving activity usually includes the work of man and is channeled through it. Certainly this is the case in the

[47] *WA* 15, 364.
[48] *Ibid.*
[49] *Ibid.*, 365.

home: "Man should and must work, but the support of the house comes not from his work but rather solely from the goodness and blessing of God. . . . You must consequently distinguish 'working' from 'providing' as clearly as heaven and earth or God and man."[50]

The sharp distinction which Luther draws here has its roots in the association which Genesis 3 makes between the sin of Adam and the curse placed upon human labor. Insofar as he is sinful, fallen man now works as a means of self-discipline. God continues to provide for all the needs of his children—the just and the unjust alike—by grace alone. Hence, if any man's labors were not blessed by God, he could work forever without any results. "For where God does not provide, men will not find anything, even if they search and work themselves to death. . . . Wherever we look, therefore, we find that all our work is nothing more than finding and gathering up the gifts of God."[51]

However, when a Christian dedicates his labors to serving his family and glorifying God's name, faith can transform a dreary occupation *(Stand)* into a meaningful vocation *(Beruf)*. This does not mean that the faithful will have any easier jobs than the unfaithful. But it does mean that they will be able to do the work expected of them free from all the gnawing doubts and anxieties about the possible misfortunes of the morrow. Confident that their work is pleasing to God and beneficial to their neighbors, Christians view their labors from a religious perspective whose motives, resources, and goals are, like they themselves, "in but not of the world." Faith provides them with both the power to perform a good day's work and the peace to enjoy a good night's sleep. In short, "God wants man to work but not so that he will have to worry and fret."[52]

Luther was convinced that this same confidence in the goodness of God should permeate a father's attitude toward his children as well as toward his vocation. It is once again solely a

[50] *Ibid.*, 366.
[51] *Ibid.*, 368.
[52] *Ibid.*, 374.

matter of the gracious gifts of his Creator for which a Christian father is to be grateful and responsible. Although God magnanimously permits man to share in the procreation of his children, it should never be forgotten that it is God alone who creates. Children are God's presents, not man's achievements, and their divine Father will see to it that they are properly provided for.

What is the use of worrying so over your domestic cares? It is not in your power to control the birth of children, born of women, which belong in a house and town. Yet were there no children born, house and town would not last very long. We see therefore that these are God's inheritance and reward, that is, gifts and presents over which men worry and yet have no control. The head of a household should assert confidently, "I will work and carry out my responsibilities, and he who created the children in the home and the people in the town will also nourish and protect them." In this way, a man can do his work in peace with no fear of its turning sour on him as long as he has faith.[53]

One cannot help being impressed by the deep faith in God's providence which underlies such a passage. Luther's confidence in the living God who is always trustworthy is simple and childlike. Realistically, though, he was also aware of the many economic considerations which were so carefully calculated by parents in his day with regard to children and their costly care. Times were bad, and many of the German peasants thought of their offspring largely in terms of providing cheap farm labor or as part of a prospective lucrative marriage deal. Others lived immorally avoiding altogether the social and financial responsibilities connected with marriage and children. Yet Luther believed with the ancient Hebrews that having many children was a sign of special divine favor, and he openly scorned those who dealt with their boys and girls as if they were commercial goods to be bought and sold according to the prevailing market price.[54]

It was precisely at the expensive point of providing their children with the education necessary for greater social service in the community at large that most of the "clever and scheming"

[53] *Ibid.,* 375.
[54] *Ibid.,* 376.

balked at Luther's social concern. They were all in favor of the Reformer's liberation of their homes from the rule of the church, but when they learned that they were being freed in order better to serve the community, that was a far different story. Yet Luther's theology of society could never permit self-contained homes to replace self-contained monasteries since secularism is no Christian substitute for clericalism. Luther conceived of Christian home life rather as a freshly flowing stream whose living waters were to provide a constant source of nourishment to the whole countryside. The self-sacrificing nature of faith constrains all truly Christian parents to help their children develop their God-given gifts for effective Christian social action.

Cornerstone of Society

The education and preparation of Christian youth for public service is an inherent feature of Luther's understanding of man's divine calling within the priesthood of all believers. If I am not called to imitate Christ's specific deeds but rather his obedience to the will of the Father (conformitas Christi), then it follows that the peculiar shape of my vocation will largely be determined by the special capacities and abilities with which I have been invested by my Creator. My talents are not to be buried selfishly in the ground when they could be directed beneficially toward meeting the needs of my neighbors. Vocational education and guidance, therefore, is not a luxury but a necessity for every young Christian steward in the community. God has fitted each of us to do what he expects of us; a well-rounded education can help us to discover just what that is.

It is considerations such as these which moved Luther to write *To the Councilmen of all Cities in Germany That They Establish and Maintain Christian Schools* in 1524. In this work he gathers together his thoughts on the relation of home and community in regard to education, a subject which had enjoyed brief and marginal treatment in his earlier writings. He feels that the time is now ripe for a full-scale investigation of education because new evil spirits are rapidly replacing the old ones which had been cleaned away by the first sweep of the Reformation.

First of all, then, we are experiencing today throughout Germany how schools are everywhere allowed to go to wrack and ruin; universities are growing weak, monasteries are declining. . . . For since it is becoming known, through God's Word, how un-Christian and devoted only to men's bellies those institutions are; and especially since the carnal multitudes see that they are no longer obliged or able to drive their sons and daughters into monasteries and cathedral schools, and to turn them out of their own houses and possessions and plant them in other people's possessions, no one is any longer willing to have children educated. "Tell us," they say, "why should we send them to school if they are not to become priests, monks, and nuns? They had better learn such things as will help them to make a living!"[55]

Luther cites this as an excellent example of how flexible and wily the Evil One is in beguiling the children of God away from his praise and service. Natural man can see only two alternatives in life: church-rule or self-rule, but never God-rule. Luther is constantly forced to disavow secularism as the only substitute for the clericalism he has helped to overthrow. Because the risk always accompanies the glory, Satan temporarily has men both coming and going. "Then he went to work, spread his nets and set up such monasteries, schools, and estates that it was not possible for a boy to escape him without a miracle from heaven. Now, however, that he sees his snares exposed through God's Word, he flies to the other extreme and will not suffer anyone to study at all."[56]

Luther assembles three strong arguments to convince the civil rulers that it is their clear and pressing duty to establish and support good schools throughout the land. In the first place, finances should not be a genuine obstacle because the Reformation has saved every Christian citizen a great deal of money which could now easily be redirected "out of gratitude to God

[55] *PE* 4, 104.
[56] *Ibid.*, 105.
[57] *Ibid.*, 106.

for his glory" toward more socially constructive goals than the former perpetuation of priestcraft.[57] Secondly, the opportunity for greater learning is now knocking at Germany's door and she had better strike while the iron is hot if she is not to share the same fate as did the Jews, Greeks, Turks, and Romans. "Now that God has so richly blessed us and given us so many men able to instruct and train our young people aright, surely we ought not to despise the grace of God and suffer him to knock in vain. . . . Germany, I believe, has never heard so much of God's Word as now."[58]

The final argument speaks with most authority of all, however, for it deals with the will of God. Above and beyond all the examples from the heathen and the animal world of caring for their young, Christians must recognize the education of their children as a God-pleasing requirement which is inherent in the parent-child relationship established by the fourth commandment. We are not the masters but the trustees of our children: "God has therefore entrusted them to us who are old and know by experience what is good for them, and he will compel us to render a strict account."[59]

Our third consideration is by far the most important of all; it is the command of God. Its importance is seen in that he so frequently through Moses urges and enjoins parents to instruct their children. . . . It is seen also in the fourth commandment, in which he so urgently enjoins children to obey their parents that he would even have disobedient children sentenced to death (Deut. 21:18ff.). Indeed, for what other purpose do we older folk exist than to care for, instruct, and bring up the young?[60]

If the councilmen object that this advice is all very well and good for parents but is no concern of theirs, Luther disagrees heartily. While education is essentially a parental responsibility, there are reasons why parents neglect their duty since many are unwilling and most are unable. "And even if parents were able and willing to do it themselves, they have neither the time

[58] *Ibid.,* 108.
[59] *Ibid.,* 109.
[60] *Ibid.,* 108-109

nor the opportunity for it, what with their other duties and housework."[61] Luther concludes that when parents neglect this vital area, it falls to the civil authorities—and not the church— to take up the slack. His rationale for this is by way of imple- menting the state's "duty toward God and man" in the kingdom on the left hand.

It therefore becomes the business of councilmen and magistrates to devote the greatest care and attention to the young. For since the property, honor, and life of the whole city are committed to their faithful keeping, they would fail in their duty toward God and man if they did not seek its welfare and improvement with all their powers day and night. Now the welfare of a city consists not alone in gathering great treasures and providing solid walls, beautiful buildings, and a goodly supply of guns and armor. Now, where these abound and reckless fools get control of them, the city suffers only the greater loss. But a city's best and highest welfare, safety, and strength consist in its having many able, learned, wise, honorable, and well-bred citizens. Such men can readily gather treasures and all goods, protect them, and put them to good use.[62]

Luther is making a strong appeal here for the best training possible for the young men in whose hands the community will find itself in the next generation. The home, the church, and the state are all in need of dedicated stewards of God's gifts who humbly acknowledge, as Luther puts it, "their duty toward God and man." Not by running from communal responsibilities, but by dedicating one's reason and common sense to meeting them, does man fulfill his calling among his neighbors. In ruling human affairs, there is no cause for Christians to engage in pious platitudes or pharisaical head-shaking when what is needed is some clear thinking and hard work. "God will work no miracles so long as men can solve their problems by means of the other gifts he has granted them. Therefore we must do our part and spare no labor or expense to train and produce such men."[63]

Turning first to preparing youth for assuming ecclesiastical

[61] *Ibid.*, 110.
[62] *Ibid.*, 111.
[63] *Ibid.*, 112.

responsibility in the community, Luther stresses to the councilmen that potential clergymen are in need of a broad liberal arts foundation to give them an acquaintance with the whole sweep of human culture and civilization. This is what made the ancient Roman citizens such "intelligent, wise, and competent men, skilled in all knowledge and experience."[64]

Luther was clearly no friend of narrow parochial indoctrination. Yet in the light of the pressing need in his day for re-establishing Holy Scripture as the sole norm and standard for Christian theology, he felt compelled to lay particular emphasis on training young men in the biblical languages so that they might cut through the Catholic maze of commentaries, glosses, decretals, and canon law, and feed directly on the Bread of Life. For Evangelicals, "it will be a great sin and loss if we do not study the languages, the more that God is now offering and giving us men and books and every aid and inducement to this study, and desires his Bible to be an open book."[65]

The education of gifted young people for social and political responsibility is of equal concern to Luther. Communities are always in need of trustworthy civil servants, particularly when there is a poor ruler. Luther pretends to hold no illusions. "You must know from the beginning of the world, a wise prince is a rare bird indeed; still more so a pious prince. They are usually the greatest fools or the worst knaves on earth."[66] As always, however, Luther will not attempt to instruct a man as to what he should actually do (as a political leader), but why and how he should act in his calling (as a Christian).

Now we want to show how civil authority should be properly exercised. I do not intend to indicate what a ruler should do in all concrete cases; this I leave to his reason. I am concerned rather with showing how love to the neighbor can be demonstrated in this calling.[67]

[64] *Ibid.*, 111.
[65] *Ibid.*, 118.
[66] *PE* 3, 258.
[67] *WA* 10^{III}, 380.

A prince's duty is fourfold: first, that toward God consists in a true confidence and sincere prayer; second, that toward his subjects consists in love and Christian service; third, that toward his counselors and rulers consists in an open and unfettered judgment; fourth, that toward evildoers consists in proper zeal and firmness. Then the state is right, outwardly and inwardly, pleasing to God and to the people.[68]

Now it is obvious that Luther's God-fearing prince would be in great need of a multitude of public officials and civil servants to assist him in the maintenance of a just and peaceful social order. Here is clearly the privilege and the opportunity for sincere Christian parents to contribute to the well-being of the community by encouraging their children to make a career out of politics. The climax of Luther's appeal to the councilmen is a stirring challenge to their preparation of a whole new generation of socially minded young people to help establish a better society under God.

It is not necessary to state here that the temporal government is a divine order; I have elsewhere so fully treated this subject that I trust no one has any doubt about it. The question is rather, how to get good and skilled persons into the government. . . . If then there were no soul, and if there were no need at all of schools and languages for the sake of the Scriptures and of God, this one consideration should suffice to establish everywhere the very best schools for both boys and girls; namely, that in order outwardly to maintain its temporal estate, the world must have good and skilled men and women, so that the former may well rule over land and people and the latter may keep house and train children and servants aright.[69]

In the main Luther conservatively accepted the feudal structure of his day as in accord with God's will.[70] To be sure, he always allowed the marginal possibility that the Lord of history sometimes raises up unusually heroic men *(viri heroici)* such as Cyrus, Samson, or Alexander the Great to act as "rods of his anger." Such men tear down existing social structures in order to chastise a disobedient people. But Luther viewed such activity

[68] *PE* 3, 271.
[69] *PE* 4, 121.
[70] Cf. *WA* 7, 378.

as highly exceptional, and steadfastly refused to prescribe such an "earth-shaking" social program for anyone (including himself) without a special calling from God. "Such a miracle is not impossible, but quite unusual and hazardous. . . . It cannot be done without grace. Therefore, first become like Samson, and then you can also do as Samson did."[71]

As early as 1519, Luther employed the traditional classification of all social life in the earthly kingdom under the three general headings of domestic-economic (oeconomia), political (politia), and ecclesiastical affairs (ecclesia). In no way was Luther thereby trying to solidify, say, a three-class society since he took it for granted that a Christian who was a baker living in Wittenberg would be in all three estates simultaneously.[72] He also encouraged intermarriage between different feudal classes, insisting that all men are equal in God's sight anyhow.[73] Moreover, educational and vocational opportunities are to be seized enthusiastically if they offer possibilities for greater service to one's fellow men.

Consequently, when Luther often employs the words of Paul to admonish man to "remain in the state in which he was called" (I Cor. 7:20), he is not so much in opposition to changes of occupation as he is against man's sinful quest for foot-loose autonomy. God normally encounters man not in isolation but in and through his community relationships. For man to leave these divine bastions in order to attempt some extraordinary good work or pattern of life is to leave the protection of God and to invite the onslaughts of the devil. Sometimes, to be sure, Luther speaks as if the class structure of medieval feudalism is permanent and inviolable.[74] More faithful to his general theological orientation, however, is his more characteristic position that it is not to but in an occupation that man is called to witness and work as a Christ to his neighbors.

[71] PE 3, 249.
[72] WA 2, 734.
[73] WA 10II, 147.
[74] WA 12, 378.

We must close our eyes to the works themselves, caring not whether they are great, small, honorable, splendid, spiritual, physical, or by whatever other name they might be called on earth. We must look rather to the command and obedience which undergirds the work.[75]

In this connection, Luther delighted in comparing the "nameless," i.e., unpremeditated and uncalculated, domestic chores which "come to hand" in the everyday life of a pious servant girl with the meticulously observed rules and regulations of the monks. "Therefore the works have no specific names so that they cannot be compared or divided up, as if you could do some and omit others. You must rather give yourself wholly and completely to your neighbor, doing whatever is necessary for him."[76] The way in which a maid cheerfully and usefully takes her life in trust and returns it in obedience is far more pleasing in the sight of her Maker than the work-righteousness of the parasitic monks.

A faithful servant girl does more good, accomplishes more, and is far more dependable—even if she only takes a sack from the back of an ass—than all the priests and monks who sing themselves to death day and night while making bloody martyrs of themselves.[77]

But a Christian's faith waxes and wanes, and often he will find himself wondering whether it was really God or perhaps "his own foolishness or the devil" which led him into his calling. This is especially true when he comes to know some of the sinful injustice which is ingrained in every human office and institution. Luther's biblical realism comes once more to the fore and he replies that though the ordinances of God are set up as dikes against the world's sin, it does not follow that man can or will live sinlessly within them. In this fallen world sin is inevitable, but the value of God's ordinances is that they provide restraints against the grosser forms of sin flourishing outside them. With but a few exceptions of inherently evil oc-

[75] *WA* 10[1,1], 310.
[76] *WA* 10[1,2], 38.
[77] *Ibid.*, 41.

cupations (crime, prostitution, priestcraft, etc.), any and all neighbor-serving stations in life may be considered legitimate places to work for the glory of God.[78] And whatever sin is incurred in the operation is covered by the forgiving love of God who graciously "looks through his fingers" at such impure costs of man's social responsibility.[79]

All this is by way of emphasizing and supporting Luther's contention that his was not a political revolution but rather a religious reformation with inevitable social and political by-products. In fact, it was not until 1528—and then only marginally in a theological treatise on Holy Communion—that Luther finally got around to formulating his view of the three "orders" or "estates" of society with some semblance of systematic consistency. "The holy ordinances and foundations instituted by God are these three: the ministry, marriage, and civil authority. . . . Service in them constitutes true holiness and pious living before God. This is because these three ordinances are grounded in God's Word and command (Gen. 1:28), and are thereby sanctified as holy things by God's own holy Word."[80]

Yet even here Luther is unwilling to classify men too rigidly for, after all, the only true significant division among men is not between classes but between believers and non-believers, i.e., in the kingdoms of God and of men.

Above and beyond these three foundations and ordinances is the general order of Christian love which constrains us even beyond the boundaries of the three ordinances to serve the needs of our neighbors by feeding the hungry, giving drink to the thirsty, forgiving our enemies, praying for all men on earth, suffering all kinds of evil on their behalf, etc. These are all good, holy works. Yet none of these ordinances and works can be used as a way of salvation. The only way in which man can be saved is through faith in Jesus Christ.[81]

As we reflect on Luther's theology of home and society we

[78] *WA* 10[I,1], 317.
[79] *Ibid.*
[80] *WA* 26, 504.
[81] *Ibid.*, 505.

are once again impressed by the inner consistency of his religion and his ethics. To employ a helpful—though limited—analogy, let us recall the relation of the physical elements to the real presence of Christ in Luther's theology of Holy Communion. Luther opposed both the radical sectarians who maintained that nothing more than bread and wine was present in the sacrament, and the Roman Catholics who insisted that the physical elements were completely transubstantiated into the body and blood of Christ. In contrast to both, Luther held that although the elements of creation remained the same, Christ himself was really present "in, with, and under" them to redeem his creatures with his forgiving love.

The same dialectical spirit permeates Luther's theology of the Christian home. Godless secularists are wrong who, in their zeal to allot the temporal order a moral autonomy of its own divorced from the law of God, separate God's redemptive activity from his creative activity.[82] On the other hand, Luther also chides godless clericalists for attempting to "transubstantiate" certain ecclesiastical offices into divine orders in which the human elements are merely "accidental" rather than substantial. Between—and against—both, Luther allows all human occupations and institutions a *relative* autonomy in the realm of creation, and yet maintains that "in, with, and under" them the living Word of God is at work transforming them into divine vocations for all who have the faith to "see." In this manner, the realms of redemption and creation are neither separated nor equated, but permitted to remain in fruitful tension until the Day of Judgment.

Concretely for the ethics of home and society, this means that the earthly kingdom must be ruled primarily by God's law and that the gifts of the Spirit—faith active in love—have only a

---

[82] The thrust of this whole last section belies those, like the Nazified *Deutsche Christen*, who tried to give a Lutheran interpretation of the "orders of creation" *(Schöpfungsordnungen)* which would make them a law unto themselves *(Eigengesetzlichkeit)*, sacrosanct sources of divine revelation parallel to and independent of God's normative self-revelation in Jesus Christ.

"helping" *(vikarisch)* role to play in this world. Love can only nourish a sick and unco-operative world intravenously; i.e., we can never directly "Christianize" politics, economics, education, etc., even though it is essential for society to have Christian politicians, economists, and educators. This is even true, strictly speaking, of the home, although the opportunities are far greater in such an intimate circle for love to replace law in the personal relations of Christian parents and children.

Once this is understood, it becomes obvious that the authority of Luther's theology cannot legitimately be used to endorse many of the unhealthy developments which have since appeared in the church bearing his name. To cite only the most notorious example, Luther could never have sanctioned a totalitarian regime ruling over a class-bound society in which a spiritually emasculated clergy could desist from any prophetic criticism of the state in return for political and social favors. The vicious attempts to discredit Luther as "Hitler's spiritual ancestor," for instance, must be denounced as theological and political fantasy —despite some deceptive Allied wartime propaganda to the contrary.

It may confidently be asserted, moreover, that the incidental character of Luther's doctrine of the "three orders" *(Drei Stände)* is in no way comparable to the fundamental importance of his doctrine of the "two kingdoms" *(Zwei Reiche)*. The former is largely time-limited to the feudal soil on which it grew; the latter is rooted firmly in the two-aeons eschatology of the New Testament. When properly interpreted and implemented, Luther's theological ethic can still provide Christians with biblical guidance and direction for the establishment of a responsible society under God.

Certainly social action was a major concern in his own life. The profound effects of Luther's reformation in the area of religion is common knowledge to us all. What is not so well known—or, at least, not so commonly acknowledged—is the impressive social reformation which Luther's theology envisioned and partially brought about in the broad and inclusive expanse of everyday activity and experience which we call the common life. Here again, Luther's contribution to a better world is incalculable. Since our own study is concentrated at the point of breakthrough in this cultural liberation—the unshackling of the Christian home—we must be content like Moses merely to scan the horizons of the Promised Land just beyond.

In his definitive essay on "The Cultural Significance of the Reformation," Karl Holl provides us with a brilliant summary of the surprisingly wide panorama of social, political, and economic interests which Luther not only held personally but which he also strongly encouraged other Evangelicals to share.[83] All of life was welcomed with a view to its potential cultivation for the service of man and the glory of God. Above and beyond his tremendous output of time and energy on strictly theological subjects (his own proper calling), Luther found the strength to throw open door after door within the various areas of cultural life for more timid men to follow. Every situation provides vocational opportunities in which a Christian can serve as a "Christ to his neighbors."

This emancipation of the common life was not so popular a crusade as it might at first appear. Constant obstacles were thrown in Luther's path by both clericalists and secularists who wanted the church either to govern all of life or else to keep its hands off completely. Luther's understanding of the Christian ethical life compelled him to combat both extremes as unevangelical. Against Anabaptists, he had to fight for the preservation of music, art, and sculpture in the worship life of the church (*Against the Heavenly Prophets*). Against Roman Catholics, he had to struggle for the opening of the monasteries and the freedom of all Christians to marry and to engage in secular pursuits without endangering their salvation (*On Monastic Vows; On Married Life*).

[83] Karl Holl, "Die Kulturbedeutung der Reformation," in *Gesammelte Aufsätze zur Kirchengeschichte* (Tübingen: Mohr, 1932), vol. 1, pp. 468-543.

Against recalcitrant parents and lax public officials, he also fought for educational reforms and the establishment of community chests to replace the illiteracy and begging so prevalent in his day *(On Keeping Children in School; Preface to an Ordinance of a Common Chest).* Against irresponsible merchants, he attacked economic injustice and proposed government controls to halt unfair commercial and labor practices *(On Trading and Usury).* Against both the reckless mobs which confused their Christian freedom with their civil rights, and the arbitrary rulers who disregarded their responsibility under God for their subjects' social welfare, Luther appealed constantly for mutual service and obedience in a community of law and order *(Admonition to Peace; Exposition of the Eighty-second Psalm).* By such continual word and deed, Luther provided his followers with social-ethical guidance, "in order that through us, too, the world may be made better. I have done my part."[84]

Conclusion

Luther does not normally conceive of the Christian's social responsibility as transforming the existing structures of society. Persons can be transformed; institutions only reformed. Men are rather to accept social structures for what they are (the Creator's dikes against sin), and to try to act as responsible Christians within them (as the Redeemer's channels of serving love). When our secular occupations are faithfully acknowledged as religious vocations under God, then love provides law with its ethical content and law provides love with its social form.

As a biblical theologian rather than a political theorist, Luther was far more concerned with the divine origin and purpose of human society than with the concrete forms of its social and political institutions. Of great importance, however, is the fact that whenever he spoke concretely of the temporal institutions of civil and ecclesiastical life, he always did so in close connection with the family and the home. Luther was convinced that

[84] *PE* 4, 125.

all earthly "dominion" was granted to Adam and Eve, and that whatever public authority is exercised in the realm of creation is derived ultimately from the parental authority and filial obedience grounded in the fourth commandment. This is true even of the church insofar as it is a social institution. By restoring the Christian home as the cornerstone of society, therefore, Luther prepared the way for liberating all of daily life from the clericalism of Rome for the service of God. "Be fruitful and multiply, fill the earth and subdue it; and have dominion ... over every living thing."

CHAPTER SIX

Marriage as Ordained by God

Before Luther was able to direct all the theological resources at his disposal to the formulation of an evangelical marriage ethic, he was forced to address himself to the existing social philosophy underlying medieval Roman society. It was always the genius of Rome to hold together two completely irreconcilable views throughout Christian history. On the one hand, it taught that the religious status of a celibate monk is higher than that of a married layman. On the other hand, it also taught that marriage is a Christian sacrament employed by God as a channel of his sanctifying grace. The logical incompatibility of these two positions did not bother Luther for long, however, since he quickly exposed both theses as unevangelical and in dire need of reformation.

It is significant that, though Luther was a celibate monk himself, the issue of celibacy versus marriage was never a primary issue in his early theology. Nor is there any evidence to support the malicious view that Luther left the Roman church in order to marry (cf. ch. 1). On the contrary, all the evidence shows that the Reformation trumpets were sounded originally on religious and not ethical grounds. Yet when the ethical repercussions of his religious protest later became more obvious and important to him, Luther was able to evaluate social issues such as marriage and divorce from the theological perspective of the Word of God. In other words, Luther was able to gain clarity on the sixth commandment (as on the fourth) only because he had begun properly with the first. Spectators like

Erasmus could glibly trace Rome's fury to Luther's attacks "on the pope's crown and the monks' bellies."[1] As an evangelical theologian, however, Luther knew otherwise.

Monastic Clericalism

It was not until 1519—fourteen years after Brother Martin had assumed his own monastic vows and two years after the posting of the *Theses*—that vows began to be questioned seriously by Luther, and then, appropriately enough, in connection with the Christian sacraments. In the *Treatise on the Sacrament of Baptism,* for example, Luther concludes his work by extolling the various civil offices and estates which have been ordained by God for the beneficial practice of man's self-discipline and service. The question then arises: "Is the vow we have made to God in baptism not greater than all the vows of celibacy, the priesthood, and spirituality? For it is now held that while baptism is common to all Christians, only the priests have accepted a special and higher calling."[2]

The unresolved tension in Luther's answer demonstrates that at this early date his ethics had not yet reached the evangelical purity of his religion. Baptism is already praised as "higher, better, and greater" than monastic vows, but the sacrificial life of the clergy is still considered superior to that of the laity.

If a man binds himself in the estate of marriage, he can discipline himself better than someone outside marriage in mortifying the flesh and preparing for death. For there are constant cares and suffering in marriage which will help chasten his nature. But if a man wishes to suffer even more and to achieve the works of his baptism and preparation for death still more quickly, he should take a vow of celibacy and join a monastic order.[3]

All this is predicated, of course, on the presupposition that faith will condition and color everything the Christian does: "If you believe, you have. If you doubt, you are lost . . . everything de-

---

[1] *WA,* TR 1, 131.
[2] *WA* 2, 735.
[3] *Ibid.,* 736.

pends upon your faith."[4] Yet Luther knows all too well from personal experience that the monastic life in actual practice does not aid, but hinders, the development of a piety based upon faith rather than works. It is not the free grace of God but the meritorious works of men which occupy the center of the stage.

Consequently, in his *Treatise on the Blessed Sacrament,* Luther appends a critical section on "The Brotherhoods" which we may interpret as a sign of things to come. These sodalities were comprised of laymen who were ostensibly dedicated to charitable and devotional aims. Luther, however, accuses them of both religious idolatry and social irresponsibility; twin charges which he was to make against the monastic life time and time again in later years. As always, Luther is suspicious of any kind of Christian piety which feels constrained to express itself outside the normal, God-created ordinances of domestic, economic, and political life. Latent in such attempts is usually the desire to earn some special merit in God's sight by the performance of so-called good works apart from the everyday responsibilities of the common life.

For there they learn to seek their own good, to love themselves, to be faithful only to one another, to despise others, to think themselves better than others and presume to stand higher before God than others. And thus perishes the communion of saints, Christian love, and the true brotherhood established in the holy sacrament.[5]

By the time Luther addresses himself to *A Discussion of Confession* in the following decisive year of 1520, he speaks with the bold confidence of one who lives the liberty for which Christ has set him free. Against the background of the commandments of God which contain his will for the ethical life of man, Luther examines the common medieval custom of taking special religious vows, a practice which Rome encouraged as an integral part of Christian piety. He comes to the conclusion that all good works must be anchored securely in the law of God and not in the imagination of men. Man's only necessary vow is taken

[4] *Ibid.,* 733.
[5] *PE* 2, 28.

in baptism at which time "we have vowed more than we are ever able to perform."[6]

The first and best plan would be for the pontiffs and preachers to dissuade and deter the people from their proneness to the making of vows, and to show them how the visiting of the Holy Land, Rome, Compostella, and other holy places, as well as zeal in fasting, prayers, and other works chosen by themselves, are nothing when compared with the works commanded by God and the vows which we have taken in baptism. These vows everyone can keep in his own home by doing his duty toward his neighbors, his wife, his children, his servants, his masters, and thereby gain incomparably greater merit than he can find by fulfilling vows to do works chosen by himself and not commanded by God.[7]

We are again struck immediately by the "ordinariness" of the Christian ethic which Luther is advocating here. The Christian becomes a saint "by faith alone" and he then lives as a saint "in his own home" by meeting the unspectacular but still important needs of his God-given neighbors. By our baptismal vow we are covered in God's sight by the mantle of the alien righteousness of Christ. This gracious acceptance of us just as we are frees us to accept our neighbors and their needs just as they are. In this way we re-enact the shape of the "suffering servant" role of our Savior. It is only in the blindness of sin that men cannot see that they are unable to vow to God anything more than to become such "little Christs" to their neighbors.

In the eyes of God there is no difference in works, and he judges works not according to their number or greatness, but according to the disposition of the doer . . . and he often prefers the manual labor of the poor artisan to the fasting and prayer of the priest.[8]

This evangelical approach to vows is developed far more comprehensively in Luther's *Open Letter to the Christian Nobility*. Matters relating to the enforced celibacy of priests and monks are treated characteristically with theological deftness, ethical sensitivity, and a pastoral concern for the bewildered consciences

[6] *PE* 1, 99.
[7] *Ibid.*, 98.
[8] *Ibid.*, 100.

of those many children of God involved in this intolerable situation. Luther refuses to depend upon scandal or sensationalism in treating the sordid dilemma which Rome has imposed upon its clergy. "Let no one accuse me of exaggeration! It is all so open that even at Rome they must confess the evil to be greater and more terrible than anyone can say. I have not yet stirred up the hell-broth of personal vices, nor do I intend to do so. I speak of things which are common talk, and yet I have not words to tell them all."[9]

The religious hypocrisy undergirding Roman morality made it possible for the church to proclaim a façade of noble ethical absolutes behind which—for a price—an endless number of exceptions, reservations, dissolutions, annulments, etc., were lucratively dispensed by experts in the casuistic nuances of canon law. Ever since marriage was suddenly included among the church's sacraments at the Council of Florence (1439), canon lawyers had the last word on all disputed marital controversies among the faithful. Most of these cases were channeled through the Dataria of Rome, a legal clearinghouse which suffered from a particularly evil reputation ever since its creation by Pope Innocent VIII (1484-1490).

Here vows are dissolved; here monks are granted liberty to leave their orders; here marriage is on sale to the clergy; here bastards can become legitimate; here all dishonor and shame can come to honor; all ill-repute and stigma of evil are here knighted and ennobled; here is permitted the marriage which is within the forbidden degrees or has some other defect. Oh! what a taxing and a robbing rules there! It looks as though all the laws of the church were made for one purpose only—to be nothing but so many money-snares from which a man must extricate himself, if he would be a Christian. Yea, here the devil becomes a saint and a god to boot . . . If that is not a brothel above all the brothels one can imagine, then I do not know what brothel means![10]

In the face of this obvious prostitution of the Christian faith, Luther addresses himself to concrete proposals of reform which

[9] *PE 2, 97.*
[10] *Ibid., 96.*

he considers necessary for "that great crowd who vow much and keep little," the celibate monks and priests of the church of Rome.[11] Luther proposes a radical reduction of the number of monasteries with a concentration of their forces in a few large centers wherein monastic divisions could be abolished, begging could be discontinued, and pious men could voluntarily enter and leave whenever they felt the need in keeping with their Christian freedom and calling. As now practiced, religious vows only impede man's quest for salvation. "I see how the vows are kept, especially the vow of chastity, which has become so universal through these monasteries and yet is not commanded by Christ. On the contrary, it is given to very few to keep it, as Christ himself and St. Paul say (Matt. 19:11ff.; I Cor. 7:7; Col. 2:20). I would have all men to be helped, and not have Christian souls caught in human, self-advised customs and laws."[12]

Luther proceeds to analyze the role of celibacy in the Christian clergy. He distinguishes first between the "ministry which God has instituted and which is to rule a congregation by means of preaching and sacraments," and the "ministries of popes, bishops, canons, and monks." Of the latter he remarks, "God has not instituted these offices. They have taken these burdens on themselves; let them bear them."[13] Although monks are thus enjoined to maintain their self-imposed vows of chastity, Luther does not feel that local priests should likewise have to bear church-imposed vows.

Certainly this was not the case in the apostolic church where the Christian freedom of every minister was respected, ". . . leaving him free choice to marry or not."[14] That some of the clergy of the early church felt personally constrained not to marry for the sake of their personal witness and calling, was no justification for the popes beginning with Siricius (A.D. 385) to

[11] *Ibid.,* 115ff.
[12] *Ibid.,* 118.
[13] *Ibid.,* 120.
[14] *Ibid.,* 119.

prohibit any clergy to marry.[15] Furthermore, for Rome to demand celibacy in order that a daily offering of the sacrifice of the Eucharist could be made by a priest "undefiled" by sexual relations was particularly offensive to the Reformer's theology of grace. Such ecclesiastical decrees were denounced by Luther as satanic: "This was all done at the bidding of the devil, as St. Paul declares, 'There shall come teachers who bring doctrines of devils and forbid men to marry,' (I Tim. 4:1ff.)."[16]

Luther's corrective to man's sinful deviation from the clear Word of God is bold and simple. "My advice is that matrimony again be made free, and that everyone be left free choice to marry or not to marry. . . . For since God has not bound them, no one else ought to bind them or can bind them, even though he were an angel from heaven, still less if he be only a pope."[17] Moreover, if this liberty is to be granted those entering the Christian ministry, it should also be enjoyed by those already within its ranks. Luther shows special concern for the burdened consciences of those many clergymen who have found it impossible to maintain their vows of celibacy and who have consequently been forced to live a public life of hypocrisy and a private life of sin. With a confidence grounded securely in Scripture, Luther advises them to "obey God rather than man" and to bring their "wives" and families out into the open.

You will find many a pious priest against whom no one has anything to say except that he is weak and has come to shame with a woman, though both parties may be minded with all their heart to live together always in wedded love and troth, if only they could do it with a clear conscience, even though they might have to bear

---

[15] More rigorous enforcement of the long-standing prohibition of clerical marriage and concubinage was begun only centuries later under the aggressive rule of Pope Gregory VII (1073-1085). It was he who declared all clerical marriages invalid in what has been described as "the greatest mass divorce in history." Cf. Kenneth Latourette, *A History of Christianity* (New York: Harper and Brothers, 1953), p. 472; Henry C. Lea, *History of Sacerdotal Celibacy in the Christian Church* (New York: Macmillan, 1907), vol. 1, ch. 14.

[16] *PE* 2, 119-20.

[17] *Ibid.,* 120.

public shame. Two such persons are certainly married before God. And I say that where they are thus minded, and so come to live together, they should boldly save their consciences. Let him take her as his wedded wife, and live honestly with her as her husband, caring nothing whether the pope will have it so or not, whether it be against canon law or human law. The salvation of your soul is of more importance than tyrannical, arbitarary, wicked laws, which are not necessary for salvation and are not commanded by God.[18]

Luther concludes by citing three arguments in support of his history-making position.[19] In the first place, most priests need wives both physically and domestically. The prevailing church practice of recognizing the latter but not the former demand only invites temptation and immorality. "It is as though one were to put fire and straw together and command that it should neither smoke nor burn." Secondly, marriage belongs to the realm of creation and not redemption and is therefore a civil rather than an ecclesiastical concern. Salvation is not endangered by a pious, God-fearing marriage, and the pope should have no jurisdiction over such "physical, external" matters which are not peculiarly Christian but common to all humanity. Very frankly, "The pope has as little power to command this, as he has to forbid eating, drinking, the natural movement of the bowels, or growing fat."[20]

Luther's final argument moves from biology to theology and places man directly in the presence of the living God. Here a clear decision is demanded between God and mammon, Christ and the Antichrist. The pretensions of ecclesiastical imperialism must bow to the dominion of the law of God. Rome has freed what is bound (faith), and bound what is free (marriage). Here every Christian priest must issue a prophetic "No!"

Although the law of the pope is against it, nevertheless, when the estate of matrimony has been entered against the pope's law, then his law is at an end, and is no longer valid. For the commandment of God which decrees that no one shall put man and wife asunder,

[18] *Ibid.*, 121.
[19] *Ibid.*, 122ff.
[20] *Ibid.*

takes precedence of the law of the pope; and the commandments of God must not be broken or neglected for the sake of the pope's commandment. . . . For Christ has set us free from all human laws, especially when they are opposed to God and the salvation of souls, as St. Paul teaches in Gal. 5:1; I Cor. 9:4ff.; 10:23.[21]

Faithless Vows

In his *Answer to Emser* (1520) Luther is compelled to defend his views against the "shocked" response of the Roman church. The invectives and insults of "Goat Emser" have drawn forth Luther's anger and he retaliates in kind. Particularly distasteful to him is Emser's purposeful misreading of his pastoral attempt to minister to the consciences of many distressed priests. He is appalled by Emser's lack of compassion for his weaker brothers and his strong insinuations that the new Evangelical teachings are merely a thin covering to justify carnal immorality: "He seeks to show that I condemn chastity and inculcate unchastity."[22] Luther's forthright reply blends sarcasm with dismay. "O holy, holy virgin St. Emser, how hath thy chastity become like iron, so unfeeling and merciless against poor sinners."[23]

"Impressed" as he is with St. Emser's "lily-white chastity," Luther presses for scriptural refutation of I Timothy 4:3 where Paul expressly denounces any religious prohibition of marriage as of the devil. Of course, Emser finds this impossible, much to Luther's angry delight. "Are you not ashamed, you great teachers of the world, that I must continually pound and press you for Scripture, with which you ought to challenge me at the very start?"[24]

After thus establishing the right of individual priests to marry if they so choose, Luther goes still further in this treatise to insist that it is the duty of the entire clergy ". . . to oppose the pope as the very devil himself" at this point, and to renounce their ordination vows of celibacy as unscriptural and

[21] *Ibid.,* 123.
[22] *PE* 3, 315.
[23] *Ibid.,* 381.
[24] *Ibid.,* 382.

anti-Christian.[25] This does not mean, of course, that all priests must go out and get married at once. But it does mean that they need not remain celibate if and when they ever should decide to marry. Luther had already made it plain that he is not condemning any Christian who privately and voluntarily decides to take a vow. Man is free to make such vows or not. Luther protests only when this private right is made into a "common and public mode of life," as in the compulsory celibacy of the priests.[26] The church has no right to demand of all what is possible only for some.

In all this, Luther also makes it very clear that everything he is saying refers only to the church-imposed vows of the priests and not to the self-imposed vows of the monks. "My advice to lessen the number of monastic houses [Emser] twists to mean: Luther has taught that monastic vows should not be kept, cowls should be thrown off, monasteries forsaken."[27] Obviously Luther is not yet willing or able to go this far because he has failed to find adequate scriptural foundations for such a position. Although Brother Martin took his excommunication from the Roman church to mean the automatic release from his own monastic vows,[28] he confessed to Spalatin as late as August, 1521, that he had not "as yet" found the theological way out for the release of his ex-brother monks.[29]

It was Luther's intensive study of Scripture at the Wartburg which provided him with the biblical authority necessary to repudiate the celibate vows of monks as well as those of the priests. Not having concrete passages at hand as in the case of the freedom of priests to marry (e.g., I Tim. 3:1-6; 4:1-6), Luther was compelled to work out a Christian solution to the problem of monastic vows which took into account all the various elements which comprised his evangelical "theology of the

[25] *Ibid.*, 385.
[26] *PE* 2, 240.
[27] *PE* 3, 315.
[28] *WA*, Br 2, 382.
[29] *SJ* 2, 52.

cross": grace, faith, justification, freedom, love, good works, reason, creation, and all the rest. After organizing his views in the treatise *On Monastic Vows* (1521), Luther's efforts pleased him so well that he considered it his "best theological work up to that time." As such it merits careful consideration.

The Latin dedicatory epistle to this work is addressed to Luther's father, but it is certainly intended more for the benefit of "the sons of many others" who were about to or had already abandoned their vows of celibacy.[30] Luther takes the opportunity to recall his own monastic motivations and experiences and concludes that his previous obedience to Rome was possible only at the expense of his fidelity to God and his God-given parents. The liberating Word of God had finally freed him from the cloister and placed him ". . . not in the false service of the monasteries, but in the true service of God."[31]

The fact that the free ex-monk did not yet choose to lay aside his own habit and tonsure until 1524, or to get married until 1525, is beside the point. He was free to do so if and when he chose. "My conscience is free and this is the most complete liberty. Therefore, I am still a monk and yet not a monk; I am a new creature, not of the pope, but of Christ."[32] Even more pertinent than his own personal testimony is Luther's careful formulation of the major theological grounds which justify and substantiate his attack on the Roman institution of monasticism and its accompanying sacerdotal celibacy.

"First, vows are not grounded in the Word of God but stand rather in opposition to God's Word."[33] Luther examines Holy Scripture and finds no biblical authority whatsoever for the monastic way of life in general or monastic vows in particular. The whole system is totally dependent upon the unevangelical invention of Roman Catholic theologians in rending asunder that which God has joined together. First they have falsely bi-

---

[30] *Ta* 263.
[31] *Ibid.,* 262.
[32] *Ibid.*
[33] *BA, Er* 1, 217.

furcated God's Word into "counsels of perfection" (including celibacy) and "general commandments," and then on this basis they have falsely divided God's people into the "religious" and "secular" classes of clergy and the laity.[34] Rome's espousal of this notorious double-standard morality must give way to the authority of the Bible in which marriage is clearly permitted as a free choice to all Christians.

Luther's second argument goes right to the evangelical core of Scripture: "Vows are contrary to faith."[35] Here Luther probes into the motivations of a person who desires to take such vows upon himself. As incorporated in the prevailing Roman Catholic "theology of glory," vows can be interpreted only in terms of idolatrous work-righteousness. Men are encouraged to assume monastic vows in order to achieve a "second baptism" on the basis of their own merit and to earn a religious status which is superior to that of the married Christian. But since "whatever does not proceed from faith is sin" (Rom. 14:23), Luther is compelled to reverse himself and to conclude that the faithless vows of monks share equally with those of the priests the condemnation of the Apostle Paul (I Tim. 4:1-3). After he has "studied the matter more closely and considered the words of Paul more carefully," Luther now attacks *all* enforced vows as "godless, pagan, Jewish, and devilish," for scorning the grace of God and trusting in the works of man.[36]

The next charge against monastic vows follows as a corollary of their denial of faith: "Vows are in opposition to evangelical freedom."[37] If the Christian receives his salvation as a free gift, he is free from having to achieve it as a good work. Evangelical freedom consists in our liberation from the law and all of its works as a way of salvation. We are judged by the faith which motivates our actions and God leaves it to our evangelical freedom as to just what particular form these works will take. Yet

---

[34] *Ibid.*, 221ff.
[35] *Ibid.*, 238.
[36] *Ibid.*, 258.
[37] *Ibid.*, 262.

this freedom in externals is precisely what Roman clericalism will not permit. To legalize and institutionalize monastic vows, for instance, denies Christian freedom by attempting ". . . to make a law out of a fact, a command out of a work, a rule out of an example, something necessary out of something nonessential."[38] As the courageous celibate, Paphnutius, was able to dissuade the Council of Nicea (A.D. 325) from legislating sacerdotal celibacy on grounds of Christian freedom, we too must keep free what God has not prohibited but rather instituted himself; namely, marriage and family life.[39]

Luther's fourth attack holds vows up to the searching demands of the Decalogue: "Vows are opposed to the commandments of God."[40] Luther had long since come to the position that faith and love, respectively, are at the heart of the commands of the first and second tables of God's law. We have already seen how monastic vows stand contrary to Christian faith. Luther reiterates this charge here and shows how vows evade the requirements of Christian love as well. He confesses, "Here my anger reaches its highest and I burn to correct this blasphemous lie and madness."[41] Luther's passion is rooted in the shameful memory of his own monastic experience where the concrete demands of needy neighbors went unheeded in the monks' selfish zeal for ceremonial work-righteousness.[42]

The parental disobedience and communal irresponsibility inherent in the recluse's severance from society also run counter to the revealed will of God. Rome has never learned that God is served best when social responsibilities are not eluded but carried out with a faithful and loving heart. Every monk should admit to his parents, as did Luther, "On your side is the authority of God, on my side is human presumption."[43] It is simply

---

[38] *Ibid.*, 282.
[39] *Ibid.*
[40] *Ibid.*, 283.
[41] *Ibid.*, 295.
[42] *Ibid.*, 297.
[43] *Ta* 260.

not true, as Rome claims, that the authority of the church's "divine service" should take precedence over the home's "secular service." According to Holy Scripture, "It is impossible that true divine service should be hindered by obedience to parents and service to neighbors. This obedience and service is true and genuine divine service in itself, even though Rome denies this by their delusive fools' play."[44] For the sake of their salvation, therefore, "All Christian wives, mothers, fathers, and relatives should seek their loved ones' release from monastic life as soon as possible!"[45]

Having exposed to his satisfaction the unevangelical character of the Roman theology undergirding monasticism and its compulsory vows, Luther concludes with a final argument which is directed specifically against the vows themselves: "Monkery is irrational."[46] Sexual desire is a matter of universal human experience, says Luther, and no man should be expected to vow the impossible. The "tyranny of the flesh" is always unpredictable and often uncontrollable. "Chastity can hardly be kept even among the most pious despite much exertion, suffering, and cross."[47] Continence for fallen man is God's gift and not man's achievement, much as he should work at it. To offer God what he himself has not yet bestowed is a logical as well as biological impossibility. "This is solely a gift from God which man may receive from him but never offer up to him."[48]

Two final questions can still be raised in connection with this position which Luther anticipates himself. First, religiously, why does this line of reasoning not also excuse man from his baptismal vow, since the keeping of all God's commandments is equally beyond his ability? Luther replies that the crucial difference lies in God's gracious promise which undergirds man's life under baptism but not his life in a monastery. Baptism is

[44] *BA, Er* 1, 299.
[45] *Ibid.*, 301.
[46] *Ibid.*, 304.
[47] *Ibid.*, 343.
[48] *Ibid.*, 357.

essentially a divine sacrament and not a human sacrifice: ". . . our vow is nothing other than a promise to accept the Christ who is being offered to us."[49]

Luther's answer to the second question serves simultaneously as a bridge to our next section. The Roman ethical charge is this: Since the divine (sixth) commandment of chastity is just as impossible to keep as the human vow of celibacy, Luther's view would serve as an invitation to wholesale immorality and licentiousness. Not so, cries Luther. Only a faithless heart would pose two such false alternatives as celibacy or fornication in complete disregard of the divinely ordained institution of marriage. "In between lies marriage; man may marry and the law of chastity will become easier for him to obey."[50]

To be sure, Luther still holds at this time (1521) that in the rich diversity of God's gifts, "virginity and celibacy are greater works and gifts than marriage."[51] But as he was to insist so often, to maintain celibacy faithfully demands special blessings of grace which are granted to "scarcely one in a thousand."[52] God has therefore provided for the protection and benefit of the overwhelming majority of his children "within the bounds of the more deeply grounded chastity of marriage."[53]

Marital Clericalism

Luther unmasked the inherent clerical presumption not only in monasticism but also in the Roman Catholic doctrine of marriage. He first addressed himself to this area in his *Treatise on Marriage* (1519), published, at least partially, to correct a spurious copy in circulation under his name. This tract still reflects the traditional Roman Catholic interpretation of marriage, although written by Luther over a year after the posting of the *Ninety-five Theses*. Clearly, his social ethics had not yet caught

[49] *Ibid,* 359.
[50] *Ibid.,* 309.
[51] *Ibid.,* 348.
[52] *WA* 15, 667.
[53] *BA, Er* 1, 349.

up to his evangelical theology and once again we are reminded how centrally religious was the initial concern of the Reformation. Once this evangelical understanding of the grace of God began to permeate other doctrines however—particularly the sacraments—it was inevitable that marriage would also have to be reinterpreted accordingly.

In analyzing the Genesis account of God's uniting of Adam and Eve, Luther lays central emphasis on the intimate ties of love which were meant to exist between a husband and his wife.[54] He considers it very significant that Adam did not go out and find his mate independently, but that God created her for him and brought her to him as his mate. "Those who want to get married should learn from this to pray avidly to God for their marriage partner."[55] Marriage is not to be entered into lightly for it is "ordained" by God himself with "counsel and deliberation." This distinguishes human marriage from all other forms of procreation although woman has also been created ". . . to be a help-mate to man in all things, especially in the bearing of children." Mutual sacrificial love "which seeks the beloved for himself alone" was meant to aid all couples to live together happily in bonds stronger than all other earthly ties.

This is what marriage was meant to be, but never is. Adam's fall has corrupted all human relationships and self-love has replaced self-sacrifice even in marriage. Whatever may have once been true in Paradise, marriage for fallen humanity has now assumed a remedial character—"a hospital for the sick"— which is superior to the grosser immorality that obtains outside its walls, but still inferior to the purer status of virginity and celibacy.

For this reason [original sin], the estate of matrimony is no longer pure and sinless. Carnal lust has become so great and furious that marriage is now like a hospital for the sick so that men do not fall into greater sin outside it. Before Adam fell it was easy to remain

[54] *WA* 2, 167.
[55] *Ibid.*

chaste and celibate. Now it is scarcely possible, and without God's grace, wholly impossible. For this reason neither Christ nor the apostles ever commanded celibacy. Yet they did advise men to examine themselves to see whether or not they could maintain celibacy. If not, they could marry; if, with God's grace, they could, then celibacy was the better choice.[56]

On the basis of this monastic-colored exegesis, Luther proceeds to develop the commonly accepted Roman (Augustinian) doctrine of marriage whose three fundamental tenets were 1) a means of grace (*sacramentum*); 2) mutual consent and fidelity (*fides*); and 3) the procreation and education of children (*proles*). [57] Luther first describes marriage as ". . . a sacrament, an external holy sign of the greatest, holiest, most worthy and noble event which ever occurred," on the basis of Paul's analogy between the union of man and wife and the union of Christ and his church (Eph. 5:32). Because of the sacramental significance of marriage, Luther goes on to add that God does not reckon the carnal lust operative in marriage to the guilt of the partners. Out of gratitude for this divine goodness, therefore, mates are encouraged to engage moderately in sexual relations as befits responsible and considerate Christians.

Luther then moves on to the second characteristic of marriage which he considers its real "foundation and true nature," namely, the lifelong covenant of fidelity which is established between the partners. This loving trust between a husband and a wife under God provides the framework in which their sexual energies can be channeled in a faithful relationship which strictly avoids any extramarital relations. As for current questions under dispute, such as the wording of the engagement vow and the problem of secret engagements, Luther confesses simply, "I still do not know." He is quite sure, however, that the choice of one's life partner is of such a serious nature that young folks should take all the advice and guidance they can get from their parents. This practice has strong Old Testament precedent (e.g.,

[56] *Ibid.,* 168.
[57] *Ibid.,* 168-169.

Isaac, Jacob, Samson) and appeals to Luther as sound filial piety.

Finally, Luther treats of the begetting and rearing of children in the fear and love of God as ". . . the true purpose and foremost function of marriage." The uniqueness of Christian marriage lies precisely here: ". . . that man seeks in marriage nothing other than the opportunity to nurture his children in praise and honor of divine service." Luther begins to pour new wine into old wineskins by declaring that this Christian education and nurture of children is a far better work in God's sight than all the current pilgrimages, sacrifices, and cultic ceremonies combined.[58] Contrariwise, parents can no more easily incur the wrath of God than to neglect the necessary religious and ethical growth of their children. These helpless little ones are "precious, eternal treasures" from God, and parents will certainly be held accountable for their welfare.

The potentialities for good and evil seem to be so great in marriage that Brother Martin can only conclude with the wondrous exclamation: "O truly a great, noble, and blessed office is marriage when kept properly! O truly a sorrowful, terrible, and dangerous office when not kept properly!"[59]

Although Luther writes of marriage again within a year, *The Babylonian Captivity* of 1520 evidences a completely new evangelical spirit in its clarified position in regard to the theological foundations of marriage. It is hard to believe that it was written by the same man. For Luther's main contention here is that marriage is one of the five Roman Catholic sacraments which does not measure up at all to the biblical requirements for a Christian sacrament. First of all, theologically, marriage is grounded in the realm of creation and not redemption and therefore, unlike the true sacraments of baptism and Holy Communion, is not a channel of God's sanctifying grace.

We said that there is in every sacrament a word of divine promise, to be believed by whoever receives the sign, and that the sign alone cannot be a sacrament. Now we read nowhere that the man who

[58] *Ibid.,* 170 [59] *Ibid.*

marries a wife receives any grace of God. Nay, there is not even a divinely instituted sign in marriage, for nowhere do we read that marriage was instituted by God to be a sign of anything.[60]

That marriage falls under the civil rather than the redemptive rule of God—i.e., in the earthly kingdom on the left hand—is apparent enough from the pre-Christian marriages of Jew and Gentile alike, long before the advent of Christ, the church, and the sacraments of the New Covenant. Jesus himself spoke of marriage as dating "from the beginning," that is, from its divine ordination and institution by God in creation (Matt. 19:8; Gen. 1:28). "Since marriage existed from the beginning of the world and is still found among unbelievers, it cannot possibly be called a sacrament of the New Law and the exclusive possession of the church. The marriages of the ancients were no less sacred than ours, nor are those of unbelievers less true marriages than those of believers, and yet they are not regarded as sacraments."[61]

Most damning of all, marriage is regarded as a sacrament by Rome "without the least warrant from Scripture."[62] The argument from Ephesians ". . . betrays great shallowness and a negligent and thoughtless reading of Scripture." In the first place, the Greek term *mysterion* means "mystery" and not "sacrament," despite the misleading Latin Vulgate translation of *sacramentum* (Eph. 5:32). Then too, the "mystery" refers to Christ and the church, not to man and wife. Rome has falsely mistranslated and inverted Paul's words here to justify another church-controlled "sacrament." The Apostle uses marriage as a human symbol of the Christ-church union. Rome, on the other hand, employs the divine union to explain the husband-wife marriage, thereby transforming a sermon illustration into a means of grace.

"So much concerning marriage itself."[63] With these decisive words, Luther dismisses the possibility of marriage as a Christian sacrament and never once deviated from this position for the

[60] *PE* 2, 257.
[61] *Ibid.*
[62] *Ibid.*, 258f.
[63] *Ibid.*, 261.

rest of his life. He firmly believed that his case against Rome was conclusive and indisputable: Marriage is a wonderful blessing of God but it is not a Christian sacrament. The resultant by-product of this position, of course, is that jurisdiction over marital matters should reside in civil rather than ecclesiastical authorities.[64] Marriage is still under the law of God but not under the wing of the church. Canons and church law must give way to magistrates and civil law if marriage is to be understood properly as a means of creation and not as a means of grace.[65]

Pastoral Counseling

Having the necessary biblical foundations firmly under his feet, Luther now sets out to destroy the clericalism which Rome unjustly exercises over marital affairs as devastatingly as he had already done with monastic issues. Taking the *Summa Angelica* of Angelus de Clavassio in hand, Luther castigates this standard work of Roman Catholic casuistry as "a book whose contents have been poured together out of the cesspool of all human traditions." Luther vents his wrath particularly on the manual's marriage casuistry, a matter which he had already begun to criticize in his *Discussion of Confession.* As for the canon law distinction between full and perfect divorce *(divortium plenum et perfectum)* and an imperfect or limited divorce which restricts cohabitation *(divortium imperfectum)*, Luther rages:

There are many who set perilous snares for married folk, especially in the case of incest; and when anyone (for these things can happen, nay, alas! they do happen) has defiled the sister of his wife, or his mother-in-law, or one related to him in any degree of consanguinity, they at once deprive him of the right to pay the debt of matrimony, and nevertheless they suffer him not, nay, they forbid him, to

[64] While always permitting civil authorities "to order and arrange marriage customs as they see fit," Luther still maintains that "should anyone desire us to bless them before the church or in the church, to pray over them, or also to marry them, we are in duty bound to do this" (*PE* 6, 226f.). In fact, he strongly encourages the practice of a public church wedding ". . . in order that young people may learn to regard this estate seriously and honor it as a divine creation and command."
[65] *Ibid.*

desert his wife's bed. What monstrous thing is this? What new remedy for sin? What sort of satisfaction for sin? . . . They put dry wood on the fire and say, Do not burn! They put a man in a woman's arms and forbid him to touch her or know her. And they do this on their own authority and without the command of God. What madness![66]

It is this same clerical manipulating of the casuistic "ocean of distinctions" which Luther condemned earlier in *The Babylonian Captivity* in his discussion of the promiscuous granting of papal dispensations to cancel all kinds of marital and monastic vows and obligations. The most notorious example is the Roman dissolution of the marital vows of those who later decide to assume monastic vows instead. "The pope decrees that a marriage is dissolved if one party enters a monastery even without the consent of the other, provided the marriage be not yet consummated. O what devil puts such monstrous things into the pope's mind!"[67]

With such concrete abuses at hand, Luther proceeds in this Latin treatise to counsel his fellow confessors how they are to evaluate the marital cases of conscience given in the *Summa Angelica*. As one who laid great weight on the church's power of the keys, Luther always distinguished sharply between the public condemnation of civil law and the private declaration of religious absolution. To punish crime is the calling of the magistrate in the courtroom; to forgive sin is the vocation of the priest in the confessional. It is no wonder, therefore, that Luther could never abide canon law in principle. By its very nature it confused God's law and gospel, the unforgivable sin of Christian theology.

Luther charges that the papists have grown "filthy and obscene" by their merchandising in "the shame of men and women" through canon law marriage legislation.[68] For instance, "Enough money can make the same woman a man's mother, sister, and wife at the same time."[69] He declares, however, that this treatise is neither the time or the place for a detailed refuta-

[66] *PE* 1, 100.
[67] *PE* 2, 243.
[68] *Ibid.*, 262.
[69] *WA* 9, 543.

tion of the "dire confusion" which obtains in the mire of ecclesiastical rules and regulations. All that he now can do is to provide some illustrations of current casuistic abuses of the general evangelical norm: "There is no hope of betterment unless we abolish at one stroke all the laws of men, restore the gospel of liberty, and by it judge and rule all things."[70]

One after the other, he examines conditions on the part of either of the contracting parties which were said to prevent them from performing a valid marriage. Luther questions the scriptural legitimacy of the vast majority of both Rome's "diriment impediments" (hindrances which make a marriage contract invalid) and its "prohibitive impediments" (hindrances which make a marriage contract sinful, though still valid). Among those condemned by Luther are: ". . . those cruel hindrances arising from affinity, spiritual or legal relationship beyond the second degree of consanguinity; the hindrance of disparity of religion; the hindrance of crime; the hindrance of a tie; the hindrance of ordination; the hindrance of public decency; etc."[71] In fact, of the eighteen impediments officially acknowledged by Rome,[72] Luther hesitatingly recognizes only three, and he admits uncertainty even about these. "Thus far there seem to me to be no hindrances that may justly annul a contracted marriage save these: impotence of the husband, ignorance of a previously contracted marriage, and a vow of chastity."[73]

Luther immediately qualifies his recognition of a vow of chastity as a legitimate marriage impediment declaring, "Still, concerning the last, I am to this day so far from certain that I do not know at what age such a vow is to be regarded as binding."[74] Aggravating his indecision here is the "foolish and stupid" desire of parents "to dedicate their children before birth or in early infancy to the 'religious life' or to perpetual chastity

[70] PE 2, 268.
[71] Ibid., 264.
[72] These are listed in WA 10[II], 506.
[73] PE 2, 268.
[74] Ibid.

. . . . I am not fully clear in my own mind whether all the things that men nowadays vow come under the heading of vows."[75] We have already learned from our previous study that by 1521, within a year after these words were written, Luther was to find penetrating clarity on the illegitimacy of vows when actuated by the desire to earn merit by good works for eternal salvation.

Before proceeding to a brief concluding analysis of those other impediments to a contracted marriage which Luther recognizes here (impotence and bigamy), it will be necessary for us to keep three factors clearly in mind if we are to arrive at a fair evaluation of his position.

1) The motivation behind Luther's concern here is avowedly pastoral. He is not addressing civil magistrates or the general citizenry on how to punish sex criminals, but is rather trying to guide conscientious priests in their pastoral care of genuinely repentant sinners. His sole aim is to provide the forgiveness and comfort of the gospel to God's imperfect children in their hour of need. He counsels in the spirit of Christ, "Neither do I condemn you; go, and sin no more" (John 8:11). To use his own words, "This I have set forth to the best of my ability, for the strengthening of anxious consciences, being desirous to bring my afflicted brethren in this captivity what little comfort I can."[76]

2) The circumstances in which Luther wrote were admittedly unfortunate. From Luther's evangelical standpoint, the legal resources for a redress of grievances were limited indeed. On the one hand were the papal courts of Rome with their literalistic and casuistic application of the hated canon law. On the other hand were the bungling and inefficient civil law courts operating then under the strange admixture of Germanic tribal customs and imported Roman civil law. The injustice rampant in both court systems convinced many of Luther's contemporaries that

[75] *Ibid.*, 243.
[76] *Ibid.*, 271.

"the less law, the more justice."[77] Certainly this was his own opinion. "The temporal law—God help us, what a wilderness it has become! Though it is much better, wiser, and more rational than the 'spiritual law' which has nothing good about it except its name, there is still far too much of it."[78]

3) Nevertheless, the content of Luther's early marital counsel, whatever the motivation and the circumstances, is naive at best and illegal at worst. As a child of his times, we can understand his unhistorical approach to Scripture, particularly in regard to the Old Testament. We can even admire his zeal to defend the character and often immoral practices of many of the heroes of the Old Testament.[79] And remembering that he was a sheltered and rustic monk who was suddenly thrust from peasant soil into an international limelight with very little social experience, helps to explain (though not justify) his ethical conservatism in general and his insensitivity to the female point of view in particular. As he himself confessed, "While I was a monk I did not know what the world was like. I had to learn it all from 1517-20."[80]

But what is least defensible in Luther—as judged by his own theological standards—is his congenital distrust of civil law and lawyers, and his flagrant disregard for public law and customs in a great deal of his marriage counsel. Here Luther is guilty of virtually separating the two kingdoms which he himself so often insisted were distinguishable but inseparable. As a pastoral counselor for troubled souls, he was so intent upon liberating men from the religious bondage of the law *(coram Deo)*, that he sometimes disregarded man's social ethical responsibilities under the law *(coram hominibus)*.

This relative depreciation of reason, social justice, and civil law in actual practice—despite his theology of society to the contrary—was particularly unfortunate in the light of his vehement condemnation of the only other legal alternative for the

[77] *PE* 1, 294.
[78] *PE* 2, 149.
[79] E.g., *WA* 9, 543; 16, 27.
[80] *WA*, TR 1, 377.

common folk; namely, canon law. Moreover, his dread of clericalism also prohibited him from issuing social or political pronouncements of his own to fill the resultant moral vacuum, much as they were in constant demand. "I leave that for the knowledge of the town council . . . Such civil matters do not fall under my jurisdiction."[81]

I know that no state is well governed by means of laws. If the magistrate be wise, he will rule more prosperously by natural bent than by laws. If he not be wise, he will but further the evil by means of laws; for he will not know what use to make of the laws nor how to adapt them to the individual case. More stress ought, therefore, to be laid, in civil affairs, on putting good and wise men in office than on making laws; for such men will themselves be the very best laws, and will judge every variety of case with lively justice. And if there be knowledge of the divine law combined with natural wisdom, then written laws will be entirely superfluous and harmful. Above all, love needs no laws whatever.[82]

In short, Luther's revolt against legalistic work-righteousness sometimes trespassed its legitimate boundaries and endangered the communal fabric of social justice. When coupled with his great respect for civil authority as an expression of the will of God, and the honor of the civil ruler as the "father of the community," the whole thrust of Luther's biblical patriarchalism was to favor wise and pious rulers over even the best of human laws. What could happen to the German people when their rulers were no longer wise and pious and their undeveloped civil laws and rights were not there to protect them, appears never to have been of major concern to Luther as part of his own calling. "I hope, however, that others have given this matter more thought and attention than I am able to do."[83]

Turning first to counseling problems in connection with sexual impotence, Luther proposes a theoretical case for discussion. Suppose, he asks, an impotent man refuses to give his wife a divorce; what could one counsel her to do? Luther offers

[81] *WA* 18, 536.
[82] *PE* 2, 263.
[83] *Ibid.*, 150.

two alternatives which are meant to "strengthen anxious consciences," but which are also given in complete disregard for the laws of the state or the moral climate of the community.

Suppose I should counsel her, with the consent of the man (who is not really her husband, but merely a dweller under the same roof with her), to give herself to another, say her husband's brother, but to keep this marriage secret and to ascribe the children to the so-called putative father. The question is: Is such a woman in a saved state? I answer, Certainly. Because in this case the error and ignorance of the man's impotence are a hindrance to marriage; the tyranny of the laws permit no divorce; the woman is free through the divine law, and cannot be compelled to remain continent. Therefore the man ought to yield her this right, and let another man have her as wife whom he has only in outward appearance anyhow.[84]

Moreover, if the man will not give his consent, or agree to this division,—rather than allow the woman to burn or to commit adultery, I should counsel her to contract a marriage with another and flee to distant parts unknown. What other counsel could be given to one constantly in danger of lust? . . . Is not the sin of the man who wastes his wife's body and life a greater sin than that of the woman who merely alienates the temporal goods of her husband? Let him, therefore, agree to a divorce or else be satisfied with strange heirs; for by his own fault he deceived the innocence of a maiden and defrauded her of the proper use by her body, besides giving her a well-nigh irresistible opportunity to commit adultery.[85]

Luther is convinced that ". . . if both be weighed on the same scales," then "unbiased Christian reason, nay, Christian charity" will lead to the kind of suggestions he has set forth. Nevertheless, he found himself hard put to convince either his friends or his enemies that this was the most expedient way for Christian

[84] *Ibid.*, 269.
[85] *Ibid.*, 270. Having no remedial recourse in either civil or canon law in such a case, Luther turns desperately to the Bible for guidance. The best he can come up with is a very questionable modification of the old Hebrew "levirate marriage." Deuteronomy 25:5-10 decrees that when a male dies without a male descendant, the widow must not marry a stranger, but rather the surviving brother of the deceased (even if he is already married). He must take her as his own wife and their first son together succeeds to the name and the property of the deceased. In Luther's eyes, the impotent male was actually "dead" to his wife as far as any possible procreation in their marriage was concerned.

liberty to express itself. Granting that Rome had created an intolerable situation by its rigorous stand on divorce, was this the best way out? That stalwart "Defender of the Faith," King Henry VIII, leaped to take Luther to account, charging him with writing that ". . . if a man cannot satisfy his wife's desires, then she should run off to another man."[86] In his treatise *On Married Life* (1522), Luther denied the immoral licentiousness inherent in Henry's condemnation, but he did acknowledge publicly that an ex-monk's first words on marriage are not likely to be as wise as they are well-meaning. "I gave that advice at a time when I was still very inexperienced."[87]

Luther next addresses himself in *The Babylonian Captivity* to the real stumbling-block in this whole area of a Christian sex and marriage ethic. This was Rome's adamant refusal to permit any legal divorce for the general public, while actively engaged in the sordid business of providing its practical equivalent for the rich and powerful in annulments, dispensations, dissolutions, and the like. While freely confessing that "I so greatly detest divorce that I should prefer bigamy to it," Luther also wonders whether divorce might not sometimes be the most loving solution possible when the only other alternative in a given situation is a faithless and loveless "union" held together publicly by the compulsion of canon law while violated privately in infidelity.

Indeed, anyone who tries to pursue a scriptural course in regard to marital problems receives little more actual guidance than reference to the "royal law of love." Hence, as Moses made concessions on divorce for fallen man's "hardness of heart," and as both Christ and Paul made exceptions in the cases of adultery and desertion, so too Luther prefers the non-legalistic approach of seeking the imperfect best which Christian love can achieve in a concrete sinful situation.

As to divorce, it is still a moot question whether it is allowable. For my part, I so greatly detest divorce that I should prefer bigamy to

[86] *WA* 10[II], 230.
[87] *Ibid.,* 278.

it, but whether it be allowable, I do not venture to decide. Christ himself, the Chief Pastor, says in Matt. 5:32, "Whosoever shall put away his wife, excepting for the cause of fornication, maketh her commit adultery; and he that shall marry her that is put away, committeth adultery." Christ, then, permits divorce, but for the cause of fornication only.[88]

I, indeed, who, alone against all, can decide nothing in this matter, would yet greatly desire at least the passage of I Cor. 7:15 to be applied here. Here the Apostle gives permission to put away the unbeliever who departs and to set the believing spouse free to marry again. Why should not the same hold true when a believer—that is, a believer in name, but in truth as much an unbeliever as the one Paul speaks of—deserts his wife, especially if he never intends to return? I certainly can see no difference between the two.[89]

Yet it is a still greater wonder to me, why they compel a man to remain unmarried after being separated from his wife, and why they will not permit him to remarry. For if Christ permits divorce for the cause of fornication, and compels no one to remain unmarried, and if Paul would rather have one marry than burn (I Cor. 7:9), then he certainly seems to permit a man to marry another woman in the stead of the one who has been put away.[90]

Luther's dismay in regard to the seeming impossibility of solving many sexual and marital dilemmas without resorting either to Roman legalism or carnal licence was rooted in his deep pastoral concern for his people. "This matter troubles and distresses me; I meet cases of it every day, whether it happen by the special malice of Satan or because of our neglect of the Word of God . . . In these matters I decide nothing, as I have said, although there is nothing I would rather see decided, since nothing at present more grievously perplexes me and many more with me."[91]

Nor is Luther convinced that he has the final answer in these vexing problems which continue to plague many an uneasy conscience down to our own day. "Herewith I hang up my harp, until another and a better man shall take up this matter with

[88] *PE* 2, 271.
[89] *Ibid.,* 272.
[90] *Ibid.*
[91] *Ibid.,* 273.

me."[92] When scriptural ambiguity and theological uncertainty combine with a pastoral concern for all the extenuating circumstances in each different case, fluidity and flexibility become an honest necessity as well as an evangelical strategy.

For example, *On Married Life* cites ". . . three grounds which may separate a man and a wife; impotence, adultery, and sexual unwillingness."[93] A fourth cause—"when a man and wife are incompatible in matters other than their marital duty" (I Cor. 7:10ff)—is recognized by Luther as a ground for separation but not for divorce and remarriage.[94] Actually, as an evangelical theologian, Luther is far less concerned with developing a new Protestant marriage casuistry than he is in attacking the unethical fruits of marital infidelity at the place where it hurts most; namely, in its spiritual roots of religious distrust. As sins express sinfulness, divorce demonstrates that ". . . the greatest sin of all—unbelief—has already taken place inwardly."[95]

On the other hand, despite this seeming liberality in the direction of the permission of divorce, Luther was also capable— under the norm of Christian love—of evaluating pertinent factors in a given case in such a way as to deny the remotest possibility of divorce. Many years later, for instance, in meeting the notorious dilemma posed by the unsavory case of Philip of Hesse, Luther acquiesced in his confidential "confessional counsel" to Philip to permit a highly exceptional secret bigamy in preference to a public marriage annullment. In this instance, unfortunately, Luther relapsed into Roman casuistry once again, employing a canon law distinction which was designed to meet the needs of an individual conscience while protecting the morals of the community at large (*dispensatio in foro interno*).[96] Undoubtedly this subterfuge was at least partially justified in

[92] *Ibid.*
[93] *WA* 10[II], 287ff.
[94] *Ibid.*, 291.
[95] *Ibid.*, 260.
[96] Cf. the explanation of Canon 1056 given in T. L. Bouscaren, S. J. and A. C. Ellis, S.J., *Canon Law: A Text and Commentary* (Milwaukee: Bruce Publishing House, 1951), pp. 508f.

Luther's own mind on the grounds that the polygamous practices of the Old Testament go uncontested in the teachings of Christ while divorce, on the other hand, is strongly condemned.[97]

The precariousness of Luther's position appears to be only compounded when we learn that he also advises Philip to tell a "good, strong, white lie" *(Notlüge)* to extricate himself from the public scandal into which his loose morals and babbling tongue had involved him.[98] Nor does Luther's case seem to be strengthened when he blandly confesses, "In like fashion, I advised several clergymen under Duke George and the bishops secretly to marry their cooks."[99]

Without involving ourselves in all the details of this 1540 situation which goes beyond our chronological scope, our purpose here is simply to illustrate Luther's conviction that, *in exceptional circumstances,* Christians may have to be unethical in men's eyes in order to be faithful and loving in God's eyes. As Abraham learned in his willingness to obey God even to the point of sacrificing his own son Isaac, men can sometimes *be* right (religiously) even as they *do* wrong (ethically) in fidelity to a God whose transmoral will is the only ultimate Christian norm. And as less heroic Christians have learned in far more prosaic circumstances (e.g. in divorce), there are times in a fallen world of fallen men when sinful entanglements become so inextricably involved that man must courageously counter Satan on his own grounds with his own weapons. "Sin bravely, but believe even more bravely" is the realistic Christian counsel which Luther offers to all who would act responsibly in a world in which sin is inevitable and service inescapable.[100] The last word in the Christian faith is not human perfection but divine forgiveness.

In reply to those moralistic and puritanical critics of Luther who take great pride in living according to the "rules of the

[97] Cf *WA,* Br 3, 703; 4, 1056, 1861; 8, 3422-23; 9, 3493.
[98] *WA* Br 9, 3513, Note 14.
[99] *Ta* 290.
[100] *WA,* Br 2, 424.

Book"—thereby demonstrating their complete misunderstanding of Christianity—it is to be emphasized that such ethical compromises do not abrogate the general norm of Christian behavior. A concrete command of God may tentatively nullify his general law *for me,* but my obedience to such a divine command is always the exception which proves the rule. No one law can cover all cases without exceptions. Where love and law do come in conflict, Luther insists that law must bow to the demands of love, its "queen and mistress." Therefore, *in an emergency,* if love for a neighbor demands a helpful lie "for his service and benefit" or even a secret breaking of the civil law, so be it![101]

God is Lord. He may annul, enact, change, or moderate any law he pleases, whether out of emergency or not. But that does not permit us to do the same, or still less to establish a right or example which validates our similar actions.[102]

Out of all this there is no right, example, or custom to be deduced for our legitimate public practice. It does not follow that what you do out of necessity, I may do as a right. A thief who steals bread in hunger is not punished. Murder in self-defense is still murder but it is not punishable. Yet such cases do not establish the right or set the example for everyone to steal or to murder. An emergency transcends all rights and examples and still does not establish a right or example in itself.[103]

It is clear that the freedom of the Christian man to discover God's will for him in a given situation under the guidance of the Holy Spirit remains Luther's *normative* rule in marital problems as well as in all other social problems. This permits the biblical ethic to remain relevant and flexible enough to confront men with the will of God under all conditions, in all societies, throughout all ages. At the same time, however, Luther also helped pastors and public officials to develop some *regulative* standards by which to govern and regulate contested marital disputes in their own sixteenth-century German situation. They

[101] *WA* 16, 15.
[102] *WA* 53, 99.
[103] *WA,* Br 9, 3513.

may be summarized briefly as follows: 1) monogamy (I Cor. 10:23);[104] 2) divorce permitted on grounds of adultery (Matt. 19:8-10) and desertion (I Cor. 7:15);[105] 3) remarriage permitted to the innocent party (I Cor. 7:9).[106]

Yet even in the two grounds for divorce officially recognized in Evangelical lands, Luther would not permit his reluctant pastoral counsel to assume the proportions of a new canon law. "Inform other pastors that they should desist from asking my opinion in all of these matters . . . or else we will soon have another papacy on our hands!"[107] Public officials are continuously reminded that marriage legislation is a civil matter under their jurisdiction as a trust from God. All true believers, however, are further admonished that a "generous exercise of forgiveness and Christian love" may well provide miracles of reconcilation completely unknown to those who are merely obeying the civil law and demanding their civil rights. On this prayerful note Luther rests his case.

For we neither encourage nor prohibit divorce but recommend that the civil authorities act in such cases in accordance with the civil laws of the community. But for those who profess to be true Christians, it would be far better to advise both partners to remain together and have the innocent partner reconciled to the other (when there is genuine repentance and desire for improvement) in the generous exercise of forgiveness and Christian love.[108]

Conclusion

Luther was convinced that a lifelong marriage union is the divinely ordained pattern of life for the vast majority of mankind. Regarding the obligatory vows of celibacy for clergymen, he came to the conclusion that this was an unevangelical demand which did violence to the Word of God, and, in turn, to the very fabric of Christian faith, freedom, love, and community.

[104] *Ta* 276.
[105] *WA* 32, 379-80.
[106] *Ta* 348.
[107] *WA*, Br 8, 3183.
[108] *WA* 32, 379.

Regarding Rome's rigidity in theory and laxity in practice in matters of divorce and remarriage, Luther espoused a more flexible approach which denied any moral double standard, and which dealt pastorally with each sinful case on its own merits in keeping with the Christian law of love.

Repudiated in the process were both fundamental tenets of the Roman Catholic marriage ethic. For Luther, the religious status of a celibate monk is not higher than that of a married laymen. Nor is marriage regarded as a holy sacrament in the realm of grace, but honored rather as a divine ordinance in the realm of creation. "For freedom Christ has set us free; stand fast therefore, and do not submit again to a yoke of slavery."

CHAPTER SEVEN

Marriage as a Christian Calling

The distinctly evangelical feature of Luther's marriage ethic is his paradoxical assertion that marriage must be kept free from the domination of the church if it is to remain free for the service of man's neighbors in community life under God. Ordained by God and served by man, it must fall victim neither to clericalism nor to secularism.

Against those who would spiritualize marriage into a Christian sacrament, Luther protests that marriage belongs essentially to the realm of creation and not redemption. It is therefore ruled by God's law and not his gospel, and, as such, is one of God's temporal dikes against sin and not a sanctifying means of grace. On the other hand, against those who would interpret this liberating message as justification for carnal lust and licence, Luther is equally insistent that marriage is rooted firmly in the creative will of God as one of his own divine ordinances. Although it is not a sacrament of the church, there is nevertheless no higher social calling in which a Christian can exercise his faith in deeds of serving love for his family and neighbors.

Marriage between non-Christians, therefore, is founded upon the law of God (even though unacknowledged) and provides society with its basic institution and social structure. Marriage between Christians, moreover, enjoys both the support of the law and the fruits of the gospel, both the fidelity of civil righteousness and the love of Christian righteousness. When transfigured by Christian faith and love, the intimate lifelong union between a man and a woman—while never sacramental or redemptive

199

—becomes the most profound human parable there is for the gracious activity of God. "This is a great mystery, and I take it to mean Christ and the church" (Eph. 5:32).

Idolatry and Adultery

It did not take Rome long to realize that if Luther could not be refuted theologically, he might best be checked politically. In a very illuminating letter of instructions to one of his agents, Pope Adrian VI cites ". . . certain things which you can say orally to the prelates, princes, and representatives of the cities of Germany, when and where you shall think proper."[1] Prominent in the suggested arguments to persuade civil authorities to oppose the new teachings of Luther is the charge that he is weakening the moral fibre of community life by an appeal to sexual license. Rulers are to beware of "the filthy German Mohammed" who is loose in their midst.

Mohammed granted men permission to have many wives and to put them away at will and take others. This man [Luther] in order to win the favor of the monks and the virgins dedicated to God, and the priests who are guilty of lustful desire, preaches that vows of perpetual continence are not lawful and binding, and that evangelical liberty, therefore, permits them to marry.[2]

King Henry VIII of England took the same tack when he urged the rulers of Saxony to put down "this madman" and his movement because ". . . no faction was ever so universally pernicious as the Lutheran conspiracy, which profanes sacred things, preaches Christ so as to trample on his sacraments, boasts of the grace of God so as to destroy all free will, extols faith so as to give license to sin, and places the inevitable cause of evils in the only good God."[3] In like fashion, Eck had earlier attacked Luther on grounds of relegating sexual morality to rather secondary importance. "Still worse are the reports of reputable persons who claim that they have heard him say in sermons that

[1] *SJ* 2, 141.
[2] *Ibid.*, 144.
[3] *Ibid.*, 162.

married folks are not saved by their fidelity to each other in marriage. He said that this very fidelity might provide the occasion for their falling into spiritual pride."[4] In fact, down to the present day, "A merry life and a blessed death" *(Lustig gelebt und selig gestorben)* is a common German Catholic caricature of the piety of Lutheranism.

To all these charges Luther replies boldly with Paul, "What shall we say then? Are we to continue in sin that grace may abound? By no means! How can we who died to sin still live in it?" (Rom. 6:1-3). As Jesus was accused of being a glutton and a drunkard, and Paul was charged with advocating ethical license, so too Luther's teachings were attacked by some of his contemporaries as being amoral if not downright immoral. Such appears to be the inevitable fate of all proponents of an ethic of grace. To those for whom God's grace is not an experienced reality, legalism or sensualism seem to be the only possible ethical alternatives. To refute these charges, we must now show how Luther condemned sexual anarchy as strongly as clerical tyranny for destroying the freedom of the Christian man.

Already in his prophetic criticism of "the failing of the temporal estate" in the *Open Letter to the Christian Nobility,* Luther roundly criticizes the laxity in German public morals. "Is it not a pitiful thing that we Christians should maintain among us open and common houses of prostitution, though all of us are baptized unto chastity?"[5] He considers it a shameful indictment of Christian social behavior that in this crucial area it even falls short of the pre-Christian practices of the ancient Jews. "If the people of Israel could exist without such an abomination, why could not Christian people do as much?"[6]

Nor was Luther satisfied to limit his criticism to vague condemnations of vice in general. Concrete, local conditions in Erfurt felt the sting of his righteous indignation when Luther measured them against the ethical demands of the law of God.

[4] *WA* 6, 583, n. 3.
[5] *PE* 2, 161.
[6] *Ibid.*

The excessive drinking and immoral practices carried on among the university students, for instance, were noted with great dismay. "Erfurt has not been much better than a brothel and beer hall. Certainly these are the two subjects the students have studied most diligently."[7]

Luther was so strongly opposed to these evil social conditions that he once took it upon himself to post a public notice at the university in which he warned all the students against the physical and spiritual dangers which accompanied illicit traffic with prostitutes.

Through special enemies of our faith the devil has sent some whores here to ruin our poor young men. As an old and faithful preacher I ask you in fatherly fashion, dear children, that you believe assuredly that the evil spirit sent these whores here and that they are dreadful, shabby, stinking, loathsome, and syphilitic, as daily experience unfortunately demonstrates. . . . Accordingly I advise you students who frequent the woods to make yourselves scarce before the prince learns of your commerce with whores . . . . Begone, I advise you, the sooner the better! Those who cannot live without whores should go home or wherever else they will. Here we have a Christian church and Christian school where God's Word, decency, and virtue are to be learned.[8]

Luther's revulsion made him wish for much stronger civil legislation to prevent and to punish sex offenders. He saw no reason, for example, why the law should be so much more lenient with them than with other criminals. "We hang a thief if he steals five or six pennies; why do we not also execute an adulterer?"[9] And as for prostitutes, "If I were a judge, I would have such venomous, syphilitic whores broken on the wheel and flayed."[10] Moreover, Luther saw it as the clear responsibility of

[7] *WA,* TR 6, 2719b. Although they belong properly beyond our scope in the period after 1525, varied materials from Luther's letters and table talk will also be cited in this last chapter (as in the first) in order to illustrate basic convictions which he held for the remainder of his life. These citations vividly demonstrate the robust and realistic wholesomeness of Luther's mature views on sex and marriage.

[8] *Ta* 293.

[9] *WA,* TR 6, 6934.

[10] *Ta* 293.

the church to help provide the proper climate of opinion in which civil authorities could reform public vice and immorality. When some citizens were urging that the newly closed brothels in the city of Freiburg should be opened again, Luther stormed:

Let those who wish to restore brothels first renounce the name of Christ and admit that they are pagans who are ignorant of God. We Christians, if we wish to be accounted such, have a clear word of God, "Whoremongers and adulterers God will judge" (Heb. 13:4). This applies even more to those who favor, protect, and support them with their aid and counsel.[11]

Coupled with the church's support of the reform activities of the government should be strong prophetic preaching which pricks the consciences of its hearers to correct persisting social evils in the community. In order for social justice to have a firm foundation, the church should provide its members with a strong faith which is acutely sensitive to the needs of the community. Social reforms should proceed "with deliberate speed," taking into careful consideration, however, the heritage of local conditions and circumstances. When Halle became Evangelical, for instance, Luther was asked whether the brothels should be closed at once by civil force. His moderate reply attempts to speak God's truth in love.

I still believe that for the present, until the gospel is more firmly rooted and the weeds are choked out, it is desirable to be patient with this matter. It may cause injury to the good if this evil is eradicated prematurely, for I believe that there is still a good deal of paganism among the Christians. However, as soon as one well can, severe measures should be taken against the evil. Meanwhile the clergy ought to preach powerfully against it in order that the honorable [town] council may be given opportunity and provocation to suppress such paganism in an appropriate way.[12]

Time and again the Reformer was also compelled to engage in prophetic criticism of men whose negligence in their public offices was an offense to the demands of God's law for a community life of decency, order, and social justice. High prices,

[11] *Ibid.,* 292.
[12] *Ibid.,* 294.

public immorality, flagrant disorder, rowdy students, drunken peasants, unjust laws, incompetent officials: these were but a few of the concrete social conditions to which the Reformer felt compelled to address himself as an ordained preacher of God's holy law as well as his gospel. When asked whether a pastor really has the authority to rebuke the government, Luther replied, "Yes, indeed! For although it is a divine institution, God has reserved the right to punish vices and correct wrongs. Accordingly, one should rebuke secular rulers if they allow the goods of their poor subjects to be drained off and ruined by usury and bad government."[13]

Nor was Luther one to give advice to others which he was not willing to follow himself. The following complaint to the Elector John of Saxony about one of his local officials is illustrative of Luther's general concern for the morals of the community at large.

I have repeatedly admonished Prefect John Metzsch in a kind and earnest fashion that he should leave off his whoring and his vicious relations with women. As a preacher I could not long endure his scandalous conduct or keep quiet about it. But in spite of everything he keeps right on, and goes so far that everybody's mouth, nose, eyes, and ears are full of his doings. In fact, he has admitted to me privately that he cannot do without women. Accordingly, I have refused for my part to have anything more to do with him and have privately forbidden him to receive the Sacrament. But he is so tied to the whores' pigtails that he shows few signs of fearing God. Inasmuch as I shall henceforth have to preach against him and condemn his behavior publicly, I humbly pray Your Grace ... to remember what I am now writing.[14]

Along with other astronomical and theological signs which seemed to point possibly to the end of the world, Luther significantly included "the new French sickness."[15] He was particularly concerned with the prevalence of syphilis among promiscuous young soldiers. Not even the pain and suffering accompanying

[13] *Ibid.*, 336.
[14] *Ibid.*, 280.
[15] *WA* 10[1,2], 104.

their diseases seemed to provide the troops with an adequate deterrent.[16] Luther believed that sexual morality and social order were inevitable casualties whenever soldiers were permitted to have their way. He deplored ". . . the immoral relations which soldiers have with their camp followers. For Turks are warriors and they must naturally act like warriors. All the poets say that Mars and Venus always go together."[17]

Realistically enough, Luther adds the priests and the monks to the ranks of those most guilty of corrupting the public standards of sexual morality. In the first place, there are many young men who feel that they are justified to take "one last fling" before assuming the vow of sacerdotal celibacy. "They live wildly enough beforehand, and wish, as they say, to 'wear out their lust,' but rather wear it in as experience shows. I find the proverb true, 'Despair makes most of the monks and priests'; and so things are as we see them."[18]

Even more injurious to the social order, Luther believed, were the notorious means by which some of the Roman priests and monks evaded the tyrannical demands of their chastity vows. Clerical sexual morality was directly attacked by Luther in his treatise *Against the Falsely Named Spiritual Office of the Pope and Bishops* (1522). In no uncertain terms, Luther charges Rome with responsibility for a godless system which results inevitably in idolatry and adultery.

Luther's religious case against enforced vows was already clear: "All religious orders and vows are against the first three commandments of God . . . They represent the spirituality of Baal."[19] The ethical case against vows of celibacy is equally damning since it is actually the other side of the same coin. Breaking of the second table of the law is the by-product of man's prior destruction of the first. "Since their Jewish faith in works destroys the chastity of the Christian faith, their reward must also

[16] *WA* 12, 594.
[17] *WA* 30[II], 126.
[18] *PE* 2, 162.
[19] *WA* 10[II], 148.

be the loss of their bodily chastity. As St. Peter says, 'Many will follow their licentiousness and because of them the way of truth will be reviled' (II Pet. 2:2)."[20]

Luther puts the possible alternatives squarely on the line: "Women must either be taken as wives or left alone completely." The evil practice of some bishops (e.g. Albrecht of Mainz) permitting their "celibate" clergy to maintain concubines—for an appropriate ecclesiastical "contribution"—is clearly denounced as of the devil. To be sure, men must give vent to their God-implanted sexual urges. To attempt to repress so powerful a natural impulse is only to invite mental or physical disorders. Man and vow notwithstanding, sex will find some means of expression. What is so abominable about the Roman clerical practice, however, is that this expression must take the form of illicit relations with private "cooks" or public whores. Because marriage has been forbidden to the clergy, bishops have become panderers in the temple of God.

Do not most bishops derive a large part of their annual income from the fees collected from the priests' concubines? Whoever desires to have such a woman is obligated to pay the bishop at least a gulden a year. From this practice originates the common saying, "Chaste priests are the bishops' worst enemies." How can the procurers become any richer than our own bishops? Who would ever have thought that our spiritual fathers could permit such sexual promiscuity and deny their priests the right to marry just for the sake of money? Truly there are many forms of madness![21]

Prophetic judgment is always concrete and Luther calls a spade a spade or a whore a whore. Yet despite his frequently crude and earthy language as well as his robust and hearty sense of humor, Luther was never once reported by any of his associates—friend or foe alike—to have engaged in the sly leer or the suggestive innuendo, the seductive glance or the double-meaning phrase. Rollicking, gregarious, fun-loving, and wholesome, Luther's spirit was as wide open and well fertilized

[20] *Ibid.*
[21] *Ibid.*, 150.

as the peasant stock and farm soil from which he came. Like the prophet Hosea, whose message and courage were so akin to his own, Luther spoke only of the fickle character of the people in order to contrast and cover it with the unchanging love of God.

Some critics, of course, seem congenitally incapable of distinguishing between nudity and nakedness despite the artist's intentions. Presumably, such prudes could never appreciate Luther's employment of the crudest of imagery to condemn the enemies of the kingdom. Luther was convinced, however, that the devil and his agents could not be handled with kid gloves. The foul-mouthed Sebastian Franck, for example, is reminded by Luther that an evil thought is like a bird alighting on one's head. "Man cannot prevent a bird from flying over his head but he can stop it from building a nest in his hair!"[22]

Luther then proceeds to castigate Franck in terms unfit for the parlor, but peculiarly appropriate for addressing one who derived his livelihood from the sale of pornographic literature on the foibles of women. "As you can readily tell from this pamphlet [of refutation] by John Freders, Sebastian Franck is like a bumblebee who goes around stinging women in the rear while gathering all the filth which the devil has ever inspired to be said or done by women through all ages of history . . . . He then holds all this dirt before our noses as if we should thank or praise him for all the stench of the devil's filth."[23]

I will give only one example to show that I have read his book and am not his enemy without reason. What do you think of an historian who writes, 'Once you douse the lights, all women are the same'? Even if he had once heard these shameful words from some wanton man, should he write them down in his book with some obvious joy and pleasure? And had he forgotten all saintly women of history, should he not at least have remembered his own mother and wife? Surely he would feel deeply ashamed of himself if there were still a spark of reason and honor or a single

[22] WA 54, 172.
[23] Ibid., 174.

drop of honest blood left in him. And then again, why are not all men the same once the lights are put out?[24]

When Paul concludes, therefore, that "no immoral man has any inheritance in the kingdom of Christ and of God" (Eph. 5:5), we may be assured that Luther is in complete agreement. The Reformer sees idolatry and adultery inseparably united: No man can love his (female) neighbor aright who does not already love his God aright. Evil thoughts and deeds grow out of sinful souls. "An adulterer has denied the faith. A filthy man has denied the faith. A proud man has denied the faith. They are all rebellious, perjurers and faithless to God . . . . Applicable to all men is the word of Christ, 'Not every one who says to me, Lord, Lord, shall enter into the kingdom of heaven, but he who does the will of my Father who is in heaven' (Matt. 7:21). Faith must be put into practice and demonstrated by good works."[25]

Remedy Against Sin

The most characteristic element in Luther's early marriage ethic is his conviction that God has not left his children unprotected in the midst of this fallen and sinful world. He has graciously provided them with a mighty dike to hold back the destructive flood of human sensuality and immorality: the divine ordinance of marriage. "Is it not a great thing that even in the state of innocence God ordained and instituted marriage? But now this institution and command are all the more necessary, since sin has weakened and corrupted the flesh."[26] As one of God's protective bulwarks in his struggle against Satan, marriage is interpreted by the early Luther, first and foremost, as a "divine ordinance and institution" which provides fallen men and women with a "remedy against sin" (remedium peccati).

Although the remedial and defensive coloration of this initial view was to be complemented after 1523 by a more positive

[24] Ibid.; cf. WA, TR 3, 2807b.
[25] WA 17[II], 210.
[26] LW 1, 134.

emphasis, it is important to note that it enjoyed virtually exclusive stress for some six years after the posting of the *Theses,* and even thereafter continued to remain prominent in Luther's view for the rest of his life. It is, however, both inaccurate and oversimplified to suggest that Luther's theology of marriage was decisively correlated with or dependent upon his own marital experience.[27] Luther is not greatly helped by this well-meaning but weak and nontheological rejoinder to the Roman Catholic charge that he "led the Protestant revolt in order to marry."

To be sure, Luther's monastic life undoubtedly colored his early view of marriage (especially regarding sex), just as his domestic life influenced his later views (especially regarding children). In the light of our study on the theological foundations of his social ethics, however, we venture the judgment that the essential features of Luther's marriage ethic were derived from his biblical understanding of the Christian faith relatively independent of his own personal experience. More sharply, it is our contention that *Luther had already arrived at an evangelical marriage ethic by 1523,* almost two years before his own marriage. In short, Luther's marriage was no more the basis of his ethic than it was of his theology; it was rather a public testimony to both.

To gain a true understanding of Luther's total view, we must begin where he (following Paul) begins. This is, of course, the universal human predicament of sin, its common personal expressions in pride and sensuality, and its remedy (religiously) by faith in Christ, and (ethically) by life in marriage. We recall at once that Luther had begun already in his *Treatise on Marriage* (1519) to emphasize its remedial role in life by describing it as "a hospital for the sick . . . so that men will not fall into greater

[27] Professor Roland Bainton's deservedly popular biography of Luther, for instance, cites the marriage year of 1525 as the crucial dividing line between Luther's early (negative) view of marriage as a "remedy against sin" and his post-marriage (positive) view of the institution as a "school for character." Cf. Roland Bainton, *Here I Stand* (New York: Abingdon-Cokesbury, 1950), p. 300.

sin."[28] This is in accord with Paul's injunction that "it is better to marry than to be aflame with passion" (I Cor. 7:9).

Luther considers it no accident that the divine commandment protecting marriage is formulated negatively: "Thou shalt not commit adultery." God's law presupposes man's sin and wars against it. Regarding salvation, of course, Christ is man's only hope. He is man's Savior, God's self-appointed "remedy" for the sin of the world.

Salutare is used by the Latins to designate that which the Savior employs to confer blessedness upon men, just as we say that food, drink, remedies, and such things are all wholesome things [*salutaria*]. In this sense, Christ is also commonly called *salutare* since he is himself the remedy by which we are saved [*salvamur*]. He is the bread which gives life to the world, and especially the doctor and the remedy through which the sins of the soul become healed and men are redeemed from all evil.[29]

We recall, however, the paradoxical nature of man's "cure" by his "remedy" in Christ. The Christian who is justified by faith still remains sinful. The righteousness by which we are saved is not found within us but is reckoned to us from without. To be sure, God also makes righteous those whom he declares righteous, but the quest for moral perfection remains unfulfilled in this life. No man ever stops sinning but by virtue of his faithful appropriation of God's grace, the Christian does not have his sins reckoned against him. When Luther views sex and marriage in the context of the radical nature of human sin, he considers the Roman attempt to sacramentalize marriage the unfortunate by-product of its Aristotelian refusal to take sin as seriously as the Bible does.

In his work *Against Latomus* (1521), Luther allows that the sophists of Rome "partially grasp" the depths of sin—"namely, an offense against God and a transgression of God's law"[30] —but where they really part company is at Rome's denial of the

[28] *WA* 2, 168.
[29] *St. L.* 4, 717f.
[30] *LW* 32, 201.

persistence of real sin in the life of the redeemed. "Of this they know nothing . . . . After baptism and the infusion of the power of God, the condition of sin is such that it is not yet entirely reduced to nothing, but it is so subjected and broken down that it cannot now do what it once could . . . . Now the issue between myself and the sophists is whether or not this sin which remains must be truly considered sin."[31]

What concerns us here is how this evangelical doctrine *(simul iustus et peccator)* affects the role of the Christian in the area of sex and marriage. Luther quotes Paul's admonition to the married Corinthians, "Do not refuse one another except perhaps by agreement for a season, that you may devote yourselves to prayer; but then come together again, lest Satan tempt you through lack of self-control" (I Cor. 7:5). In the light of this and other like passages, Luther defies Latomus to justify Rome's contention that sexual sin does not persist in the Christian marriage sacrament, to say nothing of its practice of sacerdotal celibacy.[32] In the same spirit of biblical realism, Luther later quoted the coarse proverb of his contemporaries—"If the wife refuses, let the maid come"—as a proof of man's common recognition of the fury of frustrated sexual desire and the continual danger of its extramarital expression.[33]

Luther insists that the crucial distinction for a Christian is not "sin" or "no sin," but rather "controlling sin" *(peccatum regnans)* or "controlled sin" *(peccatum regnatum)*. In the Christian life, sin is already conquered by Christ but it is not yet completely annihilated. It is therefore the Christian's ethical responsibility to establish himself within the divine ordinances of God's law—the primary of which is marriage—in which his persisting sin may be channeled and controlled by God for his own creative purposes. "We believe that the remission of all sins has been without doubt accomplished, but we daily act in

---

[31] *Ibid.*, 203.
[32] *Ibid.*, 211ff.
[33] *WA* 10[II], 290.

the expectation of the total removal and annihilation of all sin. It is those who labor toward this who do good works."[34]

It is within this biblical framework of the general sinfulness of humanity and the persisting—though unreckoned—sinfulness of Christians, that Luther integrates his view of marriage as a God-ordained "remedy against sin." Very simply, "Whoever does not feel fitted for celibacy because he has to work at his chastity should call upon God's name and enter into marriage. A young man should marry by the time he is twenty, a young girl by fifteen or eighteen."[35] Nor should it be supposed that the "remedy" of marriage will provide man with a magic cure-all for the residue of sin remaining within him. If marriages are made in heaven, they must be lived on earth by humans who are all too often all too human. This scriptural realism also informs the concluding words of Luther's early work *On Married Life.*

But in all this praise of marriage, I would not have the basic fact of sin obscured. As it says in the fiftieth [fifty-first] Psalm, all man's flesh and blood is corrupted through Adam since we are all conceived and born in sin. Nor are man's sexual relations sinless in marriage either. It is only that God embellishes them out of grace because the order of marriage is his own personal handiwork, and he preserves all the good which he has planted within it even in the midst of all the surrounding sin.[36]

Besides receiving primary stress by Luther in his early theological works (1517-1523), this view remained an abiding emphasis in Luther's marriage ethic throughout his life. Even the most cursory survey of his treatises and sermons provides us with an impressive collection of witnesses to Luther's sexual realism. Long after his monastic experiences had become a distant recollection and his happy home life with his wife and children an established fact, Luther continued to paint the demonic temptations of sex in vivid colors with marriage as the Christian's most effective remedy. We can only conclude that this abiding

[34] *LW* 32, 213.
[35] *WA* 10^{II}, 304.
[36] *Ibid.*

concern was for him far more a matter of biblical theology—"Paul's authority stands behind this"—than any personal experience.

Nature does not stop its work just because a man has reluctantly taken a vow of celibacy. Man's sexual organs remain active and fulfill the purpose for which God created them. This condition results in all kinds of emissions and secret sins which St. Paul calls uncleanness and dishonorable passions. To put it crudely for the sake of meeting this misery: If a man does not flow into a woman, he will do so into a nightshirt.[37]

The old Adam who fell in paradise and is inborn in us—that infamous bag of worms we carry around our necks—never ceases to plague us with his evil lusts and desires to commit sin and adultery. But one can control sin in the estates of marriage, virginity, and widowhood. Yet even marriage is not all pure. A married couple cannot sleep together without shameful desire even though they both want to live together blamelessly. Only when we grow old does this lust subside. But, for the sake of marriage, God does not reckon this as sin. He chooses to adorn marriage by not calling such sins sinful even though they are. Because God closes his eyes to this sin, it is forgiven in marriage.[38]

Moreover, the frequency with which Luther felt constrained to address himself to his colleagues on the importance of marriage as a remedy against sin is amply confirmed by the rather large number of entries in his later table talk and correspondence which are devoted to this theme. The following two samples are multiplied tenfold in the vast collections of Luther's sayings:[39]

After religion, marriage is the leading estate on earth. . . . Here we must look to God's order and command to beget children for the sake of the generations. And even if this purpose did not exist, we should not forget that marriage is a remedy against sin which prevents unchastity.[40]

"All things are defiled by lusts," they say, quoting words of Augustine. By God's grace there is a remedy for this, namely, marriage and the hope of marriage. But what remedial value will mar-

[37] Ibid., 156.
[38] WA 51, 51.
[39] E.g., WA, TR 3, 3120b; 5, 5264; 6, 6905.
[40] WA, TR 4, 4814.

riage and the hope for marriage have if we allow whoredom to go on unpunished?[41]

In his treatment of marriage in the *Large Catechism* (1529), Luther summarizes a decade of study on this subject with a persuasive coupling of the fourth and sixth commandments. "You must well understand and mark, first, how gloriously God honors and extols the estate of marriage, inasmuch as by his commandments he both sanctions and guards it. He has sanctioned it above in the fourth commandment: 'Honor thy father and mother'; but here in the sixth commandment he has hedged it about and protected it."[42] In various explanations of this crucial sixth commandment the Reformer frequently states his conviction that marriage is protected by the strong left arm of God's law.

In his *Brief Explanation of the Ten Commandments* (1520), Luther demonstrates how the commandments of God "contain, in a very brief and orderly manner, all the teachings that is needful for man's life."[43] Still under the influence of the format of medieval penance manuals, however, Luther provides the reader with a series of concrete examples of how the sixth commandment is both "transgressed" and "fulfilled."

Against the sixth: He who seduces virgins, commits adultery, and is guilty of incest and like unchastity; he who uses unnatural means to satisfy desires—these are the "mute sins"; he who arouses or displays evil desires with obscene words, songs, tales, or pictures; he who by looks, touch, or thoughts arouses his own desires and defiles himself; he who does not avoid the causes of unchastity, such as gluttony, drunkenness, idleness, laziness, oversleeping, and intimate associations with men or women; he who by extravagant dress or demeanor incites others to unchastity; he who gives house, place, time or help to the commission of this sin; he who does not by word and deed help others to preserve their chastity.[44]

Of the sixth: Chastity, purity, and modesty in works, words, demeanor, and thought; moderation in eating, drinking, and sleeping; and everything that furthers chastity. Here belongs all the teaching

[41] *Ta* 292.
[42] *WA* 30^I, 161.
[43] *PE* 2, 367.
[44] *Ibid.*, 362.

about chastity, fasting, sobriety, moderation, prayer, watching, laboring and everything by which chastity is preserved.[45]

The same atomistic approach is still followed in the *Short Instruction on Confession* (1519), but by the next year's *Discussion of Confession* he believes that ". . . the penitent makes so much of these trifles that he is not really able to give heed to the thing of chief importance; namely, the desire for a better life."[46] It is to this positive end that Luther devotes himself in his *Treatise on Good Works*. Herein he declares that in commanding the good work of purity or chastity, the sixth commandment makes heavy claims upon us. "Now, if no other work were commanded but chastity alone, we would all have enough to do with this one; so perilous and raging a vice is unchastity in all our members . . . . St. Augustine says that among all the conflicts of the Christian the conflict of chastity is the hardest, for the one reason alone, that it continues daily without ceasing, and chastity seldom prevails."[47]

What is so marked about Luther's treatment of sexual immorality in this work is his central insistence upon the inner resources of "prayer and the Word of God" as the faithful Christian's "strongest defense" in the struggle for purity and chastity.[48] For Luther, the corollary of faith is always freedom, and he does not disappoint us here even though this is one place where Christians have often abandoned their liberty in Christ for the "safer" way of ecclesiastical legalism. Luther refuses to issue any "blue laws" or moral codes for the Christian's sexual morality; in responsible freedom he is at liberty to act in love "as the Spirit tells him."

Some have also indicated more things which should be avoided, such as soft beds and clothes, that we should avoid excessive adornment, and neither associate nor talk with members of the opposite sex, nor even look upon them, and whatsoever else may be conducive to chastity. In all these things no one can fix a definite rule and

[45] *Ibid.*, 366.
[46] *PE* 1, 91.
[47] *Ibid.*, 275.
[48] *Ibid.*, 277.

measure. Each must watch himself and see what things are needful to him for chastity, in what quantity and how long they help him to be chaste, that he may thus choose and observe them for himself.[49]

In an extremely important advance, Luther goes on to cite husband and wife as a human analogy for the faithful relationship between God and man in which all good works are performed "cheerfully and freely . . . . content that his service pleases God." Clearly the monastic ice is beginning to thaw, for Luther is obviously thinking of marriage here in far more positive terms than merely as a remedy against sin. It is a notable sign of things to come.

This we may see in a common human example. When a man and a woman love and are pleased with each other, and thoroughly believe in their love, who teaches them how they are to behave, what they are to do, leave undone, say, not say, think? Confidence alone teaches them all this, and more. They make no difference in works: they do the great, the long, the much, as gladly as the small, the short, the little, and vice versa; and that too with joyful, peaceful, confident hearts, and each is a free companion of the other.[50]

It is clear that what Luther has said thus far about marriage has scriptural authority behind it. "Because of the temptation to immorality, each man should have his own wife and each woman her own husband. . . . For it is better to marry than to be aflame with passion" (I Cor. 7:2, 9b). Is it equally clear, however, that this pre-1523 marriage ethic is not the total biblical witness. Its partiality and coloration is due in no small part to Luther's peculiar situation. In attacking views and practices which obtained for over ten centuries in the church of Rome, it is understandable that Luther should overstate the case for marital reform at the outset for the sake of contrast and emphasis. His own monastic experience undoubtedly added more fuel to the flames of protest.

Against the Roman sacramental view of marriage, Luther insisted that marriage is a completely natural "external, bodily

[49] *Ibid.,* 276.
[50] *Ibid.,* 191.

thing," just like eating, drinking, or sleeping. Against the Roman practice of enforced celibacy, Luther was also vehement that sex is a "tyrant of the flesh" which could at best be channeled in a remedial marriage, but never overcome merely by external clerical discipline. Individually, each view has scriptural validation. Yet even when combined, both views present a rather one-sided and distorted picture of all that the Bible has to say about the Christian understanding of marriage.

For the first six years of his career as a Reformer, then, Luther's anticlericalism in this area forced him to take a quasi-naturalistic stand which was not true to the total breadth of his theology of society. In terms of his own favorite theological standard, he removed marriage from the realm of redemption (gospel) and re-established it in the realm of creation (law), *but* without at the same time accounting for the breakthrough of the vocational gifts of the Holy Spirit within marriage. In short, Luther temporarily impoverished marriage by severing in theory what he insisted must be interpenetrating in practice; namely, both civil righteousness (law-abiding reason) and Christian righteousness (faith active in love). The Christian need not consider marriage a redemptive sacrament of grace in order to believe that it is far more significant in God's sight than merely as a "remedy against sin."

Thy Nearest Neighbor

Luther's breakthrough to a comprehensive evangelical marriage ethic took place gradually following his return from the Wartburg in 1522. Up to this time he conceived of marriage essentially as a "remedy against sin," a divine ordinance in which civil righteousness could be practiced under the universal law of God. After this time, this view was increasingly complemented—not replaced—by an understanding of marriage as an "estate of faith," a Christian vocation in which Christian righteousness could be practiced as the social fruit of the gospel of God. When Luther came to view marriage both as a "remedy against sin" and as an "estate of faith," he had finally arrived at an evangelical marriage ethic which was worthy of incorporation into the organic wholeness of his theology. For as he himself later acknowledged, "This, too, is a gift of the gospel and no small fruit of our evangelical teaching."[51]

In November, 1521, some four years after the posting of the *Theses,* Luther attempted more diligently to relate Christian faith to sexual chastity. In *Against the Falsely Named Spiritual Office of the Pope and Bishops* he made a frontal attack on the clericalism of Rome in regard to sacerdotal celibacy. In his appeal for the right of marriage for the clergy, he castigated Rome for prostituting the Christian faith by its zeal for work-righteousness. Luther turns to Isaiah to support his new emphasis that faith is always prerequisite to genuine chastity. Man's relation to God is decisive in determining his relations with his neighbors, male and female alike.

To maintain chastity demands a fine, strong faith by which the Spirit overpowers the flesh and dries out its emissions like a fire. It helps men to hate this life and become angelic. As Isaiah 5 [11] says of Christ, "Righteousness shall be the girdle of his waist, and faithfulness the girdle of his loins." Faith must gird man's loins or else they will be uncontrolled.[52]

A more positive interpretation of marriage begins to emerge hesitantly in Luther's treatise *On Married Life,* written in 1522. Although marriage is still described as "an external, bodily thing like all other temporal arrangements,"[53] a whole third section of the treatise is now devoted significantly to seeing ". . . how to live in this order in a Christian and godly way."[54] In the light of faith, Luther attacks the prevailing Greco-Roman view that "a wife is a necessary evil" as ". . . the words of blind heathen who do not acknowledge that men and women are creatures of

[51] *SJ* 2, 355.
[52] *WA* 10^II, 129.
[53] *Ibid.,* 283.
[54] *Ibid.,* 292.

God. They insult the handiwork of God and talk as if men and women come into marriage unintentionally."[55]

The world says of marriage: "Brief joy and long sadness." . . . But Christians believe that it is God himself who instituted marriage. It is he who brings a man and wife together and ordains that they bring forth children. For God does not lie, and he has given his Word in order that men might be certain that the estate of marriage is well-pleasing to him in its nature, works, suffering, and everything else that belongs to it (Gen. 1:28). Now tell me, how can a man know more peace and joy in his heart than in the confidence that the nature and works of his office are well-pleasing to God?[56]

All the sacrifices and discomforts of marriage can be endured more easily if they are viewed in the faithful certainty that "they all enjoy a godly blessing more radiant than the splendor of gold and precious jewels."[57] Here we encounter another practical application of Luther's contention that faith transforms the lives of men and enables them to view historical reality from the perspective of eternity. Faith transforms marriage from a human institution into a divine calling "since I am now certain that it is well-pleasing to God." It provides men with the ethical power to meet all the daily demands of life—including even the washing of diapers to the glory of God!

See here, when natural reason, the clever whore, looks at married life, she lifts her nose into the air and says, Oh, am I supposed to put the baby to sleep, wash the swaddling-clothes, make the beds, and put up with those awful smells, stay awake nights, get up when the baby cries, and take care of the eczema and sickness? . . . Am I supposed to be a prisoner in marriage? . . . For when a man washes the swaddling-clothes or does some other menial task for the benefit of a baby, someone will undoubtedly make fun of him and take him for a fool or at least henpecked. But if he does these tasks out of faith, who really has the last laugh? Certainly God also laughs with all the angels and creatures, not because of the swaddling-clothes but because of the faith.[58]

[55] *Ibid.,* 293.
[56] *Ibid.,* 294.
[57] *Ibid.,* 296.
[58] *Ibid.,* 295-96.

Luther describes the value of marriage here as twofold. Negatively, it serves as a "remedy against sin" both personally and socially;[59] positively, it affords man the opportunity for "the noblest and most precious work of them all" which is the rearing of children in the knowledge and love of God.[60] In the Christian household, both religious and civil authority are invested in responsible parents for the nurturing of their children's filial piety.

You see how rich the estate of marriage is in good works. For into the bosom of the family God places children who are conceived from the parents' own bodies and in need of their Christian works. For example, in making known the gospel message to them, parents act as the children's apostles, bishops, and pastors. In short, there is no greater, more noble power on earth than the religious and civil authority exercised by parents over their children.[61]

It is noteworthy how the ex-monk still hedges away from too positive an evaluation of the husband-wife love relationship in marriage, and feels constrained to move back into the fourth commandment when it comes to handing out marital praise. Luther still feels more at ease talking about the love of Christian parents than of Christian mates, as he himself freely admits. What he does not admit—or even realize—is how much his views of marital love are still conditioned by his experience and teachings as a Roman Catholic monk.

In order that no one will be able to say that I am speaking about something which I have not experienced myself, and am therefore stressing the honey at the expense of the gall, I will refrain from discussing the other benefits and values of a faithful marriage such as the love and the sense of oneness which a married couple experience together. I speak confidently by the authority of Scripture rather than from the uncertainty of human experience. If anyone has experienced more goodness in marriage than I have developed here, he should be grateful and thank God all the more for his good fortune.[62]

[59] *Ibid.*, 299-300.
[60] *Ibid.*, 301.
[61] *Ibid.*
[62] *Ibid.*, 299.

Postmonastic tinges also discolor Luther's *Exposition of the Seventh Chapter of First Corinthians* (1523), although he is still moving further in the direction of an evangelical orientation. He repeats his familiar and extensive arguments against enforced sacerdotal celibacy. His general position at this point is still that marriage is good, celibacy better, liberty to choose either best of all. Yet all callings are now considered equal in God's sight when performed in faith, and it is also acknowledged that "a wife might stand higher before God than a virgin"[63] since ". . . an unhappy marriage is better than an unhappy celibacy. The latter is a total loss whereas the former is at least still useful and serviceable."[64]

It is significant that while Luther is willing to concede here that (humanly speaking) the state of virginity is superior to that of sexual knowledge, he is also insistent that when institutionalized, marriage is an office far superior to monasticism. The Roman Catholic double-standard morality for clergy and laity is not only unjustified but inverted, for actually the "spiritual monks" are carnal and the "carnal husbands" spiritual when viewed with the eyes of faith in terms of the callings of God.[65] Marriage is a place where faith can be put to work for the benefit of others. The monastery, on the other hand, is a place where "faith has no room, place, time, or work for its practice."[66]

When it comes to spelling out how this faith is active in loving service and devotion in a Christian's marriage, however, Luther still disappoints us. Very likely, the apocalyptic spirit of the seventh chapter of I Corinthians is as responsible as anything for Luther's persisting reticence. In this epistle, Paul was writing in the fervent belief and hope that "the appointed time has grown very short . . . for the form of this world is passing away" (I Cor. 7:29f.). In the light of this conviction, he counseled fellow Christians to marry only "because of the tempta-

[63] *WA* 12, 99.
[64] *Ibid.,* 117.
[65] *Ibid.,* 105.
[66] *Ibid.,* 106.

tion of immorality" if they find that they "cannot exercise self-control" and are consequently "aflame with passion" (I Cor. 7:2, 9). Otherwise, it would be better in the little time left in the world if men remained "as I myself am;" i.e., untroubled by the marital and social problems of which "I would spare you" (I Cor. 7:7, 28). Clearly, passages such as these do not lend themselves as well to the development of a responsible marriage ethic as do the later, less apocalyptic writings of Ephesians and the pastoral epistles.

This obvious shortcoming, however, should not blind us to the fact that the way has been decisively cleared by Luther for the creative operation of man's faith in marriage. The basic pattern has been completed. All that is further necessary is the inevitable infusion of its loving content. On the one hand, marriage is presented as a civil ordinance under the law of God. "Marriage is an external, bodily thing which neither hinders nor encourages faith. Hence marriages may take place between Christians and non-Christians just as a Christian could eat, drink, trade, or engage in any other form of external relationship with a pagan, Jew, or Turk."[67]

At the same time, however, marriage is also treated as a Christian vocation which offers rich opportunity for the faithful exercise of loving service to one's relatives and neighbors. "Christian faith is such a free thing that it cannot be bound to any particular estate, but is rather active in, over, and through all human estates. Therefore there is no need to take on a new office or to leave an old office in order to be saved. In whatever estate the gospel and faith find you, there you may remain and be saved."[68]

It is the *Exposition of I Peter* (1523), though, where for the first time the monastic shadowing which persisted in Luther's early marriage ethic has been completely eradicated by the illumination of the gospel. This is singularly appropriate because

[67] *Ibid.*, 120.
[68] *Ibid.*, 126.

the fruition of Luther's development of the ministry of the Christian laity—"the priesthood of all believers"—was also exhibited in this highly suggestive work.

Peter's words provide the occasion for Luther's exposition of the biblical teaching that chastity is not the work of man but the gift of God, and, as such, is far more likely to be found in the divine ordinance of marriage than in the human invention of monasticism. In striking contrast to the position of Rome, Luther correlates true chastity with marital fidelity rather than monastic celibacy. The "purity of heart" which is the source of all sexual chastity is a gift of the Holy Spirit to all those who faithfully accept their salvation by grace through faith alone.

It is a great work of the Spirit as lord over the flesh to be in control of all the evil lusts which we have inborn from our parents. For without this grace, man is unable to live chastely in marriage and avoid unchastity. Why does Peter say, "Purify your souls"? He knows that the desires of the flesh remain in us after baptism right down to the grave. It is therefore not enough to treat this at the level of works and remain a virgin externally while the evil lusts abound in the inner heart. Man must rather see to it that his soul is pure, that is, that purity must come from his inner man with his soul in deadly conflict against the evil lusts and carnal desires until they are totally defeated.[69]

Luther has now come to the full realization that chastity, like love, cannot precede or parallel faith, but must rather be the living fruit of it. As always, the inwardness of faith must direct the outwardness of works. "From inward it must proceed outward and not be forced in from the outside."[70] He contends that there is no person on earth more worthy and needful of the faith-activated fidelity and love of a Christian than his God-given mate in marriage. In a pious household where Christ is worshiped as Lord and followed as Exemplar, believers will learn from the Holy Spirit ". . . how a man and wife are to act as Christians to each other."[71]

[69] *Ibid.*, 294.
[70] *Ibid.*, 295.
[71] *Ibid.*, 341.

Addressing himself first to wives, Luther follows the general
biblical position that the father-husband is the head of the family
and that good wives should be "submissive to their husbands"
(I Pet. 3:1). Luther makes it clear that female subservience is
strictly a matter of social (*eusserlich*) rather than religious (*ynner-
lich*) significance. All of God's children are equal in his sight
but divisions and levels of authority are socially necessary for
the sake of good order.[72] Obedience to her husband's considerate
(not arbitrary) will is a God-pleasing fruit of faith. Where this
respect for a husband's authority is not forthcoming, however,
men are not to resort to physical punishment (as was common in
Luther's day) for one cannot beat a good heart into another.
But a good, pious wife will naturally be obedient, ". . . knowing
that by obeying her husband she is pleasing God by her actions.
What could make her happier?"[73]

Along with her love-motivated obedience, a Christian wife
owes her husband absolute fidelity. Peter's ideal of a good mate
is Abraham's obedient and modest wife, Sarah, and this choice
is heartily seconded by Luther. The Reformer was convinced that
a wife's life should center about the domestic tasks of the house
in fulfillment of her divine calling as a Christian homemaker.
He warns strongly against two temptations which he considers
peculiarly alluring to women: vanity and superstition.[74] An
excessive concern with cosmetics and clothing for the admiration
of others often endangers a wife's ties to her husband. A frivolous
dabbling in superstitious foolishness is likewise detrimental to a
woman's relation to God. Both whims should be avoided by
pious, industrious wives as injurious to their calling. Such
faithful and loving homemakers are truly gifts from heaven, and
Luther concurs heartily with the judgment of the ages: "He
who finds a wife finds a good thing and obtains favor from the
Lord" (Prov. 18:22).

Luther then turns to address himself to Christian husbands,

[72] *Ibid.*, 347.
[73] *Ibid.*, 342.
[74] *Ibid.*, 343ff.

admonishing them, in the words of Peter, ". . . to live considerately with your wives, bestowing honor on the woman as the weaker sex, since you are joint heirs of the grace of life, in order that your prayers may not be hindered" (I Pet. 3:7). He considers it imperative that marriage be viewed as a sacred covenant in which both partners are treated with mutual honor and fidelity. Unlike the pagans ". . . who do not know what God wants in marriage," Christian husbands are to look upon their wives with compassion and consideration as blessed instruments of God for the bearing and rearing of children and the orderly running of the home. They are to be ruled reasonably and lovingly by their responsible spouses.

The Apostle reminds us that wives are also the tools or instruments of God. For they are used by God to carry, bear, rear, and protect children, as well as running the household. These tasks the wife should do since for this purpose she was created as an instrument or vessel of God. This should be acknowledged clearly by every husband. Therefore St. Peter says that men should rule their wives reasonably rather than foolishly or inconsiderately. A wife should live in obedience to her busband's will but he, in turn, should be careful to act chastely and wisely with her, giving her all the honor due her as a weak instrument of God.[75]

Women are obviously considered to be the weaker sex by Luther, and men are advised to take this into account in their dealings with them. The exercise of brute force is once again decried as un-Christian. A pious husband must realize that he is married ". . . in order to help, sustain, and protect his wife, and not to hurt her." Each wife's unique personality must be respected and therefore Luther wisely refuses to offer any hard and fast rules for running a particular household. "Experience and practice provide the best advice in home life."[76] The inevitable problems which always arise in marriage should be approached flexibly with a strong dependence upon common sense and mutual forgiveness. As he was to advise his parishioners so often later, "One cannot give rules in such matters. God re-

[75] *Ibid.,* 346.
[76] *WA,* TR 6, 6903.

quires only that every man act reasonably with his wife in keeping with her own special needs."[77]

Adam and Eve must have scolded each other roundly during their nine hundred years together. Eve would have said, "You ate the apple!" And Adam would have replied, "But why did you give it to me?" There is no doubt that during their long life they encountered numberless evils as they sighed over the Fall.[78]

Things will not always go the way you want them to. See to it, therefore, that you play the man and act all the more reasonably to make up for your wife's behavior. Remember that sometimes you must look through your fingers in lenience and moderation as well as giving her the honor she deserves.[79]

Luther is always very realistic about the many human factors which can either make or break a happy marriage. He warns, for instance, that "It is a calamity of the first order from which many other evils follow" if a wife does not know her way around the kitchen.[80] Nor should female beauty be the main criterion for the choice of a wife. "You would gladly have a beautiful, good, and rich wife if you could. Indeed, we really ought to paint you one with red cheeks and white legs! These are the best, but they usually cook poorly and pray badly."[81]

Sexual compatability and natural love are also clearly recognized as basic and necessary for a happy married life. It is man, and not sex, which is inherently evil. Christians who have been transformed by the gospel are not to avoid sex, but to dedicate their sexual gifts—like all others—both joyfully and shamelessly to the glory and service of God.[82] In fact, the passionate devotion of a young bride for her mate is one of the richest blessings of God's creation. "I leave it to those who have ex-

---

[77] *WA* 12, 346.
[78] *Ta* 283.
[79] *WA* 12, 347.
[80] *Ta* 284.
[81] *WA*, TR 6, 6903.
[82] *WA*, TR 5, 6317. As to the recommended frequency of marital coitus, the hale and hearty spirit (if not the actual words) of Luther's sexual counsel is reflected in the humorous couplet traditionally ascribed to him: "Twice a week, hundred-four a year; should give neither cause to fear" *(In der Woche zwier, Macht im Jahre hundertvier; Schadet weder dir noch mir)*.

perienced it to describe the loving heart of a bride. But there is enough common knowledge on the subject to assert that there is no stronger or more passionate love on earth than that which a bride feels for her groom."[83]

Nevertheless, young couples are warned repeatedly that even the power of sexual love will not be strong enough to keep them faithfully united for long. Along with their bodies, their hearts and minds must also become one if their marriage is to be happy and lasting.

A bride is taken quickly; to love her for a lifetime is quite a different matter. This is difficult and needs God's grace. Whoever has received this should be very grateful to God. Before a man takes a bride, he ought to pray seriously to God in words such as these: "Dear Lord God, if it be thy will that I remain without a wife throughout life, grant me the power to keep my virginity. If not, provide for me a good and pious wife with whom I might share my life in mutual love." For merely sleeping together [*copula carnalis*] will not do it alone; there must also be unity and harmony of mind, heart, habits, and life. Each must be patient and helpful with the other for things cannot always go smoothly.[84]

In the last analysis, therefore, Luther considered piety to be a wife's best dowry. Since he humbly acknowledged God to be "the true grandfather in every home,"[85] the secular cult of romantic love was completely distasteful to Luther. To equate marital love with sexual attraction or frivolous infatuation is to deny that marriage must be lived responsibly under God. Luther's relative condescension—by modern standards—regarding the wife's role in marriage and society owed much to the masculine spirit dominating his medieval times. Sixteenth-century German women were generally considered second-class citizens, and the tenderness and sensitivity which natural love can inspire were relegated almost exclusively to the distaff side. "It is more natural for a woman than for a man to be loving and

[83] *WA* 10[1,1], 297.
[84] *WA*, TR 5, 5524.
[85] *WA* 48, 90.

kindly."[86] Consequently, when Luther reflected a great deal of the patriarchalism which he found to his liking in the Bible, his views in this regard excited very little attention in an age which, domestically at least, was far closer in spirit to first-century Palestine than to twentieth-century America.

In one particularly aggravating social problem, however, Luther steered an obstinate course dead set against the popular stream of life and thought in his day. He considered the growing number of secret engagements and marriages to be a romantic violation of the evangelical understanding of marriage. Rome held that these practices were allowable since, as a sacrament, the chief consideration in marriage was the free and unconditional willingness of the partners to take each other for life (*matrimonium facit consensus*). Luther heartily agreed with this central emphasis: "the covenant of fidelity is the foundation and true nature of marriage."[87] Yet he was equally insistent that this personal covenant should not be kept a secret by the betrothed couple.

Marriage, as we have seen, is a civil institution as well as a personal commitment. As such, it affects not only two isolated individuals, but, simultaneously, the homes from which they come and the communities to which they go. The common good of society at large is also at stake here. Viewing the sixth commandment (marriage) against the background of the fourth commandment (home and community), Luther maintained that both parental approval and public notice were prerequisite to a valid engagement and marriage. After many unhappy pastoral counseling experiences in connection with secret betrothels, Luther finally dedicated an entire tract to the subject of the reciprocal responsibilities of Christian parents and children when it comes to marriage.[88]

His argument is virtually summarized in its lengthy title: *That Parents Should Not Compel or Hinder Their Children's Mar-*

---

[86] *WA* 10[I,1], 297.
[87] *WA* 2, 168.
[88] Cf. also *WA* 7, 238-45; 10[I,1], 640-45.

riage, and That Children Should Not Marry Without Their Parents' Consent (1524). His counsel takes the two-sided stance of which he was so fond. On the one hand, tyrannical parents are warned that they exceed their God-given authority when they attempt to dictate regarding their children's prospective mates. If it comes to a showdown, the true Christian "should and must accept and obey such injustices as a tyrannical and un-fatherly father imposes on him."[89] Weaker Christians who are unable to accept this kind of martyrdom are urged to "confess their weakness before God and pray for grace and help," with public aid or leaving home as two possible solutions.[90]

On the other hand, Luther was also convinced that secret be-trothals were a clear violation of the fourth commandment and the "universal custom" of public marriage celebrations. Obedient children should respect their parents' wishes for their prospec-tive mates as did the great heroes of the Old Testament. Parents even have the right to break up secret betrothals which are un-acceptable to them unless there has already been cohabitation, in which case the union should remain intact and the lenient father "look through his fingers."[91] However, in normal cases, pious parents may be expected to help insure their children's marital happiness by their loving co-operation. "The father has power to prevent a child from marrying this or that person, but he has no power to prevent his child from marrying at all. On the contrary, he owes it to his child to provide him with a good and suitable spouse or see to it that he gets one. If the father does not do so, the child must and should provide for himself."[92]

As in all Luther's ethical advice, his concern is for the troubled consciences of those involved in the dispute. Unwilling to legis-late a new Protestant casuistry, he always attempts in such in-stances to reconcile differences in a loving judgment based upon

[89] *Ta* 265.
[90] *Ibid.*, 266.
[91] *WA* 10[1,1], 643.
[92] *Ta* 269.

the spirit rather than the letter of the law. As he characteristically wrote later on in life:

In short, in the case of young people who are attached to each other by mutual love (which is the basis of marriage), there should be no opposition without grave cause. The example of Samson should be imitated, however, and children should inform their parents. This should be the procedure especially now that the gospel has free course and marriage is held in high esteem. . . . In such cases, therefore, attention must be paid to consciences, and the circumstances must be considered according to equity [*epieikeia*] and the judgment of a good man rather than according to the strict application of rules, laws, etc.[93]

We can only conclude from all this evidence that while love plays a central role in Luther's view of marriage, the love he has in mind bears no resemblance to our modern Hollywood version of romantic love. For Luther, love is too sacred a gift of the Holy Spirit ever to become enamored with itself. Love is always directed outward in service to the neighbor in fulfillment of the "Great Commandment." It is the faith-activated Christian righteousness which knows no other law but to "love one another as I have loved you" (John 15:12).

Those who have the Holy Ghost—even if they still have and feel sin within themselves—have something far higher and better than the law. For here the law ceases. To be sure, it does not cease in the sense that it disappears or that it is no longer valid or to be obeyed—as is the case with civil and canon law. It ceases rather in the sense that a higher law has now been given which puts it to silence even as it fulfills it.[94]

The law of love is a short command and a long command, a single command and many commands. It is no command and yet includes all commands. By itself it is a very short command and easy to understand quickly with the mind. But it is a very long command in actual practice for it encompasses and governs all the other commands within itself. In terms of works it is no command at all for it has no specially named works of its own. But it is all

[93] *Ibid.*, 286.
[94] *WA* 17^1, 114.

commands as well since it is and should be the purpose and end of all works of the law.[95]

The kind of mutual love which Luther lauds as the very "basis of marriage"[96] is marked by its willingness to become incarnate in acts of service for actual neighbors at hand. It does not inspire dreamy flights from reality into an ethereal state of rose-petalled bliss. It pulls us down from such selfish escape into the everyday involvements and responsibilities of the common life. Christian love is self-giving love, and we dare not try to escape the others to whom we are meant to give ourselves.

Because "God so loved the world" he condescended in the form of a suffering servant; if we are in Christ, so must we. Over against the papists and the sectarians who deplore the practical concerns of family life as "mundane thoughts from which man should free himself in order to sit quietly and speculate about heaven," Luther insists that domestic service is divine service if it is done to God's glory. "When a man has a wife and works for her with a joyful heart, or a wife goes about doing good for her children," they are faithfully re-enacting the shape of the earthly ministry of Christ: "For he made the blind see, the dead alive, and did all kinds of other good works. In meeting the needs of God's creatures, Christ could not spend all his time solely in thoughts about God."[97]

Willing, therefore, neither to be romanticized into mist nor legalized into rules, Christian righteousness remains patterned after the loving righteousness of God in Christ. It is in this all-inclusive, self-giving sense that the Christian is to love his neighbor—the nearest and dearest of whom is his own God-given wife. A Christian husband does not love his wife for what she has, but for what she is; not for what she might become, but just as she is now. He loves her as Christ loves him; not because of her attributes but despite her shortcomings. He does not cherish and protect her for any ulterior motive, but only

[95] *WA* 17[II], 95.
[96] *Ta*, 286.
[97] *WA* 17[I], 117.

for the sheer joy of doing God's will by serving her needs. What the world calls love is ultimately selfish and fickle. "Christian love, on the other hand, should be a gushing, surging kind of love which overflows from the inner heart like a fresh stream or brook that is always in motion and never dries up."[98]

Having finally arrived at this dynamic a conception of marriage as a divine vocation, it is no wonder that Luther can confidently advise his celibate brothers to ". . . lay aside false chastity and take upon themselves the true chastity of wedlock" in his work addressed *To the Knights of the Teutonic Order* (1523). Luther now condemns enforced celibacy as a "false chastity" which is deemed unworthy of the Christian calling. The Roman Catholic equation of chastity with virginity is branded as unbiblical. All of God's children are to be chaste, whether they are virgins, married, or widowed. True chastity is the by-product of a pure heart which is a gift of the Holy Spirit to every faithful Christian. No longer, therefore, is virginity to be considered inherently superior to marriage.[99] In fact, as Luther was to write shortly before his own marriage, there is far more likelihood of a man's chastity in marriage than in celibacy—especially enforced celibacy—". . . because there is least lust and frustration to be found there."[100] Hence, "Unless God performs a miracle, there is most chastity in marriage and least in virginity."[101]

On this liberating theological basis, Luther advises the Teutonic Knights to abrogate their faithless vows of celibacy and to convert their order into a civil principality or duchy. What is of climactic importance for us is Luther's definitive formulation of an evangelical marriage ethic here—already in December of 1523—which does full justice to the twofold rule of God via law and gospel in civil and Christian righteousness. Some six years after his divorce from Rome and some eighteen months before his marriage to Katie, Luther had arrived at a theology

[98] *WA* 36, 360.
[99] *WA* 17^{II}, 157.
[100] *Ibid.*, 185.
[101] *Ibid.*

of marriage consonant with his theology of salvation from which he never deviated for the rest of his life.

On the one hand—under God's law and man's civil righteousness—marriage is a divine ordinance serving both man and society as a remedy against sin.

It is true that man will avoid married women, not because he loves chastity or serves God, as he will pretend in order to deceive the world, but that he may have an easy life and be spared the worries and difficulties of married life, and yet neither live chastely nor serve God, but be so much the freer to practice harlotry and knavery. . . . But in God's sight it is a precious and noble good work to train and educate children, to rule wife and servants in a godly manner, to earn one's living in the sweat of one's face, and to endure much misfortune and many difficulties in the person of wife, children, servants, and others. Such good does not make much show . . . but he who believes it and rightly understands it, sees how good it is for the soul, although it is an evil for the flesh and its lusts.[102]

On the other hand—under God's gospel and man's Christian righteousness—marriage is a holy calling in which a faithful and loving man can serve as a Christ to his nearest neighbor.

For this reason also God has done marriage the honor of putting it into the fourth commandment, immediately after the honor due him, and commands, "Thou shalt honor father and mother." Show me an honor in heaven or on earth, apart from the honor of God, that can equal this honor! Neither the secular nor the spiritual estate has been so highly honored. And if God had given utterance to nothing more than this fourth commandment with reference to married life, men ought to have learned quite well from this commandment that in God's sight there is no higher office, estate, condition and work (next to the gospel which concerns God himself) than the estate of marriage.[103]

Conclusion

Up until 1523, Luther conceived of marriage essentially as a "remedy against sin," an institution ordained by God in which man's civil righteousness could be practiced under the universal

[102] PE 3, 423.
[103] Ibid.

law of God. In keeping with his teaching on the persistence of sin in the Christian life and in opposition to the Roman sacramental view of marriage, Luther removed marriage completely from the realm of redemption and re-established it firmly in the realm of creation.

Following 1523, this view was complemented by another interpretation of marriage as an "estate of faith," a blessed vocation in which Christian righteousness could be practiced as the loving fruits of the gospel of God. In keeping with his teaching on the priesthood of all believers and in opposition to the Roman glorification of sacerdotal celibacy, Luther extolled marriage as the Christian's highest social calling. Already by 1523, then, Luther had arrived at an evangelical ethic which portrayed Christian marriage both as a "remedy against sin" and as an "estate of faith." "For this reason a man shall leave his father and mother and be joined to his wife, and the two shall become one."

We may now confidently conclude that Luther married as a public testimony of faith in witness to his restoration of the biblical view of marriage and home life under God. This assertion must be made boldly in the face of two common but erroneous myths in this area. First, it must be maintained against the contention in certain Roman Catholic circles that Luther left the church of Rome in order to marry. Our historical analysis proves this charge to be untrue. Second, it must also be maintained against the contention in certain Protestant circles that Luther had no consistent theology of marriage and home life to guide the social ethic of the church which bears his name. Our theological analysis proves this claim to be equally groundless. Hence, despite the scorn suffered for its daring, Luther's marriage provides evangelical Christianity with a very vivid and valid symbol of what it means to live responsibly in a Christian home under God.

Cited Works of Luther (1515-1525)

PE 2, 57-164	*Open Letter to the Christian Nobility of the German Nation*
PE 2, 167-293.	*The Babylonian Captivity of the Church*
WA 6, 595-612	*Against the Cursed Bull of the Antichrist*
LW 31, 327-377	*The Freedom of the Christian*
PE 2, 351-384	*A Brief Explanation of the Ten Commandments, the Creed, and the Lord's Prayer*

1521

PE 3, 307-401	*Answer to Emser*
LW 32, 5-99	*Defense and Explanation of all the Articles Unjustly Condemned*
LW 32, 101-131	*Proceedings at the Diet of Worms*
LW 32, 133-260	*Against Latomus*
WA 8, 255-322	*Against the Theologians of Paris*
BA, Er 1, 201-376	*On Monastic Vows*

1522

WA 10^{I,1}, 1-739	*Church Postils*
WA 10^{I,2}, 1-208	*Advent Postils*
WA 10^{II}, 93-158	*Against the Falsely Named Spiritual Office of the Pope and Bishops*
WA 10^{II}, 263-266	*Which Persons are Forbidden to Marry*
WA 10^{II}, 267-304	*On Married Life*
WA 10^{III}, 1-435	*Sermons of 1522*
PE 6, 439-489	*Prefaces to the Books of the New Testament*

1523

PE 3, 223-273	*Secular Authority: To What Extent It Should Be Obeyed*
WA 11, 387-400	*That Maidens May Honorably Leave Their Cloisters*
WA 12, 88-142	*Exposition of the Seventh Chapter of First Corinthians*
WA 12, 249-399	*Exposition of I Peter*
PE 3, 403-428	*To the Knights of the Teutonic Order*
WA 12, 400-702	*Sermons of 1523*
WA 14, 92-488	*Sermons on Genesis*

1524

PE 4, 101-130	*To the Councilmen of All German Cities*
WA 15, 79-94	*Story of How God Helped a Nun*
Ta 263-270	*That Parents Should Not Compel Their Children's Marriage*
WA 15, 222-229	*Opinion for Wolf von Salhausen*
WA 15, 348-379	*Exposition of the 127th Psalm*
WA 15, 398-810	*Sermons of 1524*
WA 16, 1-654	*Sermons on Exodus*
Ta 270-272	*To Three Nuns*

1525

LW 40, 73-223	*Against the Heavenly Prophets*
Ta 272-275	*Appeal to Reissenbusch to Marry*
WA 18, 402-411	*Why Archbishop Albrecht Should Marry*
WA 17$^\text{I}$, 1-507	*Sermons of 1525*
WA 17$^\text{II}$, 1-247	*Lenten Postils*
WA 18, 531-540	*To the Erfurt Council*

Selected Bibliography[1]

Bainton, Roland. *Here I Stand.* New York: Abingdon-Cokesbury, 1950.

———. *What Christianity Says about Sex, Love and Marriage.* New York: Association, 1957.

Beach, Waldo, and Niebuhr, H. Richard (eds.). *Christian Ethics: Sources of the Living Tradition.* New York: Ronald, 1955.

Boehmer, Heinrich. *Luther and the Reformation in the Light of Modern Research.* Translated by E. Potter. New York: Dial, 1930.

Carlson, Edgar. *Reinterpretation of Luther.* Philadelphia: Muhlenberg, 1948.

Cole, William. *Sex in Christianity and Psychoanalysis.* New York: Oxford, 1955.

Elert, Werner. *The Christian Ethos.* Translated by Carl Schindler. Philadelphia: Muhlenberg, 1957.

Forell, George. *Faith Active in Love.* New York: Association, 1954.

Köstlin, Julius. *Theology of Luther.* Translated by C. E. Hay. 2 vols. Philadelphia: Lutheran Publishing Society, 1897.

Lenski, Gerhard. *Marriage in the Lutheran Church.* Columbus: Lutheran Book Concern, 1936.

Mattes, John. "Luther's Views Concerning Continence," *Lutheran Church Quarterly,* IV (1931).

McNeill, John. "Natural Law in the Thought of Luther," *Church History,* X, 3 (1941).

---

[1] A complete bibliography, with a lengthy evaluation of secondary English and foreign works, may be examined in the author's original study entitled *Testimony of Faith: The Genesis of Luther's Marriage Ethic Seen Against the Background of His Early Theological Development* (1517-1525). Ann Arbor: University Microfilms, 1958.

Niebuhr, H. Richard. *Christ and Culture.* New York: Harper and Brothers, 1951.

Niebuhr, Reinhold. *The Nature and Destiny of Man.* 2 vols. London: Nisbet, 1941.

Nygren, Anders. *Agape and Eros.* Translated by Philip Watson. 3 vols. London: S.P.C.K., 1932ff.

———. "Luther's Doctrine of the Two Kingdoms," *Ecumenical Review,* III (1949).

Pauck, Wilhelm. *The Heritage of the Reformation.* Boston: The Beacon Press, 1950.

Pelikan, Jaroslav. *Fools for Christ.* Philadelphia: Muhlenberg, 1955.

Piper, Otto. *The Christian Interpretation of Sex.* New York: Scribners, 1941.

Prenter, Regin. *Spiritus Creator.* Translated by J. M. Jensen. Philadelphia: Muhlenberg, 1953.

Rupp, Gordon. *The Righteousness of God.* London: Hodder and Stoughton, 1953.

Troeltsch, Ernest. *Social Teachings of the Christian Churches.* Translated by Olive Wyon. 2 vols. New York: Macmillan, 1931.

Vajta, Vilmos. *Luther on Worship.* Translated by U. Leupold. Philadelphia: Muhlenberg, 1958.

Watson, Philip. *Let God be God!* Philadelphia: Muhlenberg, 1948.

Wingren, Gustaf. *Luther on Vocation.* Translated by Carl Rasmussen. Philadelphia: Muhlenberg, 1957.

Zimmerman, Carle. *Family and Civilization.* New York: Harper and Brothers, 1947.

Index

Type used in this book
Body, 11 on 13 and 10 on 11 Garamond
Display, Egmont
Paper: White Standard Antique R